BY

NORVAL WHITE

NEW YORK A Physical History 1987
The Architecture Book 1976

BY

NORVAL WHITE AND **ELLIOT WILLENSKY**

AIA Guide to New York City
1967, 1978, 1988

NEW YORK
A Physical History

NEW YORK
A Physical History

NORVAL WHITE

Atheneum NEW YORK 1987

Atheneum
Macmillan Publishing Company
866 Third Avenue, New York, N.Y. 10022
Collier Macmillan Canada, Inc.

Library of Congress Cataloging-in-Publication Data
White, Norval, ———
    New York a physical history.
    Bibliography: p.
    Includes index.
    1. New York (N.Y.)—Description.   2. Architecture—New York (N.Y.)
3. City planning—New York (N.Y.) 4. Infrastructure (Economics)—New York
(N.Y.) 5. New York (N.Y.)—Buildings, structures, etc.
I. Title.
F128.3.W48   1987   974.7'1   86-47696
ISBN 0-689-11658-6

Macmillan books are available at special discounts for bulk purchases for sales promotions, premiums, fund-raising, or educational use. For details, contact:
    Special Sales Director
    Macmillan Publishing Company
    866 Third Avenue
    New York, N.Y. 10022

Designed by Cathryn S. Aison
FIRST EDITION

10 9 8 7 6 5 4 3 2 1

Printed in the United States of America

FOR *Catherine*

Acknowledgments

Catherine Lobstein read the manuscript with care, and offered suggestions that made my sometimes complex prose clearer and more precise. Suzan Kunz organized the illustrations, took many of the photographs herself, and followed up on the loose ends that I, both lazy and busy, did and could not ravel. Additionally, she collected permissions and assigned credits with the help of Mary Flower. Tom Stewart, president of Atheneum, edited the manuscript thoughtfully, and Lawrence McIntyre, his associate editor, led it through the tortuous path to publication with careful precision. Joel Honig was a meticulous copyeditor, but more importantly a dedicated New York enthusiast. Cathy Aison, the designer, managed to give the organization of illustrations a lively presence.

I also thank those no longer with us who have, through their words, given to those who care or wonder about New York a deeper perception: the epigraphs that follow range from Thomas Jefferson to Gertrude Stein, from Walt Whitman to Saul Bellow. Thank you all you long-gone and still-present bards, for you have jointly distilled language so that all of us can better appreciate and understand this vast, vulgar, wondrous, and sometimes joyful city.

In the process of pursuing research, one name stands out as a source of sources: Isaac Newton Phelps Stokes. That gracious gentleman was thought a dilettante in his time, but his *Iconography of Manhattan Island* is perhaps the best document both attempted and realized of any city, in any country, of the world. Architect Stokes even added some buildings, socially experimental modest incomed housing, but his love of the city in an overall context makes him a latter-day Herodotus or Vitruvius, a chronicler of civilization's greatest achievement: the *city*.

New York is, and has always been, my home. My father and mother both were deeply immersed in professions that sought to solve its ills; he as a surgeon, she as a social worker. William Crawford and Caroline Taylor White set their son, Norval, on a course that did not match their own professions, but, hopefully, and in a very different way, inspired him to cull the wonders and criticize the defects of this three-dimensional architectural, urbanistic, historical, modernistic, conventional, conservative, radical, glitzy place.

Contents

The spirit of pulling down and building up is abroad. The whole of New York is rebuilt about once in ten years.
The Diary of Philip Hone,
former mayor of New York (May 1, 1839)

My city's fit and noble name resumed,
Choice aboriginal name, with marvellous beauty, meaning,
*A rocky founded island—shores where ever gayly dash the coming,
   going, hurrying sea waves.*
WALT WHITMAN
"Mannahatta," in *Leaves of Grass* (1888)

A cloacina of all the depravities of human nature.
THOMAS JEFFERSON

A sucked orange.
RALPH WALDO EMERSON

—ashes, vegetable refuse, old hats without crowns, worn-out shoes, and other household wreck, lay scattered about as a field of agreeable inquiry for a number of long-legged and industrious pigs . . .
WILLIAM CHAMBERS (1854)

I simply rejoiced in the New York streets, in the long spindling legs of the elevated, in the straight high undecorated houses, in the empty upper air and in the white surface of the snow. It was such a joy to realise that the whole thing was without mystery and without complexity, that it was clean and straight and meagre and hard and white and high.

GERTRUDE STEIN
Q.E.D. (1903)

"Who's that?" a Polish girl asks softly, staring in wonder at the Statue of Liberty.

"The American god," someone replies.

.   .   .

From this distance the city seems like a vast jaw, with uneven black teeth. It breathes clouds of black smoke into the sky and puffs like a glutton suffering from his obesity.

MAXIM GORKY
"The City of the Yellow Devil" (1906)

Here I was in New York, city of prose and fantasy, of capitalist automatism, its streets a triumph of cubism; its moral philosophy that of the dollar. New York impressed me tremendously because, more than any other city in the world, it is the fullest expression of our modern age.

LEON TROTSKY
Novy mir (1917)

New York lives by its clear checkerboard. Millions of beings act simply and easily within it. Freedom of mind. From the first hour, the stranger is oriented, sure of his course. . . .

In the store windows I saw an album published for the Christmas season by Scribner's: *The Magical City*. I reflect and argue with myself. I change it to: *The Fairy Catastrophe*. That is the phrase that expresses my emotion and rings within me in the stormy debate which has not stopped tormenting me for fifty days: hate and love.

For me the fairy catastrophe is the lever of hope.

LE CORBUSIER
When the Cathedrals Were White (1937)

New York is an ugly city, a dirty city. Its climate is a scandal, its politics are used to frighten children, its traffic is madness, its competition is murderous. But there is one thing about it—once you have lived in New York and it has become your home, no place else is good enough. All of everything is concentrated here, population, theatre, art, writing, publishing, importing, business, murder, mugging, luxury, poverty. It is all of everything. It goes all night. It is tireless and its air is charged with energy. I can work longer and harder without weariness in New York than any place else.

JOHN STEINBECK
New York Times Magazine (Feb. 1, 1953)

On some nights New York is as hot as Bangkok. The whole continent seems to have moved from its place and slid nearer the equator, the bitter gray Atlantic to have become green and tropical, and the people, thronging the streets, barbaric fellahin . . .

SAUL BELLOW
The Victim (1947)

London is a wide flat pie of redbrick suburbs with the West End stuck in the middle like a currant. New York is a huge rich raisin and is the biggest city I can imagine.

. . . A city is a place where you are least likely to get a bite from a wild sheep . . .

BRENDAN BEHAN
Brendan Behan's New York (1964)

If Westway is ever built, and the shoreline made pretty by city planners—when the city is totally renovated, when gays have restored all the tenements, garden restaurants have sprouted on the Lower East Side, and the meatpacking district is given over entirely to boutiques and cardshops—then we'll build an island in New York Harbor composed entirely of rotting piers, blocks of collapsed walls, and litter-strewn lots. Ruins become decor, nostalgia for the mud.

ANDREW HOLLERAN
"Nostalgia for the Mud"
The Christopher Street Reader (1983)

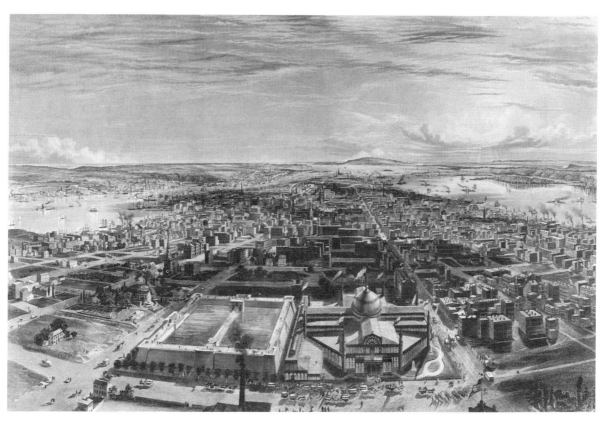

New York Viewed from Latting Observatory, 1853. A technological concert on display. The assembled waters of the Croton aqueduct are a powerful tank within the Murray Hill reservoir's battered neo-Egyptian walls. The cast- and wrought-iron Crystal Palace sits in today's Bryant Park, horsecars travel on rails up Sixth Avenue, steamboats smoke in the distant waters. And all is seen from the Latting Tower, a perch gained by a steam-powered elevator.

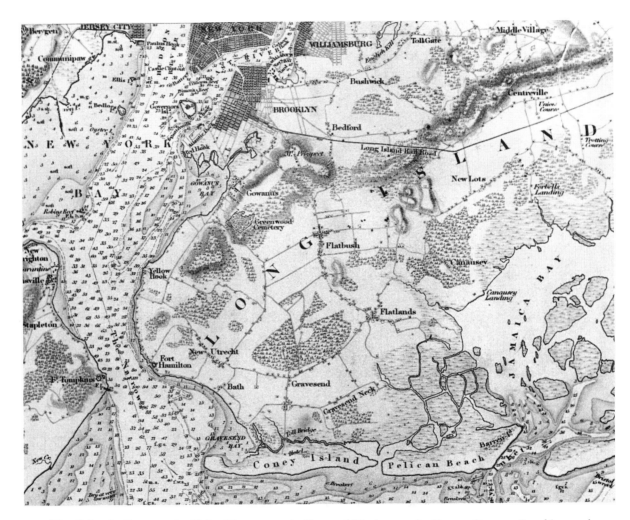

The Suburbs Became the Urbs. The scattered villages of Manhattan, the Bronx, Queens, Brooklyn, and Staten Island had a European scale of dense enclaves amid farmland. They were officially encapsulated in New York's single city by 1898 and were functionally made part of its life by the transit networks of ferry, streetcar, elevated trains, and finally subway.

Past

The Quiet must have forced itself into every nook, a conscious quiet rolling over the fertile, forested island, releasing the
small sounds of beaver, deer, and muskrat, the rustle of leaves,
the faint moccasined tread of Indians. Manhattan was a glorious
wild place of precipitous hills, deep green forests, racing streams,
and lovely salt marshes, cheeking vast rivers filled with fish, clams,
and oysters, rich in nature, rich from nature. Stand today on the
west flank of the Cloisters, narrow your vision with horselike
blinders, and peer northwest across Henry Hudson's river to the
great bluffs of New Jersey's Palisades; wipe your mind, and mind-
clear, history shelved, feel the sigh of rock, tree, water—no manmade intrusion in this narrow, censored view, the same one, near
the same place where Verrazzano paused, where Hudson toiled
north to Albany, where Adriaen Block might have wandered.

At Manhattan's flanks, away from its rock-based forests, across
the tidal waters of the East River, stretched the hundred miles of
Long Island, its western end later to join the city as Brooklyn and
Queens: vast reaches of sand and gravel, scrub and grass, with
marshlands serving as a life-generating reservoir of food and life
for the sea. The harbor's marshlands were legion, edging Man-

hattan, future Brooklyn and Queens, Staten Island and the New Jersey shore: Wallabout Bay, Jamaica Bay, the East and West banks, the Oyster Flats, mostly gone by landfill and buildings save for Jamaica Bay—happily now a wildlife preserve. The fast-moving waters of the East River flushed the harbor with influent from Long Island Sound through the narrow, tricky Hell Gate, and the returning effluent from the mixed waters of the Harlem and East rivers. These temperate lands and waters, sparsely inhabited, were a wondrous find. Fertile soil, rich waters, forests abounding with animals—all at the edge of a harbor vast and protected—combined to give seventeenth-century Europeans visions of a new Eden.

Personal Preface

Myriad books have recounted the political, social, military, ethnic, and anecdotal history of New York City. Happily, many are excellent. The chronology of political and social events does not concern us here, unless it brought physical change to the form and pattern of the city. This is a book about how manmade New York came to be the way it is, through the selfish and social efforts of man, the nature of the raw place, and the evolution of technical, engineering, social, and aesthetic constraints and stimuli. It is about *why* what New York still enjoys is *where* it is: whether a Federal house in Brooklyn, or a tenement in Harlem, or a factory in Long Island City.

I was born to an apartment on Manhattan's East Side, later lived in another, and then another afterwards, seven stories above the sidewalk, elevator-borne. Stairs were novelties. I traveled in the city by streetcar and bus, subway and elevated, but mostly on foot. The world I knew was made of asphalt and concrete, brick and limestone, brownstone and glass. An occasional tree was permitted and loved; severely trimmed grass grew in its Park Avenue band. Central Park was all the country anyone could ever need. Later I discovered that houses close to the ground were a snazzy way to live *in* the city. The elevator has been banned from my home ever since.

New York is a city that first grew in the European sense, where the speed of horse-borne and foot movement kept it clustered densely within its watered shores. Early Brooklyn, which later married New York, similarly hugged the Upper Harbor and East River. There, houses were in rows, closely and elegantly packed, with four and five stories possible by stair. These pedestrian cities later grew over a great sprawling landscape via ferries, with trains that ran both above and below the city's streets.

My world is now in such brown neighborhoods from New York's mid-history, with the nineteenth century's best buildings neatly adapted to a twentieth-century life-style. But how did I get here? How did others get to towering condominiums on Third Avenue, overpriced co-op apartments on Fifth Avenue, tenements in Harlem, lofts in SoHo, row houses in Queens and Staten Island, mansions in Forest Hills Gardens? And how were all of these residential styles of architecture and urbanism created to serve and be served by the army of vast office buildings that are New York's workplaces, the sometime fingers of its skyline, the sometime architectural icons of the city?

This book is not about architecture alone, but also the sewers and subways, water supply and ferries, technology and wealth, that created the vast fabric of the city itself. Architecture is the ever present product, from brownstones to skyscrapers, from tenements to museums, just as engineering (both structural and environmental) has been the ever present and ever changing means to make the architectural product possible. Often, as we will see, the engineers have led the parade—architects following behind, exploiting the possibilities that engineers created, and often for no greater reason than that the possibilities existed.

America at one time seemed bent on physically destroying its cities. Not only in the economic sense, due to welfare and the extra cost of compensatory education for the poor migrant. Not only because of middle-class fear-filled drift to the suburbs. Not only because of crime in the streets, drugs, dirt, and pollution. All these are highly touted ills, well advertised, stubborn, but perhaps manageable with education, imagination, and an infusion of money from a federal government controlled for half a century by people who don't like or live in cities. But times change, and although the fervor for suburbanization has not abated, a great body of the metropolitan population has rediscovered the city: a giant influx of what sociologists term "gentrification."

The care and feeding of the lawn are, perhaps, sophorifics for the unsophisticated metropolitan dweller, an escape from the burden of intellectual self-reliance in those leisure hours that, somehow, never are true leisure. Museums, theaters, staged events and happenings, great gatherings of the populace, strolling and shopping, are, on the one hand, advantages and possibilities offered by the city. Urban life at its best rises to urbanity where effortless possibility for urban intercourse, face to face, is a natural by-product of the city's dense configuration. Hunting, hiking, sailing, swimming, gardening, or just long walks in the woods are the complementary, and competing, opportunities of the country. Thoreau in his cabin at Walden Pond found possibility for contemplation in his isolation. Isolation and uncultivated nature gave freedom to soul and body from the currying, dress, and social constraints of dense urban life. The gray suburbia between is an unhappy compromise affording neither clutch of resources to its people. And when that compromise is foisted on a city, as it has been in Houston and Detroit and Los Angeles, the result is a disaster. Instead of urbane architecture there are flashy filing cabinets with exterior decoration, surrounded by amorphous space shunned by their inhabitants and neighbors, connected by smooth, richly financed but clogged highways that lead to shopping malls and office complexes, packaged simulations of the more obvious commercial aspects of urban life without its true underlying substance. New York has escaped much, if not all, of this deadly suburbanization. At its best—in Brooklyn Heights, for example, or in the blocks close to the American Museum of Natural History—it has a grace and urbanity found only in a few other places, such as Philadelphia's Society Hill, Chicago's Near North Side, New Orleans' French Quarter, Boston's Back Bay and Beacon Hill, San Francisco's Telegraph Hill, London's Bloomsbury, and the best sectors of Paris, Rome, and Copenhagen.

Manhattan, the tourists' New York, is remembered in mental snapshots, amid a vast flux of sight and sound. Even its residents are, when off their own turf, tourists in their own city, carrying their mental cameras over well-trod routes, capturing the symbolic moments of the city. To most, Manhattan is New York, the downtown of all downtowns. Even here, knowledge is excerpted from the whole: Fifth Avenue, Broadway, Greenwich Village, Wall Street, the caricatures of the chic, of bright lights, of the offbeat, of power. This passing parade bypasses New York's myriad local neighborhoods of character that house the city's personality, far from the boulevarded cliff dwellings of Park, Fifth, Third, and West End, but equally removed from the dreary banality of public (and most "middle-income") towered housing.

"Time present and time past/Are both perhaps present in time future." T. S. Eliot's lines from "Burnt Norton" are a most eloquent promise for this or any city.

The city's life is like that of an organism living on a skeleton of streets, with arteries as the pipes and drains of everyday life, with movement systems that allow timely access to work and play, and all filled with a sense of both whole and part, of downtown and neighborhood, of the ordinary and the special. Time past is here in its great skeleton and arteries, its aura of history both tactile and verbal, its early, ever present and long-growing skyline. Time present is where and what we are. Time future bears the great responsibility of creative use of both the past and the present adapted for future life and its aesthetic context. In spite of the vainglorious commentaries that have accompanied our recent past and present realities (that is, the built reality of architectural proposals), New York has survived as a whole whose sometimes raucous, sometimes banal buildings are small blemishes on the city's presence. For although New York is never thought beautiful, it is powerful and wondrous and sprawling: a place at once of tremendous vitality and serenity, of towering commerce and wealth and quiet treelined blocks of brownstones, of nouveau-riche aeries and silent private gardens (although the Cloisters offers gardens both silent and public). The huckstered towers of AT&T and its peers are more the dime-store jewelry on a sometimes tawdry but dignified matron than any serious intrusion on the whole of the city. And whether diamond or paste, new candidates for the monumental are small events in the city's vast reaches.

New York's demise has been announced by many with scorn—and with perhaps more than a hint of jealousy—a dozen dozen times. Neighborhoods have been demolished, great buildings destroyed; their replacements are frequently banal, sometimes vulgar. But the city survives in its relentless grid, husbanding handfuls of its varied past sometimes by accident, as in the poorer parts of town, and sometimes by design, as with more recent landmarks legislation. The city as a totality blossoms with its incessant vitality and occasional brilliance. But it lives. Residents savor its best, tourists flock to its towers, orchestras play, diplomats harangue, trees grow. And occasionally some owner, some builder, some planner, some architect gives us a new moment of joy.

Manhattan's Pre–World War II Skyline, 1932. When Manhattan emerged from its four-story, church-spired, eighteenth-century skyline, it produced this twentieth-century silhouette of giant finials. The flat boxes did not arise for another twenty years, when air conditioning allowed vast, artificially ventilated floors. Instead of new slender towers, stubby towers then muted this elegance.

A Historical Preview

Cities aren't created by chance, but sometimes their sites are accidentally chosen. New Amsterdam, that tip of Manhattan now coterminous with the financial district, was found by Italian sailors seeking the spices of the East Indies by a shorter route than Marco Polo's; and it was settled by sharp Dutch businessmen who valued that haphazard find: a reservoir of beaver. Seeking spices, they found fur; finding fur, they settled at the most accessible and defensible spot nearby, arranged a village from their own experience in Renaissance Amsterdam, served similarly by canals, and erected buildings like those back home, with the stepped-gable architecture that one can still find at New Amsterdam's contemporary, Curaçao. They added an early Renaissance fort harboring a governor's palace, soldiery, and barracks; the inevitable Reformed church (the Catholics discovered New York Harbor, but the Protestants settled it); and a palisade (the wall of Wall Street). And they planted gardens and orchards to fill these row-house-encircled blocks.

This lumbering, almost uncontrollable behemoth, this vibrant, dirty, beloved city, an ethnic mosaic, has endured the ladled vitriol of H. L. Mencken and Anthony Trollope, the terse love of writers from Henry James to Kurt Vonnegut, and the no-nonsense prose of E. B. White. Trollope in 1862 dyspeptically grumbled, "Speaking of New York as a traveller, I have two faults to find with it. In the first place, there is nothing to see; and in the second place, there is no mode of getting about to see anything."

And Mencken heaped further scorn on the city in a 1922 private letter, saying: "I thoroughly detest New York, though I have to go there very often. . . . Have you ever noticed that no American writer of any consequence lives in Manhattan? Dreiser tried it . . . but finally fled to California."

Why is New York City here, who founded it, and was it anything more than the chance find of wanderers seeking spices in the Indies, who fell on her doorstep? Verrazzano, Block, and Hudson were the prime stumblers. And what were the raw materials that man could alter, obliterate, take advantage of, and build upon?

Slowly, the medieval fabric unrolled northward, and in a final fateful year, 1811, the vast rolling topography of Manhattan was destined to be subjugated. Washington Irving, in *Knickerbocker's History of New York* (1809), describes what is now termed the West Side as "a sweet rural valley, beautiful with many a bright flower, refreshed by many a pure streamlet, and enlivened here and there by a delectable little Dutch cottage, sheltered under some sloping hill; and almost buried in embowering trees." The aldermanic commission of 1811 laid a grid of street and avenue over the whole island, with almost total disregard of hill and valley, lake, pond, stream, and marsh. At 155th Street—at the edge of the earth in the eyes of its creators—the graph paper halted; the city could never reach that far! If one couldn't imagine growth to that point, how could one have the more extraordinary fantasy of a Brooklyn whose population would approach that of modern Israel or Ireland? Here were engineers at work, not poets or even farsighted merchants. Poets came later and found their stuff in the counterpoint of buildings and personalities, playing in concert with this initial regimentation.

* * *

These three elements, the geology of the place, the organically grown New Amsterdam, and the commissioners' plan, respectively, set the tone for all that was to become the tourist, financial, culture-centered, international (United Nations), and fashion city that we know today: Dyckman Street to the Battery, river to river. Here are the major "palaces," monuments both ancient (by New York standards) and modern, a rich background architecture punctuated by moments of glory.

The vast reaches of outer New York City today, from Staten Island's western shores to the marches of southern Queens, from Coney Island to suburban Riverdale in the west Bronx, are the villages and towns of New York's former countryside. These were mostly captured in the consolidation of 1898 in a time of America's first muscle flexing as a world power—as in the Spanish-American War—where bigness seemed better. Brooklyn, a town before 1658, a city in 1834, and a borough of consolidated New York in 1898, was the stalwart competitor of Manhattan for the center of attention before the Civil War and a valiant second city until the very end of the nineteenth century. Harlem, a sleepy farming village of the eighteenth and nineteenth centuries, burst with an immigrant population seeking space at more modest prices along the Ninth Avenue El. The villages of the Bronx, such as Mott Haven and West Farms, later became the barracks for the urban poor, again by courtesy of elevated transit. Queens and Staten Island, on the other hand, were rural places till late, excepting such pockets as Queens' industrial Long Island City. But these two boroughs did not develop with an urban intensity comparable to their parents, Manhattan and Brooklyn, and to the annexed Bronx, until after World War II.

Ideas of planning and passing styles of architecture left their marks on neighborhoods because their time had come: the Federal and Greek Revival styles left remnants in parts of Greenwich Village and Brooklyn Heights because they were the dominant fashion when those communities developed. Gothic Revival followed closely after in these areas, but in the form of its predecessors, that is, with the same arrangements in plan and a bit of Gothic exterior fancy dress. The new commissioners' grid, of course, hard by Wall Street's flank, crept northward. Its first major body of buildings are those of present-day SoHo, with cast iron now acting as an architecture of technology to become both the generator and the resource for creating this industrial and warehousing district. (SoHo, of course, is a modern precinct name for the area south of Houston Street, emulating in name-only London's "Greenwich Village" district.)

As each neighborhood opened, it was built with the technology and in the style then in fashion and/or available. SoHo became a monolithic presence built in the newly available cast-iron technology of its time. But, in addition, the many Venetian, Palladian, and other High Renaissance facades are there because the 1850's chose those styles, reflected, in Brooklyn Heights for instance, by the Anglo-Italian brownstones of the period.

Convent Avenue north of 141st Street, on the other hand, is in a Picturesque style, akin to the Shingle style, because the pace of housing did not reach that far north until the 1880's. Here, houses with similar plans in long rows are composed into a variegated facade with towers, mansard roofs, and finials that give a serrated profile against the sky. Forest Hills Gardens is a vast sea of Tudor Revival because that was the style for the upper middle class ("Stockbrokers' Tudor," in the words of Osbert Lancaster, to be seen equally in suburbia as at Scarsdale) around the time of World War I, although in Forest Hills the construction was in the radical new material, reinforced concrete.

All the grids, plans, and cast iron in the world would not suffice to make a city grow without sewers and a supply of clear water. These arrived in 1842, the cool waters of Westchester's Croton River dammed in reservoirs, coursing through aqueducts aimed straight as an arrow at the city's population, while sewers quickly carried away the urban effluents to the deep East and Hudson rivers.

Transportation technology first caused housing to leap across the East River from Manhattan to Brooklyn (Heights) through Robert Fulton's 1814 steam ferry and, two decades later, via the new New York and Harlem Railroad, expanding urbanization to the northern Manhattan towns of Yorkville and Harlem. The Industrial Revolution brought with it first cast iron, then a practical safety elevator, and, ultimately and suddenly, skyscrapers.

Elevators, abetted by steel, could generate towers that man had never dreamed of, and the pre–World War II filigreed finials of the financial district punctuated the city's meandering streets from 1900 onward, obliterating all traces of Dutch New Amsterdam (save for the street plan) and most of English New York.

The Industrial Revolution, in capitalist style, produced wealth, and wealth was not shy about creating its own personal environment and symbols. The Medicis and their peers had performed similarly in fifteenth- and sixteenth-century Florence. New York's Medicis were the Astors, Vanderbilts, Carnegies, Fricks, Pratts, Stewarts, et alia. Their American-style palazzi festooned the city as it grew northward, first at and around Lafayette Street (remnants still extant at Colonnade Row); then along and near Fifth Avenue in the 30's (extinct) and 50's (extinct save for the Plant House, now Cartier's, and part of the Villard Houses left as a forecourt for the Palace Hotel); and then again in the 60's and 70's (still present in assorted consulates and embassies). One can see some semblance of these vast private palaces at the Frick Collection (an extension of the Henry Clay Frick house into a museum) or at the Cooper-Hewitt Museum (the former Andrew Carnegie mansion).

While all these fashionable and power-centered constructions were occurring, the further reaches of what was to become New York City blossomed as a series of rural and semirural towns. Richmondtown on Staten Island is a rare remnant village from the seventeenth and eighteenth centuries; and that same island birthed St. George, New Dorp, and Grymes Hill. The flourishing sister city of Brooklyn looked east and south to Flatbush, Bedford, Stuyvesant Heights, Gravesend, New Utrecht, and Bushwick; distinct towns with their own character and industry. Bushwick, for example, vied with Milwaukee, as a center of beer brewing. Queens started its western shores with Long Island City, Astoria, and Steinway (a company town) and crept eastward to Forest Hills and Jamaica. What was to become the Bronx included West Farms, Morrisania, Kingsbridge, and Mott Haven.

Burgeoning Manhattan must have seemed endless to those who lived on its thousands of grid blocks in the years before the Civil War. Few parks punctuated it: Washington Square, Union

Square, Stuyvesant Square, Gramercy Park, Madison Square—all provided those special neighborhoods with breathing space; but the brownstone blocks surged north relentlessly, and 155th Street no longer seemed so far away, or so improbable.

One of the greatest urban acts ever proposed, or accomplished, reorganized the whole concept of the city and provided it with a contrasting place of artificial country. Central Park was the product of a competition inspired by the poet William Cullen Bryant and won by landscape architects Frederick Law Olmsted and Calvert Vaux. This 840-acre enclave was built as the city began to surround its borders, not as an excision but as a planned place that became the navel of New York or of Manhattan. (Brooklyn's later Olmsted-designed Prospect Park serves a similar service and was built for the then-separate city of Brooklyn.) Parks, boulevards, and parkways became elements in ordering the city visually: civic leaders were inspired by the works of Paris such as the Bois de Boulogne and the Avenue de l'Opéra, the marks of Baron Eugène Haussmann, military prefect of Paris under Napoleon III and organizer of the dominant civic scene that we enjoy today. In Paris the new boulevards transformed the old medieval city into a coherent neo-Renaissance place. In Brooklyn, Ocean and Eastern parkways opened up opportunities for new construction just as Riverside and Central parks created an opportunity for construction of early flanking mansions on Riverside Drive and Fifth Avenue. Physical New York today is, therefore, the end product of an accidental find, the memories of its European settlers, a ruthless and systematic grid, all subjected to vast expansion of both density and area due to the city's booming commercial success. Happily, success came before the automobile became dominant in American urban-suburban life. As a result, New York blends the tight pedestrianism of nineteenth-century Europe with the vitality of twentieth-century architecture, while preserving in vast precincts, as well, its earlier building, to be savored, once more, by citizens of the twenty-first.

Demolishing Old Madison Square Garden, etching by William G. McNulty, 1925. Stanford White's Renaissance Revival pleasure palace (1890) fell in favor of the New York Life Insurance Company's new tower. The next Garden, architecturally innocuous, stood between 49th and 50th streets on Eighth Avenue, devouring only brownstones and tenements of Hell's Kitchen in its arrival. Its third incarnation managed to destroy New York's greatest architectural patrimony, Pennsylvania Station (by White's partner, Charles McKim). *That* Garden is itself doomed to a fourth move, having survived from 1966 to 1989. People seem to have won the longevity battle with monuments: it took ten generations to build Chartres Cathedral, which has survived for eighteen more. The Gardens will have grown and perished three times in less than a century.

Ratzer Map of New York, 1766. A meticulous British military map that precisely and eloquently describes the city's increasing urbanization. Engineering Lieutenant Bernard Ratzer's name is sometimes misspelled in history's records as Ratzen.

NEW YORK
A Physical History

The "Danckers" or "Visscher" map. A 1660 view of New Amsterdam and the surrounding farms of the New Netherlands. Note Fort Amsterdam on lower Manhattan, and the scattered houses symbolizing outlying homesteads.

1.

The Virgin Place

An ice cliff, thirty stories tall, hundreds of miles long, the glacial creep of a thousand years confronted the sea. Its crumbling, melting facade marked a frontal line from Gay Head on Martha's Vineyard past Block Island's Mohegan Bluffs, along a spine down Long Island's North Shore through Queens and Brooklyn, to New Jersey's Atlantic Highlands. The geological debris of a continent, this colossus of sand, gravel, clay, and organic matter of prehistory (a dinosaur or two perhaps?), moved in a paste of a million million tons, pressed before, and under the ice sea. It reached its crest at the glacier's last line, leaving bluffs behind as the glacier, warmed by the changing climate, melted over another aeon. The melting waters washed before it, with sand-bearing torrents forming the flat vast outreaches of Queens, Brooklyn, and Staten Island's south shores, the Great South Bay and the barrier beaches of Fire Island and the Hamptons.

In *The Geology of New York City and Environs* (1968) Christopher Schuberth describes the spectacular event that occurred 1½ million years ago, "as an almost four-thousand-mile wall of ice, perhaps as much as two thousand feet thick, spread southward across the face of Canada and out into the North Atlantic. . . . this frozen tide eventually smothered New York City and its outlying environs to the north and west under a tremendous burden. But it went no farther [i.e., the terminal moraine]. To the south, however, the frigid winds that blew off the ice sheet must have chilled the land for hundreds of miles beyond."

Manhattan and the Bronx are seated on plunging strata of volcanic rock from more ancient times: Fordham gneiss, Inwood marble, Manhattan schist, forming a tilted underground sandwich. They plunge seaward from the Heights of the Bronx to the Battery of Manhattan. They are the rock that once justified Manhattan's towered midtown to the towers' engineers. A firm foundation for true skyscrapers, the schist pokes above the ground to show its face in Central Park. Contemporary builders have conquered less firm land to build skyscrapers on soft Chicago clay or the mud of New Orleans at the Mississippi delta; but New York's earlier engineers sought the economy of rock substructures. A considerable geological symbiosis is that of the first subway (which penetrated the northern spine of Manhattan along Broadway) and City College, whose very walls are clad in the Manhattan schist torn from the cut that made the subway's route. The schist, a hard sparkling rock from volcanic times, has been a Manhattan favorite, cladding the dour walls of St. Paul's Chapel since 1766, ten years before the Revolution.

The raw land of the northeast, heavily forested, abounded in small game. It drew great rainfalls to its rugged contours, feeding creek and stream and river in a network of veins and arteries that fed plentiful fresh waters to salty estuaries and the sea. The wooded land did not give simple place for homely agriculture, and the Native American's livelihood was in the capture and collection of food animals, of wild berries and plants. But there was so much land and forest that the sparse population barely dented the natural resources. Here was a place of animal and veg-

Blasting the IRT. By 1904 August Belmont's Interborough Rapid Transit line had opened past City College's new Hamilton Heights campus, and much of the excavated Manhattan schist would veneer George B. Post's new buildings. This pairing of disposal and reuse followed the World Trade Center's excavation: that fill became part of the land of Battery Park City.

etable life lightly used and a cornucopia waiting for exploitation.

So why would any intruder more than intrude: who would want to stay? Who could foresee that the beaver and its brethren would supply European needs and found such fortunes as that of the Astors, who later invested in New York's real estate and established their own line of American "society"? The "Indians," who never saw the Indies in question, were marked with a name of a place half the world away, a tropical land where spices grew.

From James Fenimore Cooper to Zane Grey, writers have imbued American generations with a sense of space and nature that was the North America-to-be, a sense that can still be savored in the backreaches of northern New York and New Hampshire woodlands, Wisconsin and Michigan lakes, Kansas and Oklahoma prairies, the deserts and canyons of Arizona and New Mexico, and the rugged coasts of Oregon and Maine. Their writings were the fantasies of adventure, of Indians and trappers, of pioneers and cowboys, and where, incidentally, the lands these heroes dwelt in were lovingly described. Henry David Thoreau enjoyed a sense of the continent's splendid loneliness, virgin and unsullied still in great part, out of the early nineteenth-century city: "The Indian . . . stands free and unconstrained in Nature, is her inhabitant and not her guest, and wears her easily and gracefully. But the civilized man has the habits of the house. His house is a prison."

John Muir, the great naturalist whose lifework was the backbone of much of America's park system, writes that "In God's wilderness lies the hope of the world—the great fresh unblighted, unredeemed wilderness . . . the clearest way into the Universe is through a forest wilderness. . . . How hard to realize that every camp of men or beast has this glorious starry firmament for a roof! In such places standing alone on the mountaintop it is easy to realize that whatever special nests we make—leaves and moss like the marmots and birds, or tents and piled stone— we all dwell in a house of one room—the world with the

A Native American. Europeans who stayed home were more solicitous of the "Indians" than those who dealt with them face to face. They were the extraterrestrials of the seventeenth century, the mental circus of the eighteenth and nineteenth—and, from afar, neither loved nor hated but, rather, wondered at.

firmament for its roof—and are sailing the celestial spaces without leaving any track."

The urban memories of Europeans would confront vast raw nature on the North and South American continents. Their remembered tight masonry clusters of continental town and city were to be in dour contrast to the great expanse of these newly discovered lands. The magnificence and splendor of the rich and almost empty coastline were to affect the tiny bands of exploring viewers as much as did the regal innocence of the "Indians." The land along the sea was an obvious place to build for those who had come from the sea edge of Europe, a trading place where the resources of a newly found continent could be tapped. A secure and strategic site, abundant water, seemingly friendly natives, plentiful animals for food and skins, and the unprecedented possibilities of vast woodlands, farmlands, and hunting grounds beyond, together formed an ecology that later grew and blossomed into a great city.

Frances Trollope wrote in *Domestic Manners of the Americans* (1832): "I have never seen the bay of Naples, I can therefore make no comparison, but my imagination is incapable of conceiving any thing of the kind more beautiful than the harbour of New York. . . . I doubt if ever the pencil of Turner could do it justice, bright and glorious as it rose upon us. We seemed to enter the harbour of New York upon waves of liquid gold, and as we darted past the green isles which rise from its bosom, like guardian centinels of the fair city, the setting sun stretched his horizontal beams farther and farther at each moment, as if to point out to us some new glory in the landscape."

"**New York From Brooklyn Heights**" was drawn by J. W. Hill, engraved by W. J. Bennett, and published by L. P. Clover in 1837 Aquatint. It is a rooftop view from Remsen Street, spanning Manhattan as far as Wall Street on the left and Canal Street on the right. Amazingly, one can see both East and Hudson rivers and New Jersey in this low rise vista.

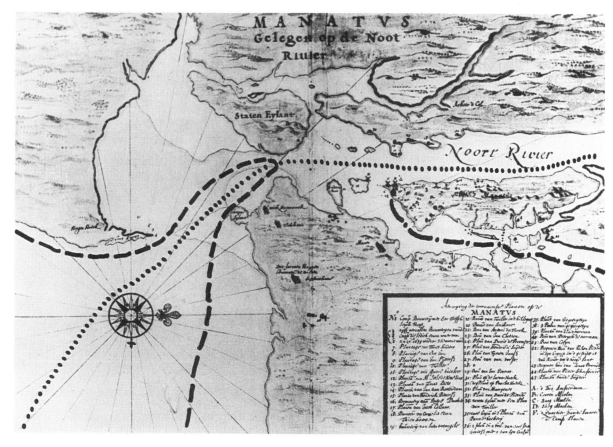

--- Verrazzano 1524
... Hudson 1609
---- Block 1614

Routes of Discovery, New York Harbor and environs. Not until the Panama Canal was opened in 1914 did the European idea of a direct westward water passage to the Indies become a reality. These three adventurers, Verrazzano, Hudson, and Block, had chanced upon New York Harbor in their own search. They mapped this and other places that did *not* penetrate the Americas. The discovered beaver replaced as a resource the spices they had sought. New Amsterdam was the resulting beachhead.

2.

Discovery

In the spring of 1401 in the Tuscan city of Florence a competition was held to design great sculptured doors for the baptistery of that see. Sculptor Lorenzo Ghiberti's winning maquette was a panel illustrating the moment that God stayed the hand of Abraham as he was about to sacrifice his son Isaac to God, a parable told in Genesis that weighs importantly in Judaism, Christianity, and Islam. The Abraham of Ghiberti was a lively human individual unlike the stylized anonymous figures of medieval sculpture. The creative break was so positive, so self-assured, that historians sometimes refer to this act, this moment in art, as the touchstone of the Renaissance, the symbolic moment of the rebirth of the individual creative man.

The Renaissance, or rebirth of humanism, after the visual and scholarly abstractions of medieval life, permeated art, science, and literature. In the course of less than a hundred years, architecture, painting, sculpture, science, mathematics, astronomy, printing, music, and geographic explorations all bloomed with the creative energies of individuals released from the group regimens of the Middle Ages. Across these many disciplines this flowering includes Brunelleschi's Foundling Hospital, Florence (1419) and his great cathedral (Duomo) dome, Florence (1436); the Gutenberg Bible (1456); the first world globe (1492); Michelangelo's Pietà (1498); and Columbus's four voyages (1492–1504). By 1492 the Strozzi Palace was under construction in Florence; Leonardo da Vinci was forty and about to begin painting *The Last Supper*.

The age of discovery meant discovery in every human sense: the discovery of new worlds of the mind, of the eye and ear, of the emotions; new worlds of literal geography, of the place of the globe in the solar system, of the universe.

Geographic discoveries were not for some abstract cause, as in Sir Edmund Hillary's yearning to conquer Mt. Everest "because it is there." Columbus's mission, financed by the merged kingdoms of Ferdinand and Isabella, Aragon and Castile, was to seek the spices of the Indies and Asia. Marco Polo had been to China in the thirteenth century, and the Portuguese had skirted Africa to India in the 1480's. Spices were as valuable as gold: Alaric the Visigoth raised the siege of Rome in the fifth century in return for pepper, for the diet of Europe in the late Middle Ages was both bland and subject to spoilage. When the Mongols severed land trade routes to the East, new stimulus was given to navigation to the Indies by sailing west around what men newly realized was a globe. How large that sphere, and how distant the Indies, were vague ideas; but the early explorers, exulting in the individualism of the fifteenth and sixteenth centuries and lured by the specific goal of the Indies, blithely and with surprising skill at navigation sailed west to find the magic route. Coursing up and down the islands of the Caribbean and along the coasts of the Americas, they charted those lands and edges in maps that show their constant attention to ways of passing through: the river mouths are penetrated and recorded in great detail, as possible passages through the landmasses, which are

Remains of Adriaen Block's ship, *Tiger*. The by-product of excavations for the Goldman Sachs office building on Pearl and Broad streets, these ribs were the skeleton of Block's burned ship. It is the earliest remnant of European man in New York.

illustrated only in linear profile. Columbus wrote in his logbook's dedication to Ferdinand and Isabella: "Your highnesses ordained that I should not go eastward by land in the usual manner but by the western way which no one about whom we have positive information has ever followed."

The historian Samuel Eliot Morison noted: "America was discovered accidentally, when discovered it was not wanted; and most of the exploration for the next fifty years was done in the hope of getting through or around it."

The first European to penetrate New York Harbor was Giovanni da Verrazzano in 1524. He sailed into the Upper Bay, sighting Manhattan and Brooklyn's shores, "in the midst of which flowed to the sea a very great river." He passed the Narrows, now spanned by a bridge named for him, and entered New York Harbor, thus becoming the first European known to have seen the lands of modern New York. Columbus was an Italian in the service of Spain. But Verrazzano, also an Italian, a Florentine, whose native city was the site of the greatest riches of the early Renaissance, represented, at 4,000 nautical miles from the Duomo, King Francis I of France. Verrazzano did not linger in New York's harbor but pressed on in a ranging exploration of the great North American landmass. That he recorded it is more important than that he was here, for many others passed by but made little note. "I did not expect to find such an obstacle of new land as I have found, and if for some reason I did expect to find it, I estimated there would be some strait to get through to the Eastern Ocean."

It was an Englishman in service of the Dutch who first penetrated and mapped the harbor and river to its navigable limits. Henry Hudson sailed to the point of present-day Albany on behalf of the Dutch West India Company. In the summer of 1609 he mapped the river that bears his name. Strangely, the Dutch termed it the Noort or North River: but the English, when in place after 1664, called it the Hudson. The South River, which defined the

A Sixteenth-Century Caravel. These tiny sailboats were the spaceships that discovered the planet America, across the unknown, subject to the vagaries of wind and water. Seeking a needle, they found only a haystack, the vast North American continent.

southern boundary of the New Netherland Colony, is the present Delaware, divider of New Jersey and Pennsylvania. Sometimes, in shipping circles today, the Hudson reads as North. Until 1985 one could see it so called in the *New York Times* ship "Arrivals and Departures" listings. But Hudson, too, was less interested in land than in water. He wanted to get *through* the continent to India and left his name as well at Hudson's Bay, another massive water-penetration of the continent.

Adriaen Block—for once a Dutchman in the service of the Dutch—became the first European to tarry on the land of Manhattan, when his ship, the *Tiger*, burned at anchor in the harbor in the spring of 1614. Landing near Wall Street, he and his fellow sailors built a small (forty-four-foot) "yacht" and set sail that summer along the coast of Long Island Sound to join another Dutch vessel that took them home to Holland. Block's tour of the north-eastern coastal waters left his name at an island between the tip of Long Island and Narragansett Bay. His brief stay was further evidence for the Dutch burghers that profit was to be made through this vast harbor.

The search for the East Indies was the compulsion that motivated Columbus and his followers. But in that process, the more perceptive and practical noted potential riches unrelated to spices, unrelated to the Orient, but equally related to profit: beaver. Pelts of the abundant beaver more than replaced the worth of the elusive spices. Furs of hat and body were compulsory for the wealthy in seventeenth-century Europe, no less than ermine and mink in our own times, for fashion, for status, for keeping up with the Joneses.

The Dutch, keepers of a canny commercial economy not dissimilar to that of the Swiss, were, and still are, a hardworking, dour, practical lot, although they were less obsessed with tidiness then than now, if we take for evidence the garbage-strewn and pig-infested streets of early New Amsterdam. The discovery of the great upper bay was a happy accident: Hudson's river (then called the North)

New York Times of May 2, 1985: "Looking improbably small against a backdrop of passing freighters and the grand facades of the Royal Naval College across the River Thames in Greenwich, a replica of the sailing ship that carried the founders of Britain's first successful colony in America lifted anchor Tuesday and set out to duplicate the historic, hazardous voyage.

"The destination is the Virginia coast at the mouth of the York River, where the original Godspeed and two sister ships, the Susan Constant and the Discovery, deposited the 104 tradesmen and farmers who founded Jamestown in 1607. That was 13 years before the Pilgrims landed at Plymouth Rock seeking religious freedom and, to the annoyance of many Virginians, grabbed the historical limelight from their more business-minded predecessors. How far the Godspeed will go toward redressing the situation is not clear yet, but Britons who have seen the ship here this week have been fascinated.

". . . The original 14-man crew contended with 39 passengers and assorted pigs and chickens in a ship just over half as long again as a New York City bus and less than 15 feet wide."

and, best of all, an island from their dreams, forested, and coursed with clear fresh water, became a defensible place from which to trade for the ubiquitous beaver.

North of New Amsterdam, discovery and immigration were the product of a search for religious freedom or, more precisely, independence from the intolerance of England, the very country that had broken nationally from the Church of Rome. Henry VIII's willful act, largely taken for his personal reasons of marriage and divorce, created a new national hierarchy, with the king or queen now not only autocratic chief of state but also becoming the autocratic head of the Church of England. Later, the English Civil War (1642–1648) had been in part a Puritan revolution against the Catholic Stuart, Charles I, and the interwoven complexities of religious posturing and persecution beset both England and Scotland, complicated by the strongly conflicting attitudes of the Church of England, the Church of Scotland (Presbyterianism), and the renascent Church of Rome. And so we have the almost mythic stories of the Puritans, Pilgrims, and Plymouth Rock, of witchcraft and Thanksgiving. The Bible of the American spirit lies in such religious and symbolic events of New England as these and, to a lesser extent, in the English colony of Virginia, where commerce (agricultural, this time) founded the colony at Jamestown, which blossomed ultimately into the great slaveowning plantation society of the South. Potatoes, corn, tomatoes, and tobacco were Virginia's equivalent of the New Netherland beaver: commercial fodder for the great markets of Europe. It is said that Queen Elizabeth I, upon receiving a potato and tobacco from Walter Raleigh, smoked the potato and ate the tobacco. If only her example had been pursued by society since then, how our health and habits might have differed.

The Dutch West India Company's directors transported the first thirty families to their New Netherland outpost at Fort Orange (now Albany) in 1624, although eight men and some cattle were left on Governor's Island (then called Nut Island) in the Upper Bay. In 1625 a large group under Willem Verhulst settled on Manhattan Island proper, and the future city was in place. On May 4, 1626, Peter Minuit, director general succeeding Verhulst, arrived. Six months later, in crafty but honest Dutch fashion, he purchased the island of Manhattan for sixty guilders worth of goods, thought by historians to be the twenty-four-dollar land deal we have all heard ballyhooed from early childhood. Land, coveted in our real-property-oriented society, bore a very different value to the Indians. They by no means felt cheated: both parties to the agreement probably considered the transaction fair and honorable. The Indians, with a very different concept of ownership, received goods in return for what they conceived to be a sharing of abundant lands—not surprising on the edge of a vast and sparsely populated continent three times the size of Europe.

Indians, of course, derive their name from the lands sought by the early explorers. So convinced were these sailors that they had found the outer islands of Asia (Columbus believed it to his dying day), that they dubbed them Indians, for India and the Indies. The English, more aptly, soon called them red Indians, to differentiate them from Oriental natives. The Indians of Manhattan Island were a friendly and peaceful lot, who cooperated until they were confronted with the greed of the colonists.

The trials of exploration across vast reaches of unknown ocean were events coequal with man's landing on the moon or his robotic exploration of other planets. The psychic situation was, of course, far more fantastic. In respect to the moon, technology had provided hard information on exactly what was there, physically, and on the rigors of the temperature, light, geology, and texture of the place. Known, too, was the absence of life of almost any variety, underlined by returned samples of the moon's surface that proved that "almost" could be eliminated as well.

In 1492 those who were serious in matters of geog-

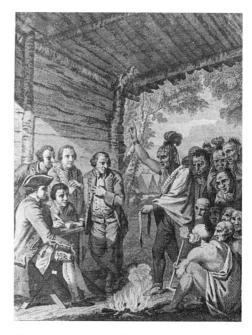

Native Americans Consorting with Europeans. The "noble savages" received the Europeans as strange animals, and sometimes as gods, enduring them as a pestilence of corruption and transmitted disease. They were never consulted with altruism but to assuage their fears with goods, as Dutch and English adventurers consumed their lands.

raphy, astronomy, and navigation knew well that the world was a sphere, but they did not know how big it was or where the various known territories were located on its surface. Columbus believed it of a smaller diameter than reality proved, a fact that contributed heavily to his belief that what he had discovered (the Bahamas, Haiti, Santo Domingo, central and northern South America) was, in fact, the outer islands of the main Japanese archipelago.

But it is perhaps more interesting to speculate on the fantasies and feelings of the first navigators: what they felt they would find, and what kinds of peoples; what they felt of the unknown and its dangers. The Italian, Portuguese, Spanish, Dutch, and English sailors, who found the integrity of the globe and mapped its surface, sailed firmly believing only one concept: that to find the Indies would make them rich. They found, instead, a totally different set of cultures, from Inca to Iroquois, whose habits and life-styles were unknown and unique. Contemporary science fiction gropes for weird and unknown creatures inhabiting strange and remote planets in other solar systems, serving other stars. But the hard reality of living Indians, very much human, physically not dissimilar to the explorers themselves, is far more difficult than a potential relationship with a one-eyed, seven-armed green Martian. In the same way that man finds solace in pet dogs and cats, he finds conflict in relating to his own near-kind. He caters to a horse with whom there is minimal emotional one-to-one relationship, while he divorces his wife and does battle with his neighbor. If Martians had been found by Columbus on San Salvador, they would have been the stars of Europe's zoos, rather than the combative enemies into which explorers and settlers later converted the Indians.

The New Netherlands was, of course, a much vaster spread than that inhabited and used by the inhabitants of New Amsterdam. Its reaches and marches were set by the two rivers and by the penetration into the landmass that the great Hudson (North) River allowed. Fort Orange (Albany) was settled a year before the West India Company set ashore its first settlers on Manhattan Island. Dutch explorers had, between 1614 and 1618, traveled west along the Mohawk River, skirting the headwaters of the Delaware (South) River, and had traveled down the Susquehanna to embrace their claimed New Netherland limits.

The restored Charles II, fresh with power after the English Civil War, and incidental to his wars with France, granted all of New Netherland (plus Long Island, Martha's Vineyard, Nantucket, and Maine) to his brother, James, Duke of York, whose agent, Colonel Richard Nicolls, ordered the capture of New Amsterdam by threat, if not by shot. "On the 26th of August [1664] there arrived in the Bay of the North River, near Staten Island, four great men-of-war, or frigates, well-manned with sailors and soldiers." (So writes the Reverend Samuel Drisius.) "They were provided with a patent or commission from the King of Great Britain to demand and take possession of this province, in the name of His Majesty. . . . The frigates came up under full sail on the 4th of September with guns trained to one side. They had orders, and intended, if any resistance was shown to them, to give a full broadside on this open place, then take it by assault, and make it a scene of pillage and bloodshed." The prudent and outgunned Dutch agreed to surrender rather than perish, and on September 9, 1664, the English moved in. New Amsterdam came to be New York and, in theory, James's personal fiefdom. Happily, James honored the properties in place, including most of the great manors established by the Dutch: Van Cortlandt, Roosevelt, Rensselaer, and others.

The first governor of the Province of New York was the duke's conquering agent, Colonel Nicolls; and in 1665 the first mayor was Thomas Willett, whose city was extended by fiat to include all of Manhattan Island, although its urban parts still barely passed Wall Street. Nicolls ruled a secure and easily accessible trading town, at the dawn of America's commercial era, a town gloriously—and fortuitously—situated to exploit the resources of a yet unopened continent.

New Netherlands. The "Fortified Toehold" has left its mark as the street system of lower Manhattan's physical presence up until this very day. Here mid-nineteenth century New York has replaced the 2½-story shallow houses of the Dutch with 5-story, deep commercial structures fronting the same blocks.

3.

The Fortified Toehold

For I. N. Phelps Stokes, New York's most exhaustive historian: "There is, perhaps, no other city in the world, having equal claims to antiquity, that can boast such a record of its early years of existence." The technology of record keeping was superb and much in line with the spirit of the newly blossoming Renaissance, as if the first moon astronauts had brought back an equivalent map of the moon from their voyage of discovery.

That portion of Manhattan's southern tip that is embroidered with the imprint of Dutch settlement remains today physically arranged precisely as it was created three hundred fifty years ago. The waterfronted surrounds, however, from Wall Street at the East River to its modern extension at the Hudson, have been filled in by successive nineteenth-century commercial ventures. All Dutch structures have been obliterated, but the space between—the streets, ways, alleys, and bowling greens—remain as memory of a city built for a different use a long time ago. The Dutch naturally built their New Amsterdam in the image of the old, imparting an architecture that may still be seen

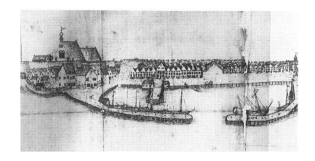

Fort Amsterdam, the "Prototype View," ca. 1650. The fort, governor's house, garrison, and church dominate the young town of 100 houses in this earliest known view of lower Manhattan's skyline.

in Holland and, more appropriately, in Curaçao, that Caribbean colony settled by the Spanish in 1527, captured by the Dutch in 1634, and rebuilt as an architectural contemporary of New Amsterdam. The Curaçao town of Willemstad presents facades of stepped Dutch gables to the street and water, as those of New Amsterdam presented themselves to the Heere Gracht (canal) that penetrated the city in the midst of what is now Broad Street.

The idea of a watered city is drawn from a variety of sources. The most renowned models are Venice, Amsterdam, and places and colonies under their influence. Holland, of course, is a low-lying alluvial country, barely above sea level in most of its parts, and frequently below. Looking back to the earlier large towns of Holland, one sees, in the richly drawn city plans by Johannes Blaeu (his atlas of 1648 in particular), that water serves simultaneously to create routes of commerce and defensive moats for the whole town. New Amsterdam, however, had but one canal, with a short branch at midpoint (Canal Street was *not* the route of another). It was necessarily in scale with the village it served. A population of a few hundred families formed here a tiny colonial outpost, a commercial trading station. It served as a place where up-country fur trappers could barter for goods from the homeland. It was from here that ships brought the pelts to Holland, and to here that they returned with supplies that could not be grown, caught, or constructed in the New World.

The best description of early New Amsterdam is that of the Castello Plan, named, oddly, not for its artist or content but for its repository: the Villa Castello, near Florence. It is apparently a copy of a plan by one Jacques Cortelyou depicting a bird's-eye view of the town in the summer of 1660, with every structure clearly delineated, including three hundred houses. The Castello Plan, combined with a list of buildings prepared by Nicasius de Sille, a local recorder otherwise unremembered, conjoins to present, in more detail than recorded for most of history's early outposts, the occupancy of every building.

Heere Gracht, or Gentlemen's Canal. The canal lived but briefly, until 1676, when its width together with the service ways to each side created the aptly named Broad Street.

On the site of the present Custom House was the fort that de Sille described as Castle Amsterdam, a four-bastioned Renaissance-walled compound that sheltered the church, the governor's house, the barracks, the prison, and the officers' quarters. The wall of Wall Street presented seven bastions to the north in an array of pointed tree trunks, or palisade, and continued down the Hudson River frontage to a point just short of the battery in front of the fort, a line of gunnery that stood at that shore. At the East River frontage, a water gate exited from the town around a bastion projecting into the river, a "half-moon" shaped projection in contemporary descriptions. And a city gate allowed formal entry from the north, at the head of Broadway.

Major monuments of the time include Peter Stuyvesant's great stone house, which later served as the English governor's mansion, renamed Whitehall by Governor General Thomas Dongan, and the source-name of the still extant street that serves it (J-1). The Dutch city hall, or Stadt Huys, faced the water across the island-edging Pearl Street (O-8 and O-9). The landing place before it, Coenties Slip, is remembered today by a street of that same name, connecting Pearl and Water streets. Oloff van Cortlandt's brewery stood on Stone Street (D-10); the Gasthuys, or hospital (E-23 and E-24), ran between Bridge and Stone streets "for sick soldiers and negroes"; the company garden (meaning the Dutch West India Company) was where the formal garden of a Jan Verbrugge, now part of the Trinity Churchyard, lay, beyond the wall (10).

In a world of developers' suburban clusters, we find streets named for trivial, sentimental, or mistakenly arty reasons: where culture is self-conscious, it is no longer culture but the contrivance of those who simulate, rather than inhabit, any true cultural experience. So streets are named Barbara or Petunia or Harvard, after one's spouse or child or alma mater, whose cachet might rub off on the local resident. New Amsterdam/New York streets were named out of the *experience* of the place, and the organic

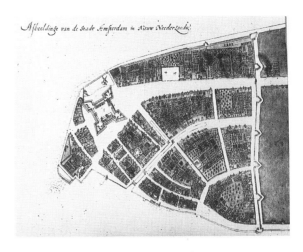

The Castello Plan. New Amsterdam recorded in 1660, four years before it became New York. This meticulous town plan located precisely every manmade modification of the island's tip: each house, public building, fort, wall, wharf, and even gallows. The sobriquet Castello refers to the museum in which it is curated, the Villa Castello, near Florence.

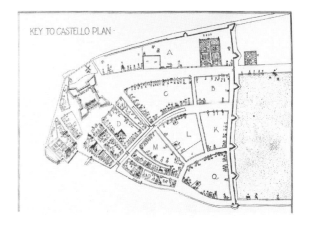

The Castello Plan "Redraft." Here the rather murky forms of the original Castello document are redrafted for clarity. Numbers and letters are referred to in adjacent text, locating significant landmarks.

Broad Street, 1797. Here Federal Hall, the Capitol from March 1789 to August 1790, now the City Hall, still dominates the street. An old Dutch house, a survivor from 1656, and several newer Federal-style ones form the street's flanks.

development of its functioning parts: the Castello Plan did not name them, but they have been surprinted on the "redraft."

The Heere Gracht (Gentlemen's Canal) most specifically described the waterway from the East River to the third bridge at Beaver Street. Beyond it was the Princes Gracht, and the branch following the future Beaver Street, the Bevers Gracht. The canal, when filled, in 1676, after the English occupation, became Broad Street, broad because of its functional history as a canal with service roads on both sides, allowing width that would not have been planned for a street or road alone. The first bridge was at, not surprisingly, Bridge Street, which was the first crossing from Pearl Street to the east. Pearl Street was the shore of New Amsterdam, a street paved with the oyster shells—mother-of-pearl, rather than pearls proper—that proliferated along those shores. The bridges allowed only barge traffic to penetrate to the commercial center of the colonial town, with goods from bulkier vessels unloaded in the harbor. The second bridge (first to be built, in 1633), at Stone Street, led to the first paved street in New Amsterdam, here with cobbles, hence Stone Street.

Broadway, again defining its own character with its own name, was, at various times, known by the same name in Dutch (De Breede Wegh) and also as De Heere Wegh (the Gentlemen's Way), the Public Wagon Road, the Common Highway, and the Great Public Road, but Broadway seems to best encapsulate its role. And, of course, Wall Street was named for its important defensive wall.

Small row houses, cheek by jowl, were a thin frame around great blocks that harbored gardens (mostly vegetable) and some orchards, but with a sprinkling of tulips and other flowers—a patchwork quilt of vegetation. Each house was a microcosm of multiple uses, often with a shop or workplace on the ground floor, dwelling space on the second, and a warehouse in the attic. The last was functionally served by the gable-fronted street facade, allowing goods, heavy or light, to be hoisted to an access door by means of an outrigged beam, an extension of the heavy-timbered and trussed-roof structure.

Streets were largely unpaved (save such as Stone), the territory of pigs and mud, perhaps inevitable in Amsterdam's country cousin, and travel was largely on foot with beaver-booted leggings above sabots, or wooden shoes. Life for the colonist was not considered hard in a society where even the king's palace at Versailles lacked central heating and plumbing; where the facade of dress, ornament, coiffure, perfume, and powder masked a body that was unbathed and unwarmed; where the smell of bodies and chamber pots was only masked by the artificially scented air, and where the smell of overripe and aged food and meat was covered by the intense flavorings of spices that had been the whole motivation for "discovering" New Amsterdam at all.

Richard Blome, an English traveler, wrote in 1672 of what was still a Dutch town: "Here is one very considerable Town, first built by the Dutch and called New-Amsterdam, which name is now changed to New-York: It is well seated both for Trade, Security, and Pleasure, in a small Isle called Mahatan [sic], regarding the Sea, made so by Hudsons-River, which severeth it from Long-Island [Blome's mistake: it is the East River's tidal flow that severs Manhattan from Long Island], which said River is very commodious for Shipping, and is about two Leagues broad. The Town is large, containing about five hundred well-built Houses; . . . For the further security of this Town, here is raised a Fort called James-Fort, which is very strong, and well Defended and Maintained with Men, and Ammunition. The town is Inhabited by the English, and Dutch, and hath a considerable Trade with the Indians, for the skins of Elks, Deer, Bears, &c. Also for those of Bever, Otter, and other Furrs; and doth likewise enjoy a good Trade with the English."

Broad Street, 1937. Nothing remains of Dutch or English history save the street's width and path. The oldest building extant is the Federal Hall National Memorial, originally the 1842 Custom House and later the Sub-treasury Building, which now, as a museum, remembers the site of Washington's inauguration in 1789.

St. Paul's Chapel of Trinity Parish, Broadway, Vesey, Church, and Fulton streets, 1766. St. Martin-in-the-Fields, London, by James Gibbs, inspired its architect to bring this piece of English style to Broadway. It is the only extant pre-Revolutionary building within the limits of eighteenth-century New York City proper.

4.

An Imported Culture

Where the doughty Dutch burghers imported their workmanlike architecture and organic sense of planning of both streets and waterways, the English, at first under the patronage of James, Duke of York, brought style. Early English architecture has been obliterated as cleanly as has been that of the Dutch, but the row housing of New York, still remaining in major areas of Manhattan and Brooklyn, is based, aside from stylistic detail, on the scale and rhythm of London of the late seventeenth and early eighteenth centuries. In such celebrated London neighborhoods as Covent Garden and Bloomsbury—both the estates of the dukes of Bedford—dense and stylish row housing was constructed from the middle of the seventeenth century up to almost modern times. No single house or building of any sort remains in the pre-Revolutionary precincts of Manhattan save the 1766 St. Pauls' Chapel of Trinity Parish. Even its parent, Trinity Church proper, was built long after, in 1846, and was the third successive building on that site. The first (1698) was burned in the great fire of

Schermerhorn Row, Fulton Street, Lower Manhattan. Chic boutiques of the South Street Seaport restoration are now housed in the rough-and-tumble dens of seamen's pleasures and shipyard needs. Chandlers were housed here, and the vast pitched roofs sheltered rope walks, where rope was woven to nautical standards. English Georgian was the parent style of these Federal buildings, later opened up to visual trade with granite lintels and wide glass storefronts.

1776; the second was demolished in favor of further grandeur in 1839.

To taste the flavor of early New York, one must look at later buildings and groups, the most prominent of which is Schermerhorn Row, on Fulton Street, now part of the South Street seaport complex in lower Manhattan, near the Brooklyn Bridge. An investment property of Peter Schermerhorn, the row was built on land filled by Schermerhorn at the river's Water Street edge on underwater lots, producing space for warehouses and countinghouses. The inevitable building style of the time was late Georgian, "Americanized," and hence a form of early Federal architecture, the first native American style. The buildings as they now exist have shop areas remodeled in later times. Original facades at the ground floor had arched entryways and a large, double-hung, many-paned window to light the interior. Granite lintels, later introduced, allowed the opening of a glassy Greek Revival storefront (which exists in today's restorations) for the practical display of commercial wares. But above the ground floor the buildings are much as they were in 1812, steep-pitched roofs, slated and many-chimneyed, that gave the silhouette of early New York a rich picturesqueness, a kind of small-scale serration in counterpoint to the many-steepled churches in the skyline.

James Birket, an English traveler of 1750, remarked: "Neither their Streets nor houses are at all Regular Some being 4 or 5 Story high & Others not above two, Not any of the Modern houses are built with the Gable End to the Street as was formerly the fashion amongst all the old Dutch Settlers, but are many of 'em Spacious Genteel Houses Some are built of hewn stone Others of English & Also of the Small white Hollands Brick, which looks neat but not grand, their houses are Generally neat within and well Furnished. Notwithstanding there Still remains too many of the Old Dutch houses which prevents its Appearing to Advantage, The Streets (as above) are very Irregular & Crooked & many of 'em much too Narrow they are Generally pretty well paved which adds much to the decency & Clean-ness of the place & the Advantage of Carriage."

James Boardman, a resident of Liverpool and self-styled "citizen of the world," remarked in 1829: "The main street, called Broadway, is two miles and a half long, in a straight line, and proportionably wide, with broad flagged trottoirs or side-walks, some parts of which are shaded by poplars and other lofty trees; but in the quarter devoted to business, canvass blinds are stretched from the shops to permanent wooden rails of a convenient height and neatly finished. The architecture of the buildings, however, does not at all correspond with the magnificent scale of the street, the greatest irregularity prevailing; handsome edifices of brick, and even marble, of four and five stories, being side by side with those of two and three, and in some parts actually intermixed with miserable wooden cottages."

The qualities of London precincts such as Bloomsbury appeared in much more than architecture *per se:* the town planning of early New York owed much to the system of street and square that Bloomsbury had refined to an elegant level. Gramercy Park of 1831 and Stuyvesant Square of 1837 bring English romantic landscape into the formal grid as elegant commons, foregrounds to the surrounding town houses, much as Bedford, Russell, and Tavistock squares do to the former town houses of Bloomsbury.

Federal townhouses still survive in lower Manhattan. A particular example, at the grand scale, is the former James Watson house, now the Shrine of St. Elizabeth Seton on State Street facing Battery Park; at a smaller but elegant scale is the Seabury Tredwell House on East 4th Street, an almost perfect example of Federal architecture on the exterior, although the interior is later. Federal houses were commonly of two or three stories, with basement and attic, the former for kitchen and service rooms, the latter for servants and/or children's quarters. Roofs were pitched to shed water, for the technology of roofing (fortunately) did not at that time permit the flat or invisibly sloped roofs that blossomed in Greek Revival and later times. The rosy

Stuyvesant Square, 15th to 17th streets, Manhattan, 1837. Bisected by Second Avenue, this pair of cast-iron fenced gardens served its neighbors in the manner of Bloomsbury squares. The sometimes manicured gardens were of the scale of Gramercy Park, Union Square, and Madison Square in this counterpart of London's streets and open space. Central Park would later supplement them as a vast common garden for most of Manhattan.

Seabury Tredwell House, 29 East 4th Street, 1832. A perfect example from early nineteenth-century New York, preserved and lovingly restored. These blocks abounded in mostly similar houses until commerce and industry moved in, leaving number 29 an orphan in a visually and aurally cacophonous neighborhood.

brick facade, with shuttered, multipaned windows, surmounts a marble stoop, with elaborate wrought-iron railings, great basketed newel posts at the sidewalk. Ionic columns flank the door, which is crowned with a delicate transom or fanlight. To each side is a narrow, slotlike window that allows surveillance of those who knock. At the spring of the pitched roof is a wooden cornice, originally carved from a single log, that completes a classical vocabulary for this rich building.

Londoners live in a city that is both dense and sprawling, a collection of urban villages packed together in the container of London County. The City of London is only the original walled medieval enclave, now largely the center of commerce and banking. Greater London, called a city, is actually a county composed of many separate municipalities: Westminster, Hampstead, et alia. Its horizontality (up to the post–World War II high-rise commercial and housing construction) is punctuated by public buildings from St. Paul's to the houses of Parliament, the many spires of Christopher Wren's fifty-one churches, and the hundred more built by the Parliaments of Queen Anne and George III. A city of street and square, graced with many parks, it was and still is a human-scaled place of urban delight.

Commerce bred London's character through the need to cluster dwellings close to business and each other, in a world of foot and carriage transportation, of simple transit. It grew as a bourgeois city, in large part financed and created as the home and habitation of the modest businessman. All these qualities were, in effect, the model for the best of what became English New York and, to a large extent, American New York. Unfortunately, one major element of London's evolution was missing: planned development of entire sectors for profit, but with an enlightened attitude. Virtue bred profit, and profit virtue, where the size of the London precinct in question, and the financial stability of the developer, made long-term investment attractive. The result was a gain for private and public sectors jointly, not the "get in and get out" speculation of the wheeler-dealer.

The most prominent developers of the urbane London we know today were the dukes of Bedford, whose great estates at Bloomsbury and Covent Garden became models for the happy marriage of finance and intelligent urbanization. Bedford's Covent Garden no longer remains, now usurped by the opera house, then filled with the vegetable market, both later activities added to the urban landscape. But Bloomsbury is like a carpet of rich weave, of rectilinear geometry, of dark, light, and gray tones, of somber, stolid earth colors; rich greens cool and transparent; hard and dark and shining. A carpet, unlike a rug, spans wall to wall, its pattern within itself. A rug is an island afloat in a sea of flooring or, in our borrowed urban sense, the town surrounded by nature's countryside. Bloomsbury's carpet is one of a series overlapping one another at slightly canted geometries, their several patterns joined at seams serving jointly their separate traffic. The carpet, within its own weave, has a life and world of its own; but with its neighbors and the joining tributaries, it forms a larger creature—in this instance, a city.

In New York, for "Bloomsbury" read "Brooklyn," for this very metaphor describes the development of Brooklyn as a city, later than New York and long after the English had lost their colony but at a time when London still served as the conscious reservoir and encyclopedia of architecture and urban design. The tapestry of Brooklyn conjoins a warp and woof that is incomparable in modern history; and no other place has assimilated so many people with such grace in housing of style as in the row-housed areas of 1814–1898.

London lasted more for its role as a model exporting scale and urban design than for its stylistic detail. Yes, the English brought style to their new New York, and, in concert, they brought *a* style, the Georgian that blossomed into America's own Federal. But that stylish urbanism was sequentially infilled in a whole sequence of succeeding

Wall Street, 1850. By 1850 Greek Revival temples of banking and other substantial commerce had replaced everything on this street, which was crowned by Richard Upjohn's Trinity Church of 1846. Today only the Custom House (with flag), now the Federal Hall National Memorial, and Trinity remain.

Maison Carrée, Nîmes, France. This Roman temple, oddly called the Square House, served as Thomas Jefferson's inspiration for a whole train of neo–Greco-Roman architecture. Jefferson's leadership encouraged many to follow this bolder Roman and Greek Revival approach; and majestic Doric, Ionic, and Corinthian columns soon appeared where only delicate Federal colonnettes had ventured.

styles: Greek Revival, Gothic Revival, Renaissance Revival (sometimes termed Anglo-Italian), Romanesque Revival, Queen Anne, Shingle, Classic Revival, Beaux Arts—all within the nineteenth century.

William Chambers observed in 1854: "At the first look, we see that New York very much resembles the most densely-built parts of London. The houses, tall and principally of brick, are crowded into narrow streets, such as are seen in the neighbourhood of Cheapside, with the single difference, that many of the buildings are occupied in floors by different branches of business, with a profusion of large sign-boards in front. . . .

"Advancing northwards . . . the elegance and regularity of the houses become more conspicuous, and at last we find ourselves in the quietude and splendour of a Belgravia. Here the edifices are entirely of brown sandstone, and of a richly decorated style of street architecture; all the windows are of plate-glass; and the door-handles, plates, and bell-pulls silvered, so as to impart a chaste and light effect."

Frances Trollope remarked in 1831 that New York "seemed, perhaps, more beautiful, more splendid, and more refined, than it might have done, had we arrived directly from London; but making every allowance for this, I must still declare that I think New York one of the finest cities I ever saw, and as much superior to every other in the Union, (Philadelphia not excepted), as London to Liverpool, or Paris to Rouen. . . . Situated on an island, which I think it will one day cover, it rises, like Venice, from the sea, and like that fairest of cities in the days of her glory, receives into its lap tribute of all the riches of the earth."

After the Federal style, American architects and builders (sometimes calling themselves merely carpenters) furthered their own development in parallel with that of Europe. The first all-American effort was in the Greek Revival. Thomas Jefferson had nurtured a great interest in Roman works and, with the help of the French academician, Charles-Louis Clérisseau, had translated the Roman temple called the Maison Carrée at Nîmes (old Gaul) into the Virginia State Capitol at Richmond (much inflated in size and purpose). More elegantly, he had used Rome's Pantheon as the core of his own wondrous mansion at Monticello in Virginia. But he also cared for things Greek— in his instance, more for the democratic ideals involved than the buildings proper. It remained for the Greek revolution of 1821, which severed Greece from the Ottoman Empire, to focus a great intensity of democratic emotionalism on the buildings of Greece, and particularly those of the fifth century B.C., the age of the great statesman Pericles: the Parthenon and Erectheum of Athens' Acropolis, the Theseum overlooking its Agora. These supplied the models for innumerable churches, courthouses, and banks (interchangeable in a society where one of the ethics of Protestantism was the work ethic). For New York, more than the lovely monumental buildings they provided, the orders of Greek architecture, mainly the Doric and Ionic, became the triumphal arches that framed town house doors. Greek Revival town (and country) houses were the major infill of early Brooklyn Heights and most of Greenwich Village, for development of those places had come at the moment when this style was blossoming.

The Greek Revival town house was born in the 1830's, when water supply and sewage were becoming a reality, and its plan, therefore, grew with knowledge of bathrooms as integral elements. The water closet's inclusion in the Greek Revival envelope added a technological base to that already stylish architecture. Simultaneously, a great demand for new houses, especially those with indoor plumbing, came from the urban upper middle class generated by the Industrial Revolution. Dozens of city blocks were so infilled. Greek Revival monuments were simultaneously spread over the nation, but in Athens itself the revival came with the revival of the monarchy. In 1832, the new king of Greece, Otto I, brought with him from Bavaria German architects who fulfilled the Anglo-Saxon Greek Revival at its very nexus. And in Athens the Greek Revival

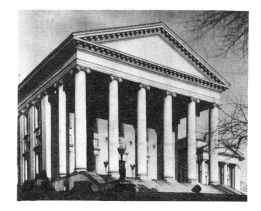

State Capitol, Richmond, Virginia. Virginia's Capitol is the Maison Carrée inflated and perforated with windows for the offices within, in a manner the Romans never dreamed of. Such classical grandeur came to New York in the temple facades of dozens of Greek Revival churches and in its Custom House, now the Federal Hall National Memorial.

Washington Square North. These Greek Revival town houses of the 1830's upped the size and scale of Federal architecture. A full top floor and almost flat roof replaced dormers or a steeply pitched roof. The stoop was higher, the basement more windowed; but the visual statement again was at the portal. Grand temple-scale classical columns embraced a bolder entrance door.

was no different: an application of decorative Doric and Ionic elements to the facades of buildings that could only have served the nineteenth century: multiroomed town houses for the middle-class family and its servants. Unhappily, Athens has been for most of its past hundred years uninterested in preserving any of its nineteenth-century past: classical Greece was so dominant that nothing else seemed to matter. Few of the great Greek Revival mansions remain; perhaps the most impressive survivors are the Benaki museum and some embassies.

The Greek Revival town house can be savored in Brooklyn Heights and Greenwich Village, Boston's Beacon Hill, Philadelphia's Society Hill, and in parts of Savannah, Nashville, and New Orleans. Evolving at the same time as the bathroom, this precocious style became America's classic urbane residence. Its plan and form continued as the template for the Gothic and Renaissance Revival styles, which made their contribution largely in the way space was decorated—with cornice, profile, and portal— rather than in the way it was shaped or used.

Styles changed in the first half of the nineteenth century in an almost whimsical way. Egypt developed the pyramid over a thousand years, and temples over another two thousand; Greece grew from the temple-megaron to the Parthenon in five hundred years; the Renaissance blossomed from Brunelleschi to Bernini in two hundred fifty years. Relentlessly, the time and rhythm of change became compressed: the nineteenth century moved from Federal to Greek Revival to Gothic Revival to Renaissance Revival in thirty years.

But style was a new element in a new nation. To think of style was to separate oneself from the hoi polloi: style became fashion, and fashion's version was to have style by being *stylish*. Once the need for stylishness became dominant, the roots of eclecticism were planted: architecture did not become the product of serious designers taking the vocabulary of the times and, with bold imagination, creating new rhythms, modified form, and enriched space, as in the vigorous architecture of the Florentine Renaissance. Rather, designers drew from the past as a vast encyclopedia of parts, concerned more with the latest fashion than with substantial questions, concerned more with applied decorative parts than with whole form and space.

Style was also imported through the education of Americans abroad, largely at the Ecole des Beaux-Arts in Paris. Richard Morris Hunt, architect of two of New York's greatest monuments (the central pavilion of the Metropolitan Museum of Art and the base to Bartholdi's Statue of Liberty) studied at the Ecole in the Atelier Lefuel and, with his studio master, designed part of the north facade of the Louvre facing the rue de Rivoli. The architecture of the Metropolitan harks back to Rome's Baths of Caracalla and Diocletian—but interpreted by the academic rules developing at the Ecole.

Eclecticism spread the elements of architectural history across the nation, but nowhere more vigorously than in New York. The work of talented architects Ithiel Town and Alexander Jackson Davis ranged from Gothic country houses to Greek temples of business; from Grecian Protestant churches to Italianate villas. Their Lyndhurst, a neo-Gothic minicastle (1838, remodeled and extended 1864), was later renowned as railroad magnate Jay Gould's country house at Tarrytown. The Federal Hall National Memorial at Wall Street was originally built as the Custom House (1842) in the style of Athens' Parthenon; and the Edwin Litchfield mansion (1857), now surrounded by Brooklyn's Prospect Park, is an Italianate villa, as if set on the hills of Fiesole overlooking Florence.

Using the town house in its evolving styles, developers created neighborhoods of character. Greenwich Village, Brooklyn Heights, Chelsea, Hamilton Heights, Bedford-Stuyvesant, and Crown Heights are, in large measure, the products of nineteenth-century speculation: in land, for the most part in Brooklyn Heights; in buildings for sale at Chelsea's old (now gone) London Terrace or in many Greenwich Village blockfronts.

Gothic Revival House, 36 Pierrepont Street, Brooklyn. The pointed arches here are emblematic of Gothic Revival on a house the workings of which are unrelated to its fancy dress. The style decorated the entrance, window, and fence as the latest dress, hat, and shoes adorned the wearer.

Samuel Ruggles, one of New York's first remembered real estate speculators, wisely took a look at the Bloomsbury experience and in 1831 arranged lots for sale surrounding a common park, to be owned and enjoyed by the houses that faced it. Gramercy Park is still a private, elegant, and exclusive green forecourt to property that now includes apartment buildings, two grand mansions (now clubs), and a Quaker meetinghouse now converted to a synagogue. The style and use of architecture can indeed change within a continuing and delightful urban-design context.

But in Brooklyn, still a village, the owners had sagely subdivided their lands almost as soon as the new Fulton Ferry went into service in 1814. The most sophisticated of these was Hezekiah Pierrepont, whose surveyors, Thomas Poppleton and Charles Lott, platted his land into approximately three hundred 25-by-100-foot house lots in 1819. The Heights, as a result, became an encyclopedia of nineteenth-century style, developing slowly with a great proportion of independently designed and built houses. Here this spate of stylistic changes was effected within an urban system more important than its separate parts, producing great variety within discipline—in contrast, for instance, to the regimentation of Haussmann's 1860's Paris.

Federal Hall National Memorial, Town and Davis, 1842. Built as the Custom House, this Athenian temple serves well the memory of Thomas Jefferson's classical revival. It now is a museum remembering the national Capitol, Federal Hall, on this site, and the history that surrounded that era.

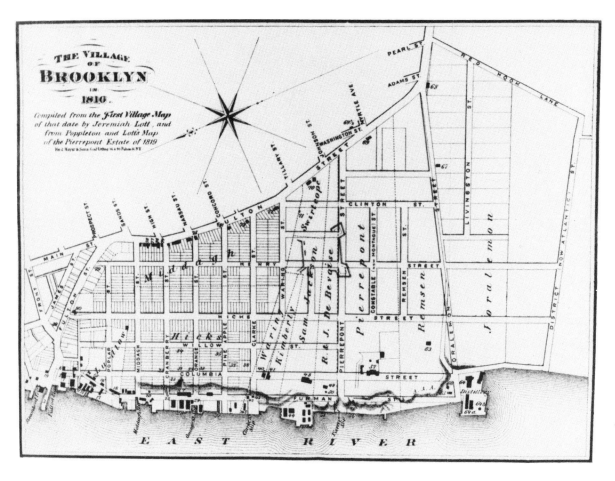

Brooklyn Heights Subdivisions, 1818. Land development and speculation has always been a particularly American enterprise, whether in quarter-square-mile homesteads offered free to those who would develop the West, or in the lure of rising lot prices. America has been cutting a patchwork of land continuingly, and here in the Heights the ferry made land a developer's gold mine.

High Bridge, the Croton Aqueduct. These proud arches carried the waters across the Harlem River in 1848, six years after they reached City Hall through pipes laid on the river's bed. The bridge-aqueduct was, therefore, a symbol more than a necessary route. Its multiple arches formed a river gate that emphasized the powerful topography of both northern Manhattan and the west Bronx. Jasper Cropsey painting.

5.

Pipes and Drains

The campus of the City College sits on the crest of Hamilton Heights, near a point where the great Croton Aqueduct was introduced into Manhattan in 1842. But for the massed buildings blocking its view, it would overlook New York's largest and most modern sewage-disposal plant, a million-square-foot behemoth (North River Water Pollution Control Plant) permanently moored on piles over the Hudson between 135th and 145th streets. On the college's south boundary, across from the North Academic Center, at 135th Street and Convent Avenue, stands the 135th Street gatehouse of the Croton (river, reservoir, and aqueduct) system, that point at which the aqueduct proper was separated into cast-iron pipes to lace through the island to the south. The gatehouse began operations in 1890, during the expansion and upgrading of the Croton system.

By default the college, since its relocation to Hamilton Heights in 1907, has been inextricably involved, mostly as neighbor but sometimes as participant, in the infrastructure of transportation, water supply, and sewage effluents that makes modern New York possible. This is apparent not only in its interlocking lands with the facilities of the Croton system, and the construction in its neighborhood of a vast modern sewage disposal facility, but also in its neo-Gothic quadrangle, built of Manhattan schist excavated from the cut for the Broadway–Seventh Avenue IRT route opened in 1904.

Water is civilizing, a balm, a place for sun and sport, essential matter for life of animal and vegetable, a route for ships, a cloud, precious stuff. Water's role is assumed, a given fact of urban life, taken for granted except during the occasional crises when reservoirs are reduced to mud flats. Water is, with bread, the staff of life, and sometimes its enemy and destroyer. Although water is plentiful worldwide and endlessly recycled, more often than not it is in the wrong place for both urban and rural needs. Water comes in pipes and leaves in drains.

The Nile Valley held a civilization watered by water, soiled by water, with water the natural highway that provided the route of trade, and the boating of stone to move and make the temples, tombs, pyramids, and obelisks. Los Angeles would be a modest city, not a great one, but for the watersheds of the Sierra Nevada—and, much more important—but for the pipes, ducts, and reservoirs that transport the waters of mountain streams to the desert shore.

Water's great engineers were both users and modifiers, using the annual inundation of the spring Nile for irrigation, fertilization, and construction; and elsewhere leading the water (aqueducting) from mountain sources to new cities, or to old ones that outgrew local supplies. The Romans and the Persians first engineered aqueducts in places as disparate as Syria, Turkey, France, and downtown Rome itself. The Romans also sent the used effluents to sea (at Rome) through the Cloaca Maxima—what comes in must go out—the Tiber River became a sewer's helper and the aqueduct a soaring separated water supply.

Pont du Gard, Nîmes, France. Scarcely a bridge in the normal usage, the Pont du Gard is a Roman aqueduct spanning the River Gard on its way to water all Gauls. Roman structural and sanitary engineering allowed concentrations of population never before possible.

* * *

In the beginning, primitive dug wells served New Amsterdam's growing population, which, at the time of the English "conquest" in 1664, had swelled to 1,500. For drinking and minor washing, buckets were sufficient to serve the household needs of those relatively unwashed times. When the density of people was modest, waste and sewage were poured into the ground—through slops in the earthen streets, the waste going into gardens, sewage into privies. For seeming aeons, such simple ecology served well but could not support density. Waters were polluted, and typhoid and other diseases of the intestine were common first, rampant later. It was clear by 1790, when the city of 33,000 breached the level where multiple wells could serve as local and personal water supplies, that a central water system was needed.

In early New Amsterdam the virgin Collect Pond welled forth its clear issue from deep springs fissuring the surrounding bedrock. Its overflow ran north and west, and meandered down to the Hudson River. This placid pond (filled in 1817) sat, overlapping modern Centre and Worth streets, a squishy bottom for the courthouses and jails that now border that great traffic maze at Foley Square. Buckets and carts drew from the pond's waters for the early New Amsterdamer. But the surge of population, and the less than sanitary habits of its citizenry, caused its early poor taste and, later, true pollution. Dug and even drilled wells suffered sometimes from similar local pollutions but, more seriously, from the seeping saline water from adjacent tides in the Hudson and East rivers. Water that did not tend to be virulent perhaps just tasted bad.

One of the more fetid wells was that at Trinity Church, aside its graveyard. There the underground pool tapped from the street above was filled by rainwater strained through the bodies of buried citizens, a grisly thought in retrospect, an unknown, or perhaps ignored, fact at that time. No one complained.

The most famous early well was from a spring at Park

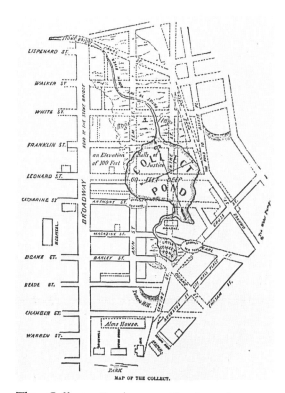

The Collect, Freshwater Pond and Springs. The original freshwater source of New Amsterdam and New York, its overflow meandered into the East River until disciplined into the canal of Canal Street. It has vanished from the surface world, its springs piped away to storm sewers so that the Criminal Courts may rest in place.

Row between Baxter and Mulberry streets. Termed the Tea Water Pump (read "spring" for "pump"), its waters were both sold in surrounding "gardens" straight and made into the tea of its name. But, more important, barrels of this clear and tasty liquid were peddled all over town in a somewhat aggressive fashion by toughs who carted it door to door at what would seem to a moralist an outrageous profit, if you can rise to the notion that a price of a cent a gallon could contain any profit at all. Tea Water became suspect, and then increasingly putrid, after the middle of the century, due to the same groundwater contamination that did in the Collect. This sorry and haphazard state of affairs showed remarkable insensitivity to the dominant role of pure water in a safe and growing urbanization. Public sources, in the sense of prolific wells with pure water, were cared for with almost religious fervor in more ancient societies, such as India, Persia, and Babylon.

New York's first central, if not public, water supply was that proposed by Christopher Colles, an entrepreneur who in 1774 embarked on a waterworks near the Collect Pond that had its own, unpolluted, spring-fed sources. Colles is also credited by some with conceiving the idea for the Erie Canal. A reservoir was started on high ground to harbor two and a half million gallons, an amount meaningful only in a place that had never had a reservoir. In today's water affluence, New York's "droughts" have meant merely less water affluence, not water poverty: 150 gallons per person per day is the normal consumption, for a total of a billion and a half gallons a day citywide. Colles' scheme included piping of hollowed pine logs joined together, a plan that was never consummated; the Revolution intervened, and New York remained under British rule until the Treaty of Paris in 1783. At that time, the city was in shambles, not only because of wear and tear, and deprivation in the war years, but also because of the great fire of 1776. Almost 500 houses and the Trinity Church of its time burned to the ground, a horrifying and recurring holocaust in the combustible cities of the time.

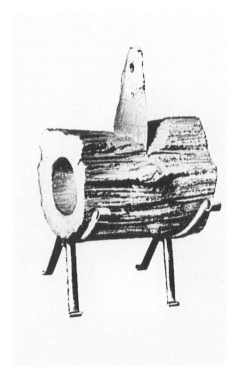

Pipes from Hollowed Logs, early nineteenth century. Christopher Colles, the city's first entrepreneur of water, planned to use hollowed logs as aqueducts. Burr's Manhattan Company followed this plan, tarring them, however, for tightness and longevity.

But the water for drinking, for bathing, and for fire fighting came to New York not because of public pressure, not because of patrimony, paternalism, or philanthropy, but as a product of Aaron Burr's successful venture to create a competing bank to Alexander Hamilton's Bank of New York (chartered 1784). With Machiavellian finesse, he stage-managed a bill in the state legislature that, today, we would term a red herring, a dreadful boondoggle that would have created a public water system. Burr arranged for his own minions to lead the opposition. And when the weary legislators were at their weariest, he substituted a bill (1799) to protect the public purse by authorizing a private water supply company, the Manhattan Company, which, incidentally, was empowered by this very bill to conduct business as a bank. The Bank of the Manhattan Company still lives as a component of the Chase Manhattan Bank, a seemingly eternal remnant of Burr's political and financial maneuvers.

Manhattan Company Reservoir, Chambers Street between Broadway and Centre Street, Manhattan. Aaron Burr's water company set the style for the later 42nd Street Croton Reservoir with its Egyptian-style battered walls.

The Manhattan Company created the first true water supply system of New York, with a reservoir at Chambers Street's north side opposite the present New York County ("Tweed") Courthouse. This was festooned with a Greek Doric portico crowned with a bronze statue of Aquarius. Water was piped (the birth of "pipes and drains") through hollowed tree trunks, as Colles had envisaged, that were coated with tar inside and out. The service was limited both by the size of this still small town and by the wonts of Burr and Company to keep the water business minimal, allowing the corporate structure of the Manhattan Company to fulfill his real purposes.

At its maximum, the Manhattan Company served fewer than two thousand houses through twenty-five miles of piping. Drawn from the original wells dug by Colles near the Collect, the water was impure and bad tasting, if not downright polluted. This was water for the well-to-do, who were badly served by a company that cared only to maintain the fiction of public water service while protecting its banking operations, a fact burned into history when the company continued to maintain its half-empty reservoir and a minimal amount of piping long after the Croton water had entered and served the whole city.

The pollution of groundwater through its seepage into the Manhattan system, and into the strata from which most other wells drew, undoubtedly abetted the several epidemics that ravaged Burr-watered New York: yellow fever in 1819 and 1822, cholera in 1832 and 1834.

Plentiful water within a realistic distance of the city was available from the Croton River in Westchester County, north of New York, and in 1835 the city held a referendum to approve a master plan exploiting that source. Dams to create a reservoir from that river were meant to (and did) serve a great underground, masonry-roofed aqueduct that tilted, straight as the proverbial arrow, downward from its high ground in Westchester to the city thirty miles south. At first, pipes were laid across the Harlem River in its deep valley to connect the northern aqueduct to that of Manhattan. In an effort to maintain the navigability of the river, the ultimate plan connected the broken arrow with High Bridge, six years later, becoming Manhattan's first physical connection with the mainland. It was an aqueduct in the Roman sense, worthy of Pope Sixtus V's Acqua Felice of 1588 or those wondrous ruins from Libya to France, left by the Roman Empire's urban engineers, as at the Pont du Gard near Nîmes. It was important to have a symbol worthy of the Croton system's power and merit, and that first symbol was High Bridge. The first receiving reservoir, in Yorkville, is little remembered and is now only a transit point on the water's route to the city. But the Croton (or Murray Hill) distributing reservoir at 42nd Street, on the site of the present New York Public Library, was built not only in the Egyptian style but also on a scale worthy of Egypt. Little Dendur, modern Egypt's gift to the United States for its financial aid in raising the rock-cut temple of Ramses at Abu Simbel, and now set in its glassy envelope on the Metropolitan Museum's northern flank, gives no hint of Middle Kingdom Egyptian monumentality, which

The Murray Hill, or Croton, Reservoir, 1842. Karnak on Fifth Avenue, this neo-Egyptian reservoir for the new Croton system gave a monumental sense of power to Croton's image. Perambulists sauntered at its top, viewing Manhattan's building boom. Egypt, the land of eternal aridity watered by the fecund Nile, brought that strangely contrasting metaphor unconsciously to New York.

one can confront at the pylons of Karnak and could savor vicariously at 42nd Street.

High Bridge and the Murray Hill Reservoir were the great monuments of the Croton system, but later gate-houses, which monitored and modulated the aqueduct's flow, were significant minor and local monuments. Among these, the most prominent is that at the edge of City College's Hamilton Heights campus. A product of the expanded aqueduct system of the 1890's, it served as the terminus of the aqueduct proper. Receiving tunneled water from the north, it divided and spread it through a network of cast-iron pipes to various way stations to the south. Little brothers, built the same year as that terminal gatehouse (1890), served as end-guard houses to a revived short stretch of masonry aqueduct along Amsterdam Avenue between 113th and 119th streets, the oldest manmade structures extant in the neighborhood, save for the Hamilton Grange, Alexander Hamilton's country house, on Convent Avenue north of 141st Street.

Diarist and citizen George Templeton Strong wrote on August 1, 1842, "There's nothing new in town, except the Croton Water which is all full of tadpoles and animalculae, and which moreover flows through an aqueduct which I hear was used as a necessary by all the Hibernian vagabonds who worked upon it. I shall drink no Croton for some time to come. Post has drunk some of it and is in dreadful apprehensions of breeding bullfrogs inwardly."

The Croton Water celebration of July 5, 1842, followed the arrival of water into the 42nd Street reservoir on the fourth, flowing from there to great fountains at both Union Square and City Hall Park. The jets produced were reminiscent in spirit, if not in form, of the fountains of Rome, not so much the baroque and romantic Trevi as those of workaday places that more simply honored the water system, as did the Acqua Felice.

Two months later Strong wrote: "Took a walk uptown. Looked into Union Square. I find the fountain there is to be, as well as one can judge from its present appearance, just like that in the [City Hall] Park, viz., a circular basin with a squirt in the middle, and nothing more. A squirt of three or four inches in diameter and rising fifty or sixty feet will be a pretty thing, but we ought to have one or two fountains, at least, like those we commonly see in pictures, where the water is carried up nearly to its greatest height in a pipe, and then falls from two or three basins successively." Strong's wishes were fulfilled only with the erection of the Pulitzer Fountain at the Grand Army Plaza in 1910.

The water passed over High Bridge proper in 1848 and then, in an expanded aqueduct, passed through extended pipery on the bridge in 1890 (the year of completion of the various gatehouses). In 1923, the Italo-Roman aqueduct design of multiple arches on tall piers was drastically modified by the still present cast- and wrought-iron span that removed multiple piers to open the waterway below to the new Harlem River ship canal of 1893. The remnant bridge is still an elegant monument to the water system that made possible the expansion of New York from a city of 300,000 in 1830 to a city of 3,500,000 after the turn of the century. No longer used for water's course, High Bridge is equally shut to pedestrian traffic —the only other traffic it was ever intended to bear— because of its isolation in a less-than-secure part of the city.

During construction of Central Park, a vast new receiving reservoir was built as part of the plan: a romantic, free-form lake that replaced the two bulky stone structures originally placed there by the Croton commissioners. The Croton system could not keep pace with the fantastic growth of the city and, in particular, with its consolidation in 1898 with the City of Brooklyn (the western Bronx had been added in 1874, the eastern Bronx in 1895, Queens and Staten Island in 1898). Brooklyn, close behind in population to New York (then Manhattan only), together with the new Queens Borough (assembled from a collection of

Queens County villages and towns), almost doubled the city's population at one stroke.

Water collection, first from dug wells, then from drilled wells to deep aquifers, was extended by the Croton water system into the watershed of the Croton River, lands comprising several thousand acres and situated a safe forty miles from the polluting density of the city. Ninety miles to the northwest lay the Catskill Mountains and a network of ebullient streams. In a stroke of great planning foresight, the city bought vast areas of these forested hills and the watershedding rights to many more; dammed streams into multiple reservoirs; and, incidentally, created one of the great symbiotic environmental acts in urban-service history. The collection of rain over unsullied mountains and hills, drained to the reservoirs and sent to the city, provides to this day a great safe breeding ground for the natural flora and fauna of the region. The Catskill system incorporated rock-hewn tunnels (later lined with concrete), twelve to fifteen feet in diameter, that meandered up and down to remain within integral rock strata, that dove a thousand feet under the Hudson, and then wandered beneath the city at depths of 200 to 750 feet below the surface. Catskill Tunnel 1, starting from the city's Hill View Reservoir in Yonkers, penetrated and served Manhattan and continued to Brooklyn, opening in 1917; Catskill Tunnel 2, branching from the same reservoir in 1936, crossed the Bronx, ducked under Long Island Sound, passed under Queens, and ended in Brooklyn, with a later, annexed tunnel under the Narrows to Staten Island in 1965. Tunnel 3 will, when finished, act as a source to supplement both previous tunnels, but its principal function will be to permit the other two to be shut down for repairs. Without the visual architectural magnificence of a High Bridge or a Murray Hill Reservoir, all three aqueducts serve, or will serve, their required functions magnificently, with hidden power fueled by lakes some 280 feet above sea level (the lowest Catskill surface). This magnificent effort has been compared to that

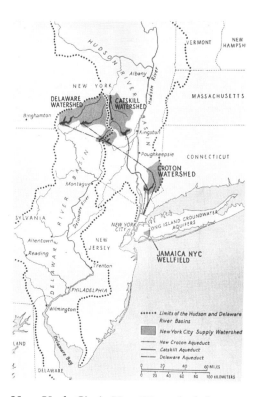

New York City's Vast Watershed System. Water from the Croton River was supplemented first by the Catskill system, then by that of the Delaware River watershed. It is comparable in scale to watering Paris partially from Chartres and partially from the Swiss Alps.

of the construction of the Pyramids at Gizeh and the Panama Canal, but it must remain, in a kind of X-ray symbolism and memory, one of the city's great invisible engineering monuments.

The availability of water, of course, taxed people's imaginations as to how to use it, or conversely, it made possible a level of civilized habit and behavior impossible previously. In a parallel to the paradox of post–World War II highway construction, the more highways one built, the more traffic was on all of them; the more water that was available, the more was "needed" per capita in domestic use. And, of course, industries that relied on fresh water could situate at its convenient source, the same locale where the density of population could provide low cost, or specially skilled, labor for that industry's work force.

The most popular bonus made possible by the new Croton water was the bathroom, whose advent was coincidental with the Greek Revival town houses of New York and Brooklyn and was therefore intertwined with that style in the planning of space and room. Abetted by the new Croton water, bathrooms with tubs, basins, and the new water closet became as important a social badge in the 1840's as might be a Hamptons beach house or a Mercedes-Benz sports car in the late twentieth century.

Talbot Hamlin, in *Greek Revival Architecture in America*, states that "New York's shortage of water up to the time of the completion of the Croton aqueduct undoubtedly had much to do with this (i.e., 'in the common use of water closets and plumbing generally New York was more backward than Philadelphia'). Privies at the rear of the back yard, often connected with the house by attractive wooden colonnades or trellises or porches, were standard even in large and expensive New York houses until the 1840's."

Prior to the Croton's coming, water for washing and other household uses was collected through leaders from the roof, which emptied into underground backyard cisterns. Unfortunately, the nearly contiguous privy per-

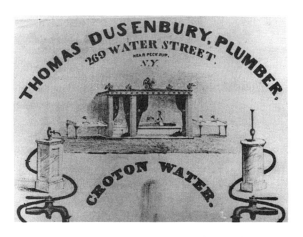

A Croton Bathroom, 1845. The first needs for bathing and plumbing had necessarily to fit into existing architecture. A hall bedroom could be converted with these prefabricated Greek Revival assemblies.

meated the ground, sullying these private reservoirs. Drinking water was bought from itinerant vendors whose tank carts delivered door to door from such venerable sources as the old Tea Water Pump. Baths of the tub variety were portable metal containers and were not placed in rooms of their own but were tucked into convenient nooks from which they might be drawn out by servants and laboriously filled. Washing was of the pitcher-and-basin variety, and the slops of both basin and tub were dumped into the street. Fortunately, the streets were not paved like a membrane as they are now, so there could be percolation into the permeable soil directly through the earth bed or between the closely packed cobbles or granite paving blocks. After the arrival of Croton water the cisterns became redundant, and in many instances roles were reversed, as cisterns became cesspools, the place where sewage might be disposed. With Croton water, therefore, the scary proximity of influent and effluent was, for a time, solved, as the pollution of groundwater became unrelated to the quality of the freshwater supply. To imagine the difference in the quality of urban life, before and after Croton, is difficult in our own times, which assume bathrooms to be a minimal part of our urban culture. But on a cold and snowy night, say, in January 1820, the trip down three flights of stairs from an attic bedroom to a backyard privy must have taken the glamour out of urban life, however elegant one's chamber pot.

Drains, the way out of the liquid waste of urban life, were dealt with more simply, casually, and much later in history than the pipery that brought the water in. Simplistically, soil and waste pipes were collected into sewers that conducted them to the river and surrounding tidal waters. Untreated, raw matter that had little impact at first with the small pre–Civil War population of New York flowed into the deep, fast-moving waters of the Hudson or the swiftly moving tides of the East River. Sewage treatment, both in the cosmetic and medical sense, was a late-blooming event, easier to postpone in this deeply watered city

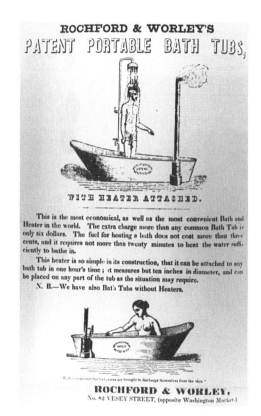

The Architecture of the Bathroom. The design of bathroom fixtures was a challenge to Vitruvius' ideal of "Commodity, Firmness, and Delight." The newly termed cast iron was ideal for the plastic shapes and structural needs of a bathtub.

and harbor than in a dense, landlocked place. Even today, and until the North River Pollution Control Plant is fully operational, the sewage of all of Manhattan's west side, from Greenwich Village to the northern tip at Spuyten Duyvil, is dumped raw into the Hudson. Moreover, as New York's sewers are "combined," meaning that storm water collected from the streets and paved areas passed through the same pipes and ducts, heavy rains cause sewage to flow into the river and bays, as vast liquid quantities cannot be handled through treatment plants.

The hardware of bathing became, after Croton's magic flow penetrated the city, as fascinating as electronic equipment became in the late twentieth century. Taps from which water flowed at a whim, and toilets that flushed, brought to their owners a power that can be little appreciated in a world that assumes these realities as obvious. When does the hardware of civilization become merely a substitute for true urbanity? "Civilized" life came to mean—overwhelmingly in the minds of some and subtly in the minds of all—the brick and paraphernalia of the urbanized environment, rather than the sophisticated business and intellectual interchange of civilized people.

New York's water remains the best of any major city, blended from the wholly owned, and partially shared (with Westchester County), Croton and Catskill systems and the shared Delaware River watershed, which also feeds part of New Jersey and Philadelphia. The chemically laced waters of Philadelphia are drawn from the Delaware downstream from New York's tap and upstream from Philadelphia. That river's flow is partly a function of how much New York draws from the common watershed. But the Croton cocktail is not, to some, ill named, for it merits some honorific title more lofty than water, a name that implies only an obvious, scanty necessity or a taken-for-granted essential. Bread and water, the prisoner's classic fare, might seem the very essence of life to some, where the absence of either half of that staff-set-of-life causes life's end.

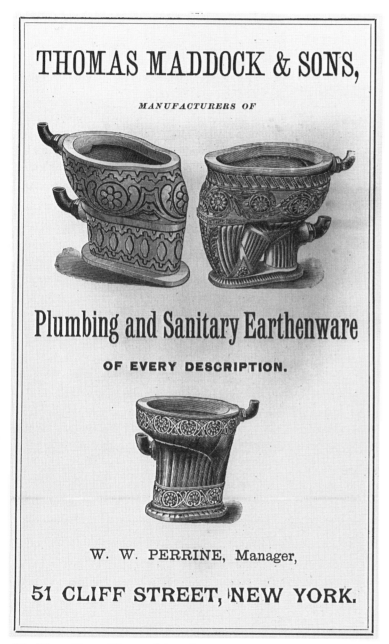

The Water Closet. Water and the Industrial Revolution brought plumbing into the heart of architecture. Toilets were not only privy to the creation of a water*closet* and bath*room*, but became objects adorned, and mass-produced.

Columbus, or Ninth Avenue, Elevated. Seemingly vanishing in its great straight length, these early tracks bore steam engines aloft on the city's first engine-powered transit line. This was the next transit landmark after Fulton's 1814 steam ferry to Brooklyn.

6.

Movement

Preautomobile American cities—Boston, New York, Chicago, Philadelphia, and San Francisco—like the admired capitals of Europe, originated as dense pedestrian enclaves and grew out from such early urbanity on armatures of public transit. Bearing commuters to and from these downtowns were horsecars, trains both elevated and at grade, ferries, and ultimately subways, all hopefully rapid, but often just plodding movers of quantity. The only thing moving rapidly in Rome of the 1660's, the time of New Amsterdam's conversion to New York, was the water in its glorious aqueducts, ancient engineering updated by Pope Sixtus V's architects and engineers. Rome, astonishingly, with a walled area of less than 1/25 of modern New York City, contained over a million people in A.D. 200, whose densely packed lives were afforded one special grace—that of easy movement on foot from dwelling to work or civic place; while the speedy waters slaked their thirst and washed their bodies. New Amsterdam's citizens were equally compacted, and early New Yorkers were, up to the mid-nineteenth century, densely settled on the southern quarter of

Manhattan (with, in 1840, 300,000 on six square miles of land south of 40th Street). It all began with boats.

The boats were ferries by oar or sail and—the ultimate fulfillment of ferries—by steam, Fulton's engineering that revolutionized movement in and out of the city. South Ferry, a present subway stop at the end of the island, was the pier to which one walked from business in order to sail or row to what would eventually be Brooklyn. The Fulton Ferry, doubly memorialized by its connection of Fulton Street in New York to Fulton Street in Brooklyn, plied the quickest, shortest route, almost identical to that later taken by its great technological successor, the Brooklyn Bridge. The bridge allowed great pedestrian masses and simple wheeled vehicles to cross the tidal East River "on dry foot." Ferries were, therefore, the colonizers of outland New York; and when their access became speedy, powered by steam, they allowed Brooklyn, Queens, and Staten Island to be reached as quickly as the developed areas of lower Manhattan. Greenwich Village, for example, was an hour's walk or an hour's ride on the indomitable omnibuses, those creaking wooden vehicles that brought commuters home as if in a Conestoga or Studebaker wagon.

Ferries might well have taken a half-hour to cross the East River and were subject to the whims of wind, storm, and tide, but Fulton's steamboat, the *Nassau*, made it across in twelve minutes, with the assurance of a true schedule and reliable landfall. Commuting was born.

Movement with some speed and reliability created the suburb in its original sense, the lesser or annexed urban place, sub-urban to the *urbs* of Manhattan. This fast and relatively precise transit movement was abetted by Hezekiah Pierrepont, a brewer and inherited landholder who backed Fulton's franchise and company, being assured that his great tracts at and south of present Pierrepont Street would command high prices from New York merchants who decried the city's noise and commonness as a place to live. Pierrepont's land was subdivided into an offset grid,

The Fulton Ferry Docking at Brooklyn. The ferry in 1840 had matured to these flat planes atop more typically shaped hulls. Note the horse and wagon, exemplifying the equal use of ferries for people as well as potatoes.

more interesting than that of Manhattan, as it served in many cases to close vistas in an urbane fashion and to limit the possibility of traffic speeding through on many streets, most appreciated now in retrospect in a world of swirling cars. His surveyor, an Englishman, Thomas Poppleton, of Poppleton and Lott, drew 25-by-100-foot lots in blocks 200 by 400 feet, lining 60-foot-wide steets. The streets actually seemed wider as the houses are, for the most part, set back ten feet more on each side.

Diarist George Templeton Strong wrote in 1865: "The situations on the Heights [of Brooklyn] overlooking the bay can hardly be matched in any great city of Christendom. How often have I wished I could exchange this house for one of them, and that I could see from my library windows that noble prospect and that wide open expanse of sky, and the going down of the sun every evening!"

Transit, whether by ferry, omnibus, horsecar, or train, was operated by private investors, whose only concern was that of providing sufficiently satisfactory service that their operations would produce a profit. Obviously, Fulton's steamboats were a bonanza for both the ferries' investors and the land speculators of Long Island. Like contemporary taxis, the omnibuses were more competitive, but with large groups rather than with two or three fares. The builders of the elevated systems were authorized to construct trestles over routes of public land by the rapid transit commissioners, but they owned both the structures and equipment and operated them. Subways were built with city funds, but equipment and operation were in private hands. This sequence of free enterprise allowed New York to develop by the interplay of transit and land speculation, without any master plan save the street system—an evolution that a fervent capitalist might term organic and democratic. Planners such as Haussmann in Paris would shudder.

Ferries, at their apogee, crossed the East, Hudson, and Harlem rivers, traversed the Upper and Lower har-

Horse Cars, 1831–1917. Travel on tracks was smooth and reliably fast, while omnibuses bumped slowly and noisily over cobblestones. Whether cars were horse-, cable-, steam-, or electric-powered, tracks were the true technological breakthrough. The fastest run in the West for a while was on the railroad worker's handcar.

bors, and even penetrated Long Island Sound in a snaky movement to the villages consisting of what was eventually to become the Borough of Queens. Because ferries to most places other than Brooklyn Heights had much longer travel times, they produced little commuting population movement and relied largely on long-term excursioning and the transport of freight and produce.

If the Fulton Ferry created Brooklyn Heights, and thence downtown Brooklyn's core, then the New York and Harlem Railroad opened up northern Manhattan to others. Before the Harlem, northward movement was limited by the perception of time thought reasonable for travel by foot, carriage, omnibus, or horsecars (by 1832, as far as 14th Street for commutation from the business center). Haarlem, the original rural village, a namesake of its Dutch homeland city, was almost eight miles north of Wall Street, an hour and a quarter ride by private carriage and unreachable within reason by the doughty omnibus. At the very beginning of the nineteenth century, Alexander Hamilton traveled to the Grange, his country house, by carriage, a time-consuming journey that made it as remote from his office as the drive from Madison Avenue to an East Hampton beach house. The scale of urban life, and the scale of the macrocosm that made and make the urban-suburban-rural relationships now and then, are, of course, a function of travel time. The mind boggles at the scale-jump that has allowed the whole Boston–Washington megalopolitan axis to infill its length, creating a single linear urbanization. Air travel had become a local transit by the 1970's, sending the middle class thousands of miles distant for summer, and even weekend, rest or recreation or research, to the cities of Europe, or the ski slopes of the Andes, or the islands of the Caribbean.

From 1832 the New York and Harlem Railroad was horse-drawn in its southern segment from Chambers Street near present City Hall north to 26th Street. From there, starting in 1837, steam-powered trains rode tracks up Fourth Avenue (now Park Avenue and Park Avenue South) to

Haarlem. This steam line, the "Northern Pacific of New York" in effect, opened the north island for more suburban colonization, bringing passengers to and from way stations at Yorkville and Haarlem at a speed that made the idea of commutation plausible. Similarly, in the 1870's the Northern Pacific proper would open the northwest of America to settlement, just as Fulton's ferry had previously created such possibilities by water for Brooklyn. The urge to develop (and frequently that merely means sell) land is often the impetus for suburban transit development, where the landowners back and finance the transit to multiply their property values (as Pierrepont did with Fulton's ferry). This dynamic is in contrast to the transcontinental routes, where traffic was fostered for rail revenues by attractions at route ends and along the way. Hence came railroad entrepreneurs with eager support of national parks such as Yellowstone, the Grand Canyon, Banff in Canada, and eager invention of resorts, such as Sun Valley, which Averell Harriman thought to induce people to travel to on his family's Southern Pacific Railroad. The New York and Harlem, however, was at first interested primarily in freight, bringing produce *from* its own markets at 27th Street to the more rocky, forested northern portions of Manhattan and, later, to Westchester. The road was supported, however, by those who sought to "develop" northern Manhattan, and, particularly, Harlem, by selling plots, and/or building on them within the empty 1811 planned grid. Such combined motives, however, helped populate not only Harlem but also the growing towns of the Bronx.

At the very beginning, in 1831, a horse-drawn ride to Yorkville took a half hour and cost 12½¢, equal to eight dollars today, a sum that would not encourage commuting by any but the wealthy. By 1837 stream-drawn trains made the trip both quick and economical for the ordinary country-seeker and well-to-do commuter.

The terminals of this infant railroad system migrated northward as the city's grid was slowly infilled. The first major congregation, that of the New York and New Haven

Harlem Temporary Railroad Trestle, 1874. On the way to Grand Central, Vanderbilt's railroads joined in this line down Fourth (now Park) Avenue. Work underway in 1874 was depressing the line, bridging the cross streets over it. This timber viaduct is now supplanted by a stone wall worthy of a medieval fortification.

system with that of the New York and Harlem, was between 26th and 27th streets, across from the northeast corner of Madison Square Park. This site is now occupied by the New York Life Insurance Company's gilt-pyramided tower. From there the trains traveled northward by surface, and through a cut later covered to become a tunnel, between 33rd and 40th streets. When the Grand Central Terminal was created by Commodore Vanderbilt (grandly termed Commodore because of his onetime ferryboat empire) in 1871, the route south of 42nd Street was ceded to streetcars, first horse-drawn and then electric, as the 26th Street station had equally been served from 1837 to 1871.

Grand Central, not surprisingly, was both grand and central. Vanderbilt's control (1876) of all three major New York–based railroads (the New Haven, the Harlem, and the Hudson lines) gave opportunity for their joint terminal to become a whole greater than the sum of what might have been only parts. Exiled in 1854 by the city to its then northern edge, the new terminal implanted itself so firmly in the structure of street and buildings that it is still rooted there, as if from a time before living memory. A service started at Chambers Street, which had then housed its steam trains at 26th Street, was now firmly stationed at 42nd, straddling the Fourth Avenue right-of-way first given by the city only to the Harlem line. Northward from the terminal, toward northern Manhattan and Westchester, the route still ran on grade, ducking into a tunnel through Lenox Hill (59th to 76th streets) after 1875 and finally totally submerged in a cut to 96th Street in 1884. This remains today, now covered with the park of Park Avenue, that gracious fringe benefit of electrification of the trains.

The local traffic was carried within the short confines of the old city by cable cars. These were later converted to an electric drive by the introduction of a power source in the cable's route. Stephen Crane describes them most eloquently in "In the Broadway Cars" of 1896: "The cable cars come down Broadway as the waters come down at

Train Shed, Grand Central, 1871. Cast and wrought iron and glass sheltered the steam trains that arrived down Fourth Avenue—later to become the covered Park Avenue we know today. Paris and London still enjoy similar train sheds, and Penn Station offered an even more elegant crystalline place of arrival until 1966.

Lodore. Years ago Father Knickerbocker had convulsions when it was proposed to lay impious rails on his sacred thoroughfare. At the present day the cars, by force of column and numbers, almost dominate the great street, and the eye of even an old New Yorker is held by these long yellow monsters which prowl intently up and down, up and down, in a mystic search.

"In the grey of the morning they come out of the uptown, bearing janitors, porters, all that class which carries the keys to set alive the great downtown. Later, they shower clerks. Later still, they shower more clerks. . . . Ten o'clock comes, and the Broadway cars, as well as elevated cars, horse cars, and ferryboats innumerable, heave sighs of relief. They have filled lower New York with a vast army of men who will chase to and fro and amuse themselves until almost nightfall.

". . . On past the Post Office the car goes, . . . until Battery Park appears at the foot of the slope, and as the car goes sedately around the curve the burnished shield of the bay shines through the trees.

"It is a great ride, full of exciting actions. Those inexperienced persons who have been merely chased by Indians know little of the dramatic quality which life may hold for them. These jungles of men and vehicles, these cañons of streets, these lofty mountains of iron and cut stone—a ride through them affords plenty of excitement. . . .

". . . From the forward end you hear the gripman uttering shrill whoops and running over citizens. Suddenly the car comes to a curve. Making a swift running start, it turns three hand-springs, throws a cart wheel for luck, bounds into the air, hurls six passengers over the nearest building, and comes down a-straddle of the truck. That is the way in which we turn curves in New York.

"Late at night . . . the cars themselves depart in the way of the citizen, and for the few hours before dawn a new sound comes into the still thoroughfare—the cable whirring in its channel underground."

Grand Central Terminal. The conning tower of a vast subterranean world of double-decker tracks and sprawling yards under the buildings flanking Park Avenue north to 59th Street.

The traditional surface railroads received an airy set of neighbors, the elevated railroads, or the El, as it was colloquially known, in the early 1870's. Charles Harvey's experimental single track up Greenwich Street, an elevated cable car powered by a stationary steam engine, was the touchstone of the Ninth Avenue El, and it was expanded slowly northward through the West 70's and 80's, and then rebuilt and electrified after 1900. Joined to the Sixth Avenue El by a spur at 53rd Street, the pair provided truly rapid transit, in comparison with any other form of movement up the West Side. The New York and Harlem, east of Central Park, was scaled for limited stops, for its mission as it grew into maturity was longer-range: to connect the city with distant and suburban places in Westchester and Connecticut by way of its sister road, the New Haven. The Harlem and the New Haven now jointly served to spread a carpet of freestanding houses over the lands to the north and east of the city, a carpet with a state of mind and a state of wealth that drew on the city's economic life but stood at arm's length in relation to its urban structure.

The El became the Els, and the Ninth and Sixth soon were joined by lines atop Second and Third avenues, connecting the island on four parallel routes in its southern half and three in the northern half, with arteries fast-moving and many-stopped. The Els largely served, as had the Harlem road initially, the land speculators, who now seriously filled the great Manhattan grid laid out by the commissioners in 1811. Such development moved across the island, save for the area that had become a postcommissioners excision, Central Park, a vast new garden of English Renaissance landscaping that happily had been consummated before the urban explosion swept about its flanks, creating the East and West sides. Each side of the park developed with its own identity, and each was served by its own Els.

The East Side and parts of the West Side were filled with brownstones and brickfronts on the common streets, with private palaces on the grand streets far from the Els.

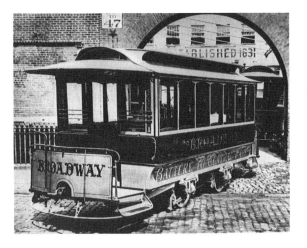

The Broadway Cars, 1889. Cable slots in the street allowed central, steam-powered engines to draw cable cars, in which brakemen gripped and ungripped their connection to the whirring cables below. San Francisco's still exist; but New York's, later electrified through the same cable slot and called merely trolleys, have now vanished.

Along the El routes themselves sprouted tenements, the walk-up apartment buildings of the middle to late nineteenth century that housed vast immigrant populations: the Irish of the 1850's, the Sicilians of the 1870's, the eastern European Jews of the 1890's. Mostly described pejoratively, these mid-Manhattan multiple dwellings were dank and unhappy only with the careless use and overcrowding that could destroy any social envelope, whether tenement, Federal town house, or Fifth Avenue apartment. The El streets proper were shadowed in the steel grillage and wood ties of these aerie railroads, and were also filled with the noise and dirt of the grinding, clanking trains that spouted steam and ash. Here were the real sites of economy housing: ten to twenty families in a 25-by-100-foot building served by the El, which made the location of these sites desirable and economically possible. The side-street tenements were classier locations and truly the residence of the American petite bourgeoisie. The rich were not loath to ride the Els; they simply did not wish to live near them.

The first Els preceded the subways by some thirty-five years, and they were abhorred by their neighbors because of their noxious presence, although with electrification (1885–1903) the soot and steam diminished. But electrification made possible something never reasonable before, underground rail travel, which caused vast changes in the city decades before the Els proper were demolished. Electrification brought not only the subways but also the depression of Vanderbilt's railroad to Grand Central into a cut along its Fourth Avenue route, a cut that was covered when electric-powered trains no longer needed to be open to the sky. Park Avenue had got its park.

The glory and grandeur of Park Avenue is that it was conceived, designed, and largely built in a short period of time (1913–1930), with architectural ideas that were strong and consistent without being flamboyant. The restructuring of Fourth Avenue, and its incarnation as Park, occurred when the "American Renaissance," as classical historian

Charles Harvey's Experimental Elevated, 1867. A single photograph left of an epic event, the first movement of a prototypical cable-drawn elevated. The top hat is appropriate: elevated travel had a certain elegance when it was born.

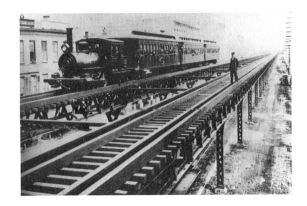

Third Avenue El, 1880. The elevated train of its time, no different than the Union Pacific on a bridge or trestle. Electrification would soon quiet these monsters and erase the smoke and soot, but true peace and light came only after the trains went underground in 1904.

Henry Hope Reed, Jr., so aptly put it, was at its zenith. The influence of the Parisian Ecole des Beaux-Arts on the training of American architects rose to such a peak in the 1870's and 1880's that the Chicago World's Fair of 1893 (also known as the World's Columbian Exposition, in honor of the four hundredth anniversary of his second voyage) brought organized civic grandeur to American cities. At Park Avenue, high-rise Italian palazzi, subdued by English Regency architects and inflated by Americans, lined the broad way, cornice to cornice, with limestone cut and quoined and rusticated, an architecture of grandeur rising within a sober discipline. And here were to move great numbers of the near-rich unable to afford the palazzi of Fifth Avenue, and even some of the rich-rich who were happier in the more secure anonymity of a fifty-room triplex penthouse than in a freestanding Loire Valley château. The movement of trains created it—a railroad's restructured engineering combined with grand social and architectural ideas. What did we do before we had Park Avenue? Little remembered for his vision was the chief engineer, later vice-president of the New York Central, William J. Wilgus, the intellectual father of this urban symbiosis of trackage, terminal, and urban development. Wilgus saw the virtues of electrification as a step far more significant than merely eliminating noise, smoke, and danger: it was the way a central city might fulfill a grand plan. To a great extent, Park Avenue is his memorial.

Els in their earliest guise were often quite grand, with gas lights, mahogany paneling, velvet upholstery, and brass fittings. Today's grimy cattlecars thundering under Lexington Avenue and Broadway are not even comparable. Els served all classes, rich and poor alike, in a time when even the lowliest saloon was equally paneled, padded, and polished. Grand lawyers, from the many-maided private houses near Madison and Fifth, would walk to the Second Avenue El and ride downtown—which at that time meant only the Wall Street area—each morning, but at a much later hour than the common man and woman, a social

Uniformly Scaled Facades along the new Park Avenue, 1913. The streets north of Grand Central are actually elevated over the railroad yards and right-of-way. Here the underworld is revealed before the voids were filled with apartment buildings. All, including "parks," float over railroad space. North of 50th Street the right-of-way becomes a pair of vaulted tunnels flanking the median park strip.

stratification in time. Els later made possible the development of vast sections of the Bronx and Brooklyn, again long before the internal-combustion engine made any mark on mass movement.

As the Fulton Ferry had created downtown bourgeois Brooklyn in concert with land speculation, the Els helped develop upper Manhattan, the Bronx, and further reaches of Brooklyn for the middle class and poor. The Els also incidentally created islands of wealth as they passed by, islands attracted by water's edge and park surrounds, such as the land surrounding Brooklyn's Prospect Park. The Fulton Street El reached eastern Brooklyn in 1889, making possible the creation of Brownsville, an alternate tenemented enclave for the Jews from the Lower East Side immigrant influx. But the Els couldn't span the East River. The Brooklyn Bridge (opened 1883), the first crossing, bore cable cars that connected the El terminus at City Hall Park to terminals in downtown Brooklyn across the river. It was up to the subways to tunnel underground and underwater everywhere, a feat plausible only with the practical application of electric-motor-driven trains, although the London subway system, first in the world, was driven at first by steam-engined trains in 1863.

The Els were electrified first, because they were already in place, bearing conversion from steam to electric power. Proposed subways soon brought great competition, delivering population next door to its desired quarters, rather than blocks away. The subway was not noxious, at least to the street traveler and house resident adjacent, because it could speed inconspicuously under any avenue (as, after 1910, the railroads sped under Park Avenue).

The first subway, the Interborough Rapid Transit Company (IRT), leased its tunnels and track from the city that had built, starting in 1900, the route of the system before its means of operation had even been decided. A $38 million contract was let to John McDonald and August Belmont for construction of the line, anchored by a loop in front of City Hall, passing under Centre Street, Lafayette

The Elevated arrived in the Bronx with monumental brick foundations—invaders marching between these pleasant wood row houses, as if from another planet.

Place (now Lafayette Street), and Fourth Avenue to Grand Central, then turning westward along 42nd Street to Times Square, and proceeding northward along Broadway to 145th Street. Opened in 1904, the line was extended in 1908 to the Brooklyn terminus of the Long Island Railroad at Flatbush and Atlantic avenues, by tunneling under the East River. Now part of the IRT system, the route's Grand Central–Flatbush section is the route of the Lexington Avenue line (4, 5, 6 trains today); the crossover at 42nd Street is now the infamous Times Square shuttle; and the line north from Times Square is part of the Broadway–Seventh Avenue line (1, 2, 3 trains today). The Lexington Line did not become the Lex until it was severed from the 42nd Street shuttle-to-be and extended north from Grand Central to 125th Street in 1918. Traveling up Fourth Avenue to that point, it was forced to offset to Lexington to avoid the station and yards of the terminal and the Central's own route up Park Avenue. Severed also was the West Side line (Broadway/Seventh Avenue), similarly extended to the financial district. Together with the shuttle and Lex, it now forms a great H in plan, rather than the original S.

The IRT's lines penetrated Brooklyn and dominated the Bronx, first under rivers in true subterranean fashion, and then sometimes continued through those boroughs on elevated structures. Nevertheless, they were still called subways, as the Els proper were entirely elevated and the subways became elevated only in the city's less populous outer reaches. In special cases, as at the Manhattan Valley at 125th Street, where the land dropped precipitously and rose again along Broadway's spine, a great bridge, worthy of Gustave Eiffel, was created, causing trains to soar, leap, and burrow again as the route continued to the north.

Brooklyn's BRT (Brooklyn Rapid Transit), later renamed BMT (Brooklyn Manhattan Transit), was nurtured in Brooklyn and later threw its network across the East River up Broadway and Seventh Avenue to 60th Street, then back across the river into Queens. The final subway, the IND (Independent) System of the 1930's and '40's,

Subway Construction, IRT, 1905. "Cut and cover" was the method largely used for New York's subways. The streets then became platforms over what were, in effect, deep ditches. The resulting chaos of traffic could be experienced briefly in the early 1970's during the construction of the ill-fated Second Avenue subway through east Harlem.

created Sixth and Eighth avenue routes to replace the now demolished Sixth and Ninth avenue elevateds. They bear commuters from the furthest ends of Brooklyn (Coney Island) through Manhattan to the end of Queens (Jamaica). The IRT's small-diameter tunnels and small cars keep it physically independent and incompatible with its two brother systems; but the BMT and IND have now been blended, their railroad-sized tracks and rolling stock interchangeable, their separate corporate names vanishing as routes interlock and overlap: A, B, C, D, E, F, G, H, J, K, L, M, N, Q, R, et alia.

As the Els colonized northern Manhattan, the Bronx, and parts of Brooklyn, subways later opened up other great new sectors of the city for development. The outer marches of Brooklyn that sprawled over the plains left by the washout of the last glacier's terminal moraine, such as the aptly named Flatlands, or Canarsie and Coney Island, were all first served by the BMT and later reinforced by the Independent's F, or Sixth Avenue (Avenue of the Americas), line. The Independent's other end reached Jamaica only after World War II, stimulating in-city medium-density suburbia. One great project made more accessible by this line is Fresh Meadows (1949), much honored for its planning mix of high-, medium-, and low-rise housing, unfortunately with dull architecture.

Fulton's ferry made Brooklyn Heights New York's first suburb. Built on developer's blocks laid out in 1819, the houses were those of that era: Federal, then Greek and Gothic Revival, then Renaissance townhouses, all stylistic events of forty years of development. Transportation triggered a unified stylistic and planning event.

The elevated system brought the poor to areas where there might be "affordable housing" in the tenements of the upper and very upper West Sides and in the enclaves in Brooklyn such as Brownsville and East New York. Tenement architecture, founded in the Lower East Side, was thus exported northward and to the southeast.

Transit, in other words, structured the placing and

Henry Hudson Parkway, north of George Washington Bridge. One of the most beautiful sections of any New York City parkway. The driver's view of the Palisades, George Washington Bridge, and surrounding parkland are handsome and dramatic.

style of city sectors throughout New York's history up to the end of World War II. But after that war, the tight and sometimes elegant form of buildings and streets was lacerated by the incursion of auto routes dissecting the city, disjointing its parts, dislocating its residents, and competing for space, time, and scale with the pedestrian city that they confronted. The early "parkways" around New York were mostly routes to the country and suburbs, away from New York; but the East River Drive and Brooklyn–Queens Expressway (BQE) impinged on the nature of the existing city. The former dominates an edge exclusively for cars, with one exception, keeping the pedestrian from the waterfront. The exception is the decked park at Carl Schurz Park that allows a high overview at the water's very edge. The BQE, on the other hand, was at one point turned into a plus, its triple-decked structure providing, in front of Brooklyn Heights, a scenic pedestrian promenade over two levels of one-way traffic. Here the expressway, originally intended to split the Heights down Henry Street, is tamed and becomes a pedestrian asset created to enhance, rather than destroy, the fabric of the neighborhood. But to the south, through Cobble Hill, a poorer and less politically aggressive neighborhood, the BQE is in a cut running down Hicks Street, effectively isolating the harborward portion physically, visually, and socially from its sister streets to the east.

The Cross-Bronx Expressway's heavy destruction of local neighborhoods left a record that caused violent opposition to Robert Moses' plans for a midtown crossway at 30th Street and a lower Manhattan expressway at Broome Street. The latter would have destroyed much of what is now termed SoHo, that handsome cast-iron district of the 1860's and '70's, built as warehousing and in large part taken over by artists—both real and would-be—and the art galleries and restaurants that followed.

Marshall Berman in *All That Is Solid Melts Into Air* (1982) describes the 1950's: "But then, in the spring and fall of 1953, Moses began to loom over my life in a new

Brooklyn Heights Promenade, 1951. The pedestrian lid here is a 3,000-foot-long allée overlooking the harbor, lower Manhattan, and the Brooklyn Bridge. The view, day or night, seems a sort of postcard myth but real, present, and overwhelming.

way: he proclaimed that he was about to ram an immense expressway, unprecedented in scale, expense and difficulty of construction, through our neighborhood's heart [the Bronx].

"For ten years, through the late 1950s and early 1960s, the center of the Bronx was pounded and blasted and smashed. My friends and I would stand on the parapet of the Grand Concourse, where 174th Street had been, and survey the work's progress—the immense steam shovels and bulldozers and timber and steel beams, the hundreds of workers in their variously colored hard hats, the giant cranes reaching far above the Bronx's tallest roofs, the dynamite blasts and tremors, the wild, jagged crags of rock newly torn, the vistas of devastation stretching for miles to the east and west as far as the eye could see—and marvel to see our ordinary nice neighborhood transformed into sublime, spectacular ruins.

"In college, when I discovered Piranesi, I felt instantly at home."

Expressways (even when called parkways or by other euphemisms) are no longer acceptable to urban planners, and the locals have recaptured the streets of the city. In-city expressways, for the most part, do not solve urban traffic problems—they aggravate them. And when this aggravation is coincidental with the destruction of the urban architectural fabric, there is deep trouble. The urban freeways of Los Angeles or Detroit or Denver are creatures of developing suburbanization: they create the suburbs, rather than impinge upon them. The freeways of Boston, New York, San Francisco, New Orleans, Philadelphia, or Chicago are aggressive intruders into a context that finds them alien and destructive.

After World War II, the federal government, in fulfillment of its warriors' wants, guaranteed the mortgage money that made possible suburbia, the voted and polled Nirvana of the lower middle class. And in New York politics, through the ego-interpretation of Robert Moses, self-appointed reshaper of the hated city, parkways were built with public money to allow auto access to such newly financed, freestanding private suburban nests. A bit of the middle class was allowed to flee, therefore, at government expense and instigation, over highways, to Long Island. This package of highways and available low-cost mortgages destroyed the county as a rural resource for the city, paving and housing it with wall-to-wall suburbia. Nassau County originally included what is now Queens as well as the present Nassau; when the city consolidated to include Queens in 1898, Nassau's present boundaries were what was left over. Quantitatively, much of Nassau County is a dreary non-urb, stolen from the city; although qualitatively, it holds many distinguished places and houses, mostly those of the affluent.

Preindustrial cities, whether trading centers, military and political bastions, or religious enclaves, were disciplined in size by the energy and speed of foot travel. Only in the nineteenth century did transit evolve with horse and carriage—the omnibuses of London and New York. The movement of populations over greater distances became possible only with the development of steam power, creating the ferries and trains that opened Brooklyn and the Bronx to an in-city suburbia. The auto suburbias of Nassau, Westchester, and Bergen counties came later. They are a different breed than the suburbs that created most of Queens and Staten Island and much of Brooklyn, for movement to sites as scattered as those of the 1950's through 1980's cannot be accomplished by transit alone, but only by car or by transit and car combined. The auto has, therefore, generated a kind of urban place that is a city only by its density, not by its quality and character. Such is the case when the auto is dominant, as in Los Angeles and Detroit. Happily, the virtues of transit and concentration in a central place, or within multiple urban clusters, have become not only understood but popular. The novelty of the auto has waned, as the attraction of convenient urban life becomes more apparent to a greater segment of the population. The issues of movement thus return to the issues of transit. A renewed, vigorous, and inexpensive transit system must be incarnated, once more with ferries and subways and streetcars, to balance and reinforce the renewal of urban New York.

Chrysler Building, 1930. Seen from the rising steel frame of the Empire State Building. The steelworker was as romantic as the spires he erected. Here the view from a tower still underway to its (now lower) rival expresses the essence of the skyscraper spirit. The stock market collapsed as the towers soared.

7.

Elevators and Iron

On revisiting New York in 1904, Henry James, born near Washington Square and a permanent resident of London, described "the multitudinous sky-scrapers standing up to the view, from the water, like extravagant pins in a cushion already overplanted . . . the new landmarks crushing the old quite as violent children stamp on snails and caterpillars . . . the special sky-scraper that overhangs poor old Trinity to the north [with] a south face as high and wide as the mountain-wall that drops the Alpine avalanche, from time to time, upon the village, and the village spire, at its foot."

The Iron Age brought to Europe a technology of hard metals that could perform functions impossible with lovely but softly plastic bronze. It gave man materials for making tools hard and stiff, useful for cutting, slashing, carving. By 800 B.C., ironmaking, which had blossomed in the lands of the Hittites (present-day Turkey and Syria), swept through Europe to provide material for agricultural implements, axle hubs, swords, pikes, helmets, and halberds, both forged and tempered. But it was not until the Industrial Revolution that iron would be cast. The technology of casting brought to the art and science of building possibilities for both technical and aesthetic feats not practicable before, because the revolution was one of applied quantity, the marshaling of energy that once could make only a knife, now, in concert, could create a whole bridge.

A year before our Declaration of Independence, an extraordinary bridge was constructed in the English iron-making town of Coalbrookdale. The structure became a landmark of cast iron, touchstone for architectural historians of the whole genealogy of iron-building that eventually created great architectural enclaves in New York's SoHo and Tribeca, and it laid the foundation for the later development of the bones of modern towers: steel. The Coalbrookdale Bridge, a prescient event, crossed the Severn River by 1779, designed by architect Thomas Pritchard in 1775 and built by the great early works of Alexander Darby (Reynolds and Darby) between 1777 and 1779. Arthur Young, eighteenth-century English chronicler of the new technology, had written in 1769: "when agriculture, manufacture, and commerce flourish, a nation grows rich and great; and riches cannot abound, without exciting that general industry, and spirit of improvement, which at last leads to performing works, which, in poorer times *would be thought wonders.*"

Iron Bridge, Coalbrookdale, England, 1779. An icon in the history of structural iron and steel, this bridge was one of the ancestors of cast-iron and then of steel buildings. Here technology took a strong hand in further architectural evolution.

Cast iron is both brittle and weak in tension. These factors make it terrific for structural columns that bear a superposed load, but terrible as a material for beams that flex under the floor load they carry and that need, as they flex, tensile strength to fulfill their role. To sustain the beam's function in a marriage with cast-iron columns, wrought iron, pressed between great rollers, spanned from column to column, from wall to wall. Wrought-iron beams were first developed as a fringe benefit in the creation of technology to make rails for the vast railroads that penetrated the continent and opened America's west to settlement. And so, Peter Cooper, inventor and iron maker, was party to a number of technological feats that changed the nature not only of New York but of America and the world. In partnership with Samuel F. B. Morse, the painter and equally prolific inventor, he commissioned the first transatlantic cable; but earlier, based on his success in the Canton Iron Works in Baltimore, he helped bring steel to iron by commissioning the Tom Thumb locomotive. In northern New Jersey, at Ringwood, his iron mines, furnaces, and rolling mills created rails that ultimately did far more than carry wheeled traffic: they served as beams in his great philanthropic venture, Cooper Union (The Cooper Union for the Advancement of Science and Art). Here rails, resting on brick walls, bore between their bottom flanges shallow brick vaults that supported the building's original five floors. Here, in 1857, industrial capitalism brought technology to the service of a major urban public building, its brownstone face above the street simple Renaissance Revival columns, pilasters, and arches. At grade, cast iron allowed the sinuous structure to reveal the merchandise of the ground-floor shops that served the fashionable Lafayette Place neighborhood nearby and subsidized the education above.

Cast iron gave promise to a whole building facade of glass and bones anticipatory of the glass-and-metal curtain walls of the 1950's and 1960's. The anticipators were far classier than their descendents, for the cast-iron facades of Greene Street, of the old John Wanamaker store, of myriad buildings of SoHo and Tribeca, are a forest of Corinthian, Ionic, Tuscan, and combined orders—columns of classical virtue so numerous that all of Rome, Greece, and their colonies were pikers. Palladio's sixteenth-century Venice is recalled in a thousand paired columns and arches marching across a dozen dozen facades. These rich faces wear well in contrast to the pallid facades of lower Park Avenue that give nothing to the street save their bland detail, though the forms and urban spaces of Lever House and the Seagram Building bring a three-dimensional interplay of solid and void to the city street, even though their bodies are simplistic.

Cooper Mills sketch. The railroad rail evolved into the first structural beams. The rolling equipment could easily be modified from the rails produced in Peter Cooper's mills (center, and used as beams in The Cooper Union), to the more efficient structural shapes here sketched at the left and right.

The partner of iron (and its later maturation into steel) in the growing concentration of building was the elevator. Elevators existed as early as 1846, but in 1853, in the Latting Observatory tower on the north side of 42nd Street, a steam elevator brought viewers to a platform 225 feet above the street, overlooking the Crystal Palace, New York's first world's fair, inspired by the much larger and grander Crystal Palace of London. New York's short-lived Crystal Palace succumbed to fire in 1858, giving lie to the theory that cast iron was fireproof: though it did not burn, it buckled in the face of flames, its members becoming limp under the intense heat. And the elevator of the Latting tower and others were unsafe in the sense that, if their cables broke, they would plummet to the ground with an impact that would most often kill all their occupants. It remained for Elisha Graves Otis to demonstrate, and then install in 1857, the first safety passenger elevator in, happily, a cast-iron building at the northeast corner of Broome Street and Broadway, the Haughwout Building. Safety was assured by the use of automatic brakes that were released if the cab dropped, binding the elevator to its guiding rails. From then on, the partnership of iron and elevators was unstoppable. Iron grew to steel, and steel provided the possibility of structuring buildings of twenty, then forty, then eighty, then one hundred stories, with elevators making their use efficient and practicable.

Steel, a lithe skeletal material in building, is equally fragile in fire, losing its stiffness under intense heat. To shield it, therefore, it was encased first in tiles, later in concrete, and now often in sprayed asbestos, all insulators that prevent the action of heat from drawing strength from its frame. The fireproof building came into being in the 1880's, supplanting, in the riskier higher-rise buildings that succeeded cast iron, an exposed iron structure. Here steel was within an encasement producing a structural symbiosis not unlike the bones and flesh of the human body.

Steel, of course, gave rise to those aptly named build-

Cast-Iron Building, Tenth Street, Manhattan. Not all of the cast iron is in SoHo, but most is at or below 23rd Street, for those parts of the city were being developed when iron columns became economically available (1848–1875).

ings that bloomed first in the 1880's in Chicago: the sky-scraper, shafts that reached to what seemed, at first, heavens. The boxy forms of early modern Chicago architects Root and Burgee, engineer William LeBaron Jenney, and of Louis Sullivan expressed the cagelike forms of their steel frames and, particularly in Sullivan's case, were decorated with ornament invented to enrich this new modern architecture. New York's early skyscrapers were equally boxy but fronted with Renaissance detail largely inspired by the aesthetic counterrevolution of the World's Columbian Exposition (Chicago World's Fair) of 1893, which commemorated the four-hundredth anniversary of Columbus's second voyage. Burnham's Flatiron Building of 1902 is a gorgeous inflation of a Florentine rusticated palazzo. Park Avenue in the 1910's and 1920's applied this same aesthetic to the creation of a grand boulevard, after the New York Central trains were depressed and covered. But the true *sky*scrapers were the children of the boom of pre–World War I America blossoming into a world financial power, the Woolworth Building (1913) and the now demolished Singer Tower (1907) being notable examples. Similarly, during the boom of the late 1920's that spilled building completions into the early 1930's, after the crash of 1929 deflated that boom, a number of landmark skyscrapers were built: 40 Wall Street (1929), Chanin Building (1929), Chrysler Building (1930), City Bank Farmers' Trust Company (1931), Empire State Building (1931), 70 Pine Street (1932), Irving Trust Company (1932).

Steel and the elevator provided the possibility of densities never before imagined and a real estate bonanza to boot. The Equitable Building at Broadway and Pine Street (1915) placed thirty acres of floor area on a one-acre plot. If it were housing of moderate-sized apartments, twelve hundred families or thirty-six hundred people would live on one acre—no problem if that acre were surrounded by a vast park in the manner of Le Corbusier's Ville Radieuse, but here the Equitable Building is contained on all sides by densely packed competition. The possibility of

Condict Building, 1898, Bleecker Street, Manhattan. Louis Sullivan's only New York venture, this backwater from stylish office enclaves has had a renaissance of tenancy, as sophisticated commerce gentrifies old commercial sectors in a parallel to residential gentrification.

unlimited high-rise density became a threatening license, choking light and air from neighboring buildings and turning streets into dark canyons, in an era when mechanical ventilation and air conditioning were a thing of the future. Today, of course, the occupants of many prominent office buildings occupy interior space, with no natural light or view, due to the balm of artificial environments that are air-tempered, cooled, humidified, dehumidified, brilliantly lighted, and equipped with telephones and computers to communicate with other cellmates in like cells everywhere.

The finial-towered profile of lower Manhattan, crowned with the aeries of corporate chairmen, was obliterated by the advent of air conditioning: thick, fat buildings, harboring vast interior reaches for the bulk corporate population, were possible. In contrast, the RCA Building (1934), perhaps New York's greatest skyscraper, was planned on the notion that no occupant should sit more than twenty-seven feet from a window and that air conditioning was provided by opening that window. The slender slab that resulted is of an elegance foreign to the blocky structures that have infilled the voids between elegant finials in both mid-Manhattan and the financial district. Steel, which allowed the possibility of a skyscraper, now serves to create vast grids, endless jungle gyms harboring working hives.

Reinforced concrete creates, in effect, cast-in-place buildings, formed not unlike bronze statues or cast-iron columns but on an immense scale. The medium joined the architecture of cities soon after 1900. Tony Garnier, son of the great beaux arts designer of the Paris Opera, Charles Garnier, gave vision to concrete in his unbuilt Cité Industrielle of 1904. And he pursued that vision as architect of Lyons, where he, by necessity, had to earn a living. Auguste Perret, his contemporary, however, built his 1905 apartment house at 25 bis, rue Franklin, in Paris, with an aesthetic of concrete equal to its structural radicalism. Here the cage frames, not unlike those of fireproofed steel, expressed themselves as the facade, the walls' infilling ornamented with a bas bas-relief of Art Deco florality.

The Flatiron Building, 1902. Twenty-one stories of skyscraping steel dressed in Renaissance stonework, this is the grandest relic of those American Renaissance years when the new technology was clad in the old clothes of fifteenth-century Italy.

Concrete played a small role in New York until after World War II. Steel was an efficient and dominant industry before and during that war, but concrete with beams, columns, and floors (using a reinforcing of steel bars) became, in combination of labor and materials, economically competitive after the war. The more compact floor heights of concrete construction also allowed more floors to sit within zoning height limitations, and the flush undersides of construction could merely be painted to become the ceilings of the apartment below (rather than having suspended ceilings to conceal structural supporting paraphernalia). The flat slabs that were the building's concrete floors could serve as the total structure without supporting beams projecting downward. In a sense, the beams were within those six- or seven-inch thick planes, with iron bars invisibly concealed like the bones in one's body. Without beams, the floors could be closer together. In older buildings, such as most of those on Park Avenue, the structure was steel, with heavy beams, and ceilings were hung below that structure, umbrellas of plaster decorated over the rooms below.

But to the casual observer, structures of concrete, and those of steel encased (fireproofed) in concrete, seem similar visually, and they are right: the buildings of Mies van der Rohe, principal aesthetician of the steel-cage-expressed, are in fact steel frames encased in concrete, with an exterior cladding of metal structural shapes that seem to be the structure and that express the idea of structure within, in a manner not dissimilar to a Halloween skeleton suit. Structure as an architectural support, and structure as an architectural expression, are not necessarily coincident, as one can see upon further reflection on Burnham's Flatiron Building and Mies's Seagram Building.

The Industrial Revolution created fossil fuel–powered industrial machinery that both permitted and required vast work forces to produce even vaster products, giving urban employment to a greater number of people and creating the need to house and serve them. The products of that revolution, including iron and steel, gave promise

Apartment House, Rue Franklin, Paris. Reinforced concrete was first used for an apartment house by Auguste Perret, architect, and his brothers, both acting as contractors, near the Palais de Chaillot. The tiled infill bears lush Art Nouveau decor.

of a means of fulfilling this new urban population's needs. In fact, for New York until the late 1930's, high-rise apartment houses were assets of the upper-middle-income citizen and the rich, and the poor and middle-income man and woman lived in low-rise, wood-framed, brick bearing-wall buildings.

The Industrial Revolution created the possibility of ferryboats and trains, their engines, rails, and bodies; and it provided the structural bones of cast iron and steel, the vertical transportation of elevators, the wires to communicate by telegraph and eventually by telephone. All these provided impetus to increase the building density and height of the two-centered city, at Manhattan's midtown and its financial district. But the suburbanites, in most of Manhattan's northern reaches, in Queens, Brooklyn, and Staten Island, enjoyed the Industrial Revolution largely at their workplaces and in the technological wonders of the subways and elevateds that brought them there and back. The Industrial Revolution was, therefore, in large part an economic lever that provided bulk jobs, infilling the cities with the job fillers and creating immense personal wealth for the lever wielders, the nouveaux riches of the latter nineteenth century: Rockefellers, Carnegies, Fricks, and their ilk, whose wealth had grown from the need for steel to build buildings, oil to heat them, and fuel to power the varied systems of transit.

In retrospect, the new cities of the South and Southwest are by-products of the Industrial Revolution, high riders on its fruit: they use energy as a basis for their very auto/air organization, creating dispersal as an innate necessity, consuming land without either efficiency or style. Dallas and Los Angeles sprawl, admittedly, over arid lands, of limited value to the farmer, grazer, or gardener but of immense value to those who would rest under that sun—the resident who may tap that climate for his personal pleasure, often at great expense to the nation's resources, necessitating importation of water over vast distances from watersheds that resent its movement and loss. The idea

that climate might determine where man might live is an
idea that suffers poorly in any rational ideology and perhaps
supports the notion that Nobel Prizes are most often awarded
to the residents of cool places.

Crystal Palace and Latting Observatory, 1853. The Latting Tower's steam-powered elevator predated
Elisha Graves Otis' first "safety" elevator by four years. It provided a perch for spectacular views, firsthand
or drawn.

Immigrants Landing at the Battery, 1847. A cosmopolitan scene and event, as Europeans debark near what was soon to be the immigrant landing depot (old Castle Garden). No Statue of Liberty, no Ellis Island for another forty years.

8.

Immigration

Liberty, the harbor lady, now more than one hundred years old, has come to symbolize the sometime open immigrant door. No other society has ever admitted mass quantities of humanity vaguely commensurate with those arriving in New York in the nineteenth century.

The shape of New York, therefore, owes much to the population available to organize and service the city. When citizens cared for their own quarters, life was conducted on a small scale in both size and quality of living space. But the Industrial Revolution gave to many an opportunity for wealth, or certainly affluence, and simultaneously left a mass unskilled population as a vast labor pool for domestic service. The Irish potato blight and famine of 1845–1849 stimulated an added wave of emigration from Ireland of the young and unskilled, who on arrival in America became candidates for positions as maids in the increasingly grand mansions of the nouveaux riches. Federal town houses that had been, prototypically, thirty-two hundred square feet, now ballooned in Renaissance Revival times to eight thousand square feet, space that not

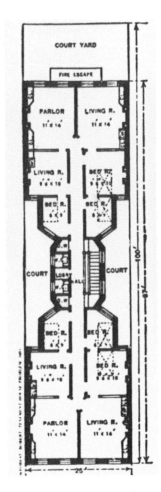

Tenement Plans. "Tenement" to many connotes a squalid building in an overcrowded slum; it was in fact the common name for early walk-up apartment houses. They filled most of the lot, and had limited light and air, but were a vast improvement over the packed quarters of degentrified houses and commercial buildings used until this true multiple dwelling was developed. Apartment buildings for the middle class were a Parisian import of the late nineteenth century.

only had to be cared for but also had to house the new resident caretakers. The style of building was, therefore, not merely another visual event in the fancy dress of facades but a social and functional event in the style of life: great spaces could create the scene for great parties and the need for servants to serve, clean, and maintain the parties' environment.

For the young Irish woman, domestic service was both a burden and a boon, a boon because the alternatives were both meager and oppressive. The sweatshop grew as a basic textile industry in New York because of the availability of a vast pool of untrained, immigrant labor of both sexes, sometimes further limited—being other than Irish or English—by language. The English, Irish, and Germans of the 1840's and 1850's were followed and reinforced by the eastern Europeans of the last half of the century. This later wave became the catalyst for architecture of a very different sort: the tenement. Tenement is a loosely defined, most often pejorative word for a small walk-up apartment house, which between 1840 and 1929 came to be the bulk housing of the poor and lower middle class. Densely packed on Manhattan's cross streets and unfashionable avenues, they were widely spread in the Bronx and eastern Brooklyn. Tenements multiplied with the burgeoning elevated train system of the 1870's and permeated the whole fabric of Greater New York with the subway's arrival in 1904. Most often on 25-by-100-foot lots, the early models filled almost the entire site, leaving five or ten feet behind to the property line. Tenement commissions in the 1840's, '50's, and '60's regulated them in theory, giving cubage required per person and limiting maximum coverage of a lot (65 percent in 1879), but a true tenement house act to regulate light, air, and sanitation did not go into effect until 1901. By then, more than 2 million New Yorkers lived in prelaw tenement buildings, in a total population of 3.4 million. By the 1960's there still remained more than 800,000 tenement housing *units* out of a total of 3 million units in New York.

After the worst abuses of sanitation and safety were corrected by legislation around the time of the Civil War, the tenements produced were criticized largely because of inadequate light and air. Laws concerning air (cubic feet of interior per person) were shortly effected. Light and ventilation, or movement of air in and out of contained space, were the bottom line for kitchens and bathrooms in particular. The sweltering New York summers must have been awful in those early tenements: rooms strung together like railroad cars (and hence "railroad flats") ninety feet from front to back, offering no air movement, no privacy. Paradoxically, the same buildings remodeled in modern times, with interior, mechanically ventilated kitchens and bathrooms and air-conditioned living spaces, are frequently quite liveable apartments.

"Slum" denotes dense population and squalor, certainly characteristics of many tenement precincts. But the converse is not necessarily the case. Much of the tenement construction in Harlem, for example, was for the white middle class. Modest, admittedly, it later housed a black population in the next generation. But it was built with substantial quality. In effect housing becomes a slum by the poverty of both tenants and services and by fantastic overcrowding, not necessarily by its intrinsic form and plan.

The Melting Pot turned out to be more of a blending-in, a bouillabaisse of the Irish, Jews, and Italians, who maintained their identities within the rich blend of populations. And slums, as physical entities, were more the sumps of those last in, the transitions from European poverty to a place in this Horatio Alger world of America, where the pins and needles of Jewish garment workers were transformed into the sutures, couches, depositions, and calculations of Jewish surgeons, psychiatrists, lawyers, and engineers (and for Jews, substitute and add Irish, Italians, and now Southeast Asians).

Immigration through New York was in large measure the intersection of many cultures, the sieve that allowed the foreigner to pass through a place of transition and to

The Italian Colony, Mulberry Bend. Many Italians fleeing poverty became laborers, later famed for construction of streets and buildings. Here they were packed into the narrow streets of the Lower East Side.

Hester Street, Lower East Side, ca. 1900. The image of the pushcart is redolent of eastern European market towns, from which most of these new arrivals had fled in poverty. The crowds and cacophony are viewed in retrospect as the milieu of the lowest classes. In fact Europeans vitalized the staid streets of New York.

be integrated socially (if not immersed) into the possibility of American life: that includes the Scandinavians of Wisconsin and Minnesota, the Czechs of Nebraska, the Hispanics of Florida, New York, and California, and so forth.

City College (affectionately remembered by its original name, CCNY, for City College of New York), now the senior member of the city university system, has traditionally been the educational conduit to higher learning for the most recent influx of immigrants. Founded in 1847 in what then was northern New York City, it became an urban migrant itself, moving from 23rd Street and Lexington Avenue to its Hamilton Heights campus (George B. Post, architect) in 1907. Its neo-Gothic walls, and mini-campus quadrangle, housed a population of Jews for the first half of the twentieth century that generated a panoply of graduate degrees, then Nobel Prizes unequaled in the nation, save for Harvard. And all this was located at the end of the West Side IRT, the cut for which created stones later piled into CCNY's neo-Gothicism. Here an immigrant, largely eastern European population celebrated the road to learning in what to their seamstress mothers in a Lower East Side sweatshop would be considered an architectural temple of learning. Now, the population given new opportunity is from many third world lands, as well as from the economic ghettos of black and Hispanic Harlem, the Bronx, and Brooklyn. And their world has expanded into an annex megastructure, the North Academic Center, that is twice as large as the parent neo-Gothic campus and that looms over Hamilton Heights a little like the visiting American aircraft carrier in Hong Kong harbor.

Immigration also brought craftsmanship that made some architectural events richer or more refined. The masonry, stucco, and plasterwork talents of immigrant Italians are to this day an essential resource for the restoration of buildings with complex neostylistic architecture. Migration of Indians from northern New York State and Canada brought self-balancing humanity to the "high wire" of open steel construction. The Mohawk was a brave erector at the

Empire State Building, more than a hundred floors above the street. And many a northern European, Scandinavian, and German has carved what could not be economically carved by ones American-born.

Joseph Mitchell and Meyer Berger were writers for New York's *World Telegram* and *Times* respectively. Berger's 1950's column, "About New York," reveled in the people of the city. About Mohawks, he said: "Most of the Indians putting up the . . . steel are from the Indian reservation near Montreal. They don't think there's much truth to the legend that they're better on high-steel because they're more sure-footed than whites. Des-Hu-Wagana, a young stalwart generally called Aleck, though his name means 'Look At Me,' says he thinks his tribe got into the trade years ago because the reservation is near the Dominion Bridge Company at Lachine, Quebec, and made a handy labor pool.

"Most of them spend their weekends around Red Hook in Brooklyn, which has an Indian steelworker colony of 700 to 800. They take their firewater, generally, in a Nevins Street groggery they call the Wigwam."

Mitchell interviewed "Orvis Diabo . . . whose Indian name is O-ron-ia-ke-te, or He Carries the Sky. 'I heated a million rivets,' he says. 'When they talk about the men that built this country, one of the men they mean is me.' "

Perhaps the most remarkable immigrants were those who saw the economic possibilities of New York and those who, with a fresh dispassion, saw its weaknesses. In this respect, two men stand out: August Belmont, the financier and entrepreneur, and Jacob Riis, the social activist and photographer. Belmont (born Schoenberg) exampled what an educated European financier, with opened opportunities in this new capitalist land, could accomplish in New York. His most wondrous effort was in creating, with partners, the first subway, then just *the* subway, now remembered as the IRT. Riis, on the other hand, an immigrant Dane, served as a police reporter and observed, involuntarily and with passion, the poverty, crowding, and disre-

Bandit's Roost, Mulberry Street, 1888. Jacob Riis photographed this eerie lot, which seems more a stage set for Maxwell Anderson's *Winterset* than real life. Today this would be a precious mews.

pair of the slums. He recorded this in words and photographs and, with the help of allies such as Theodore Roosevelt, founded neighborhood houses to give a decent center of social activities and advice to the ill cared-for slum dwellers.

Immigrants, of course, at one time or other comprised almost everybody. Special mention, however, should be given to those unique individuals whose arrival and presence modified New York's physical development and future. The financial talents of Belmont moved the subway from concept to reality, as the reporting, both verbal and photographic, of Jacob Riis helped to forge the chain of events that, having exposed severe social ills in awful physical surroundings, ended in the design of experimental tenements and eventually in public housing financed and subsidized by the city and later by the state and federal governments.

Architects, engineers, and builders whose presence in New York caused impact include a range from John McComb, Jr. (City Hall and Castle Clinton) to Cesar Pelli (Museum of Modern Art Tower and the World Financial Center at Battery Park City); from John Roebling (the Brooklyn Bridge) to Othmar Ammann (Whitestone, Triborough, and Verrazzano bridges). McComb, along with Thomas McBean and Richard Upjohn, James Renwick and Andrew Jackson Downing, Calvert Vaux, Minard Lafever, and others were from the British Isles or of similar background. A few continental Europeans, however, made their mark in this Anglican society, most prominently Pierre L'Enfant, the French officer and engineer who drew the master plan for Washington, D.C., and designed the alteration of City Hall at Broad Street into Federal Hall (which, ironically, served as the nation's capitol for one year, 1789–1790).

Grace Church Nave, Broadway at 10th Street. James Renwick, a Scottish engineer, won the competition for this, the ecclesiastical center of New York Society. English neo-Gothic architecture housed an Episcopalian population: English architecture, English liturgy, and, hopefully, English snobbery.

The Great White City, Chicago, 1893. An instant city of an architecture that might be described as vulgar or overdressed Renaissance. As a world's fair, it attracted millions and put Chicago back on the map as a place to visit after the Great Fire of 1871.

9.

The City Beautiful

Francis Baily, president of the Royal Astronomical Society, noted in 1796 that: "a battery, now converted into a public walk, . . . the only public walk the New Yorkers can boast of; of course, it is very much frequented, particularly on a summer's evening; it may then be compared to Temple Gardens in the City [of London]."

Felix de Beaujour remarked four years later that "New York has a more smiling aspect [than Philadelphia] and appears more like a European town. . . . The esplanade called the Battery, standing on the saliant angle formed by the Hudson and the sea in their junction, presents one of the most beautiful points of view that can be imagined."

Organic architecture is, by definition of its namers, that which grows from the nature of the place, site, situation, or occasion, as the species of Darwin have evolved from the nature of their environment and interplay with their peers. In such fashion grew Dutch New Amsterdam, and such was the evolutionary source of myriad European cities, certainly including London, Paris, and Rome. The present plans of all these cities, however, were grossly

Piazzo del Popolo, Rome. Pope Sixtus V created diagonal boulevards in sixteenth-century Rome to link the arriving traveler with the city's pilgrimage churches, and those with each other. This bold urban design inspired nineteenth-century Paris and, more modestly, nineteenth-century Brooklyn.

Eastern Parkway, Brooklyn. Napoleon III's great new boulevards of the 1860's inspired this and Ocean Parkway as handsome routes with tree-lined allées. Unfortunately the supporting buildings never attained the grand continuity of their Parisian models.

modified at different times by events and decisions that "remodeled" them into imageries that anticipate what we in America eventually termed the City Beautiful.

London's fire of 1666 changed more the nature of architecture and construction than the city plan. Christopher Wren eventually built fifty-one churches for the Crown, including St. Paul's Cathedral, replacing those destroyed in the fire. He proposed a new city plan that would have turned London into a variation on a continental Baroque image. Coincidentally, Pope Sixtus V (1585–1590) with his favorite architect, Domenico Fontana, had slashed straight boulevards through Rome, connecting great monuments, punctuating the eye's travel with obelisks borrowed from Egypt and giving the tired, architecturally classical, but urbanistically disorganized, city a visual structure, turning its body into a comprehensible system. Paris had to wait somewhat longer, in fact long after New York had committed itself to the commissioners' grid but contemporary with Olmsted's Central and Prospect parks, Ocean and Eastern parkways. In Paris, Napoleon III's prefect, Baron Haussmann, created avenues and boulevards that, even more intensely than Sixtus' Rome, organized a largely medieval city into the visions we see today of an ordered, formal, neoclassical city comprising, in fact, shallow buildings and facades overlaid against a medieval patchwork. New York grew northward for 147 years—its development reached roughly as far north as Greenwich Village—before a master grid was laid over the whole island of Manhattan to 155th Street. The Commissioners' Plan, presented in 1811, is in large part the street system of Manhattan today.

Thus, a town that flowered organically spread northward as an engineered discipline, much maligned in the past for its relentless geometry but, happily, a great success in modern reality. The avenues, acting as arteries together with the major two-way crosstown streets, are largely the major travel routes and commercial places. And the streets themselves are the residential infill acting in neighborhood concert with the avenues. In the original plan First through Twelfth avenues, and First through 155th Streets, were barely relieved by a few open spaces interspersed: Central Park was not even proposed until 1852. A great "Parade" was shown between 23rd and 34th streets, Third and Seventh avenues; and four squares—Harlem, Hamilton, Bloomingdale, and Manhattan—as well as an Observatory Place, were the only relief in the grid's network. Madison Square is a remnant of the great Parade, and the Museum of Natural History with its Hayden Planetarium sit on Manhattan Square, the only complete remaining open space of the Commissioners' Plan.

The commissioners were not thinking of amenities: in their own words: "That one of the first objects which claimed their attention, was the form and manner in which the business should be conducted; that is to say, whether they should confine themselves to rectilinear and rectangular streets, or whether they should adopt some of those supposed improvements, by circles, ovals and stars, which certainly embellish a plan, whatever may be their effects as to convenience and utility. In considering that subject, they could not but bear in mind that a city is to be composed principally of the habitations of men, and that straight-sided and right-angled houses are the most cheap to build, and the most convenient to live in. The effect of these plain and simple reflections was decisive.

"It may, to many, be a matter of surprise that so few vacant spaces have been left, and those so small, for the benefit of fresh air, and consequent preservation of health. Certainly, if the City of New-York were destined to stand on the side of a small stream, such as the Seine or the Thames, a great number of ample spaces might be needful; but those large areas of the sea which embrace Manhattan Island, render its situation, in regard to health and pleasure, as well as to convenience of commerce, peculiarly felicitous; when, therefore, from the same causes, the price of land is so uncommonly great, it seemed proper to admit the principles of economy to greater influence than might,

Baron Georges Eugène Haussmann. He made New York's "power broker," Robert Moses, seem a gentle amateur. His boulevards, parks, sewers, water supply, transit, markets, and churches gave Paris its still dominant image.

Commissioners' Plan, 1811. The right angle is so obvious in our planning that we forget that it fell into disuse after ancient Rome's engineered cities—and became repopularized in the nineteenth century. It is particularly appropriate that New York, founded as a commercial enterprise to trade in beaver skins, should plan itself as the world's most vast land speculation.

under circumstances of a different kind, have consisted with the dictates of prudence and the sense of duty.

"It did not appear proper, only it was felt to be indispensable, that a much larger space should be set apart for Military Exercise, as also to assemble, in case of need, the force destined to defend the City. The question, therefore, was not, and could not be, whether there should be a Grand Parade, but where it should be placed, and what should be its size. And here again is it to be lamented, that in this late day the Parade could not be brought further south, and made larger than it is, without incurring a frightful expense.

"To some it may be a matter of surprise, that the whole Island has not been laid out as a City; to others, it may be a subject of merriment, that the Commissioners have provided space for a greater population than is collected at any spot this side of China. They have in this respect been governed by the shape of the ground. It is not improbable that considerable numbers may be collected at Haerlem, before the high hills to the southward of it shall be built upon as a City; and it is improbable, that for centuries to come the grounds north of Haerlem Flat [let alone Washington Heights or the Bronx] will be covered with houses. To have come short of the extent laid out, might, therefore, have defeated just expectation, and to have gone further, might have furnished materials to the pernicious spirit of speculation." In spite of their faltering spirit and lack of vision as to the potential expansion of New York, the plan was filled to its limit and beyond by the turn of the century.

O. Henry spoke vehemently in "A Bird of Baghdad" (1905): "Fourth Avenue—born and bred in the Bowery—staggers northward full of good resolutions.

"Where it crosses Fourteenth Street it struts for a brief moment proudly in the glare of the museums and cheap theatres. It may yet become a fit mate for its highborn sister boulevard to the west, or its roaring, polyglot, broad-waisted cousin to the east. It passes Union Square;

and here the hoofs of the dray horses seem to thunder in unison, recalling the tread of marching hosts—Hooray! But now come the silent and terrible mountains—buildings square as forts, high as the clouds, shutting out the sky, where thousands of slaves bend over desks all day. On the ground floors are only little fruit shops and laundries and book shops, . . . And next—poor Fourth Avenue!—the street glides into a mediaeval solitude. On each side are the shops devoted to 'Antiques.'

". . . With a shriek and a crash Fourth Avenue dives headlong into the tunnel at Thirty-fourth and is never seen again."

San Francisco, whose magnificent hills still remain (New York's were largely obliterated in the process of economical development), is also overlaid with a grid. There the virtue of this geometry is particularly expressed, for down streets and avenues one has a constantly changing view of the harbor and sea. The topography assists this by the many high vantage points that the pedestrian enjoys in his normal travels through the city. In New York this virtue is muted, for the vistas frequently are only of sky at the street's end, but in some parts of town, such as Hamilton and Morningside heights (the campuses of City College and Columbia), the vistas of the Hudson and the Palisades are magnificent. In any wise, the grid has fulfilled, rather than destroyed, the possibilities of Manhattan.

In May 1844 Edgar Allan Poe described the fall of nature before the surveyors' relentless work. He wrote in a letter to the *Columbia Spy*: "I have been roaming far and wide over this island of Mannahatta. Some portions of its interior have a certain air of rocky sterility which may impress some imaginations as simply *dreary*—to me it conveys the sublime. . . .

"On the eastern or 'Sound' face of Mannahatta . . . are some of the most picturesque sites for villas to be found within the limits of Christendom. These localities, however, are neglected—unimproved. The only mansions upon them (principally wooden) are suffered to remain unre-

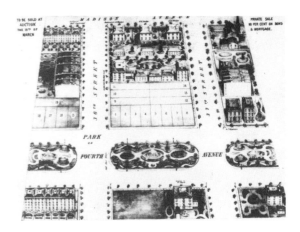

The Grid Exploited. As the commissioners clearly knew, "straight sides and right-angled houses are the most cheap to build, and the most convenient to live in. Undisciplined charm [meandering Greenwich Village] here must give way hopefully to organized grandeur."

paired, and present a melancholy spectacle of decrepitude. In fact, these magnificent places are doomed. The spirit of Improvement has withered them with its acrid breath. Streets are already 'mapped' through them, and they are no longer suburban residences but 'town-lots.' In some thirty years every noble cliff will be a pier, and the whole island will be densely desecrated by buildings of brick, with portentous *facades* of brown-stone, . . .

"A day or two since I procured a light skiff, and with the aid of a pair of *sculls* . . . made my way around Blackwell's [now Roosevelt] Island, on a voyage of discovery and exploration. The chief interest of the adventure lay in the scenery of the Manhattan shore, which is here particularly picturesque. The houses are, without exception, *frame*, and antique. . . . I could not look on the magnificent cliffs, and stately trees, which at every moment met my view, without a sigh for their inevitable doom—inevitable and swift."

Before the City Beautiful movement proper blossomed in the inspiration of the World's Columbian Exposition (Chicago World's Fair) of 1893, New York and Brooklyn's principal architect of grandeur was the landscape architect Frederick Law Olmsted. As the grid was infilled by the reality of streets and buildings, the seeming endlessness of it all became more and more apparent. The commissioners' brave words turned out to be more euphemistic than precise: "those large areas of the sea which embrace Manhattan Island render its situation, in regard to health and pleasure . . . peculiarly felicitous." The island's accessible edges became filled with shipping and the service and storage buildings of shipping. From 1820 to 1840, the population of New York had grown from 124,000 to 313,000. Four years later, in 1844, the poet William Cullen Bryant warned that "Commerce is devouring inch by inch the coast of the island, and if we would rescue any part of it for health and recreation it must be done now. . . . All large cities have their extensive public grounds and

133rd Street Near Lenox Avenue, 1882. Like the children's game of connecting the dots, the invisible grid was infilled by dotting the connects, or lines of streets. These scattered clusters waiting for neighbors to make a street were an eerie sight.

gardens, Madrid and Mexico their Alamedas, London its Regent's Park, Paris its Champs-Elysées and Vienna its Prater." And the next year he wrote that "the population of your city, increasing with such prodigious rapidity, your sultry summers, and corrupt atmosphere generated in hot and crowded streets, make it a cause of regret that, in laying out New York, no preparation was made, while it was yet practicable, for a range of parks and public gardens along the central part of the island or elsewhere, to remain perpetually for the refreshment and recreation of the citizens during the torrid heats of the warm season. There are yet unoccupied lands on the island which might, I suppose, be procured for the purpose, and which, on account of their rocky and uneven surfaces, might be laid out into surpassingly beautiful pleasure-grounds, but, while we are discussing the subject, the advancing population of the city is sweeping over them and covering them from our reach."

The plea was reinforced by America's first great landscape architect, Andrew Jackson Downing, who wrote in 1849 in the *Horticulturist*, of which he was editor: "A large public park would not only pay in money, but largely civilize and refine the national character, and increase knowledge of, and taste for, rare and beautiful trees and plants. . . . The true policy of republics is to foster the taste for great public libraries, parks and gardens, which all may enjoy." This was a time when writers such as James Fenimore Cooper were lauding the wilderness and its Indian inhabitants, and painters were outdoing nature, "improving" it to make it more picturesque. Thomas Cole, leader of what came to be known as the Hudson River school, and his friend, Asher Durand, created visions of a nature of fantasy, wild and rampant, that inspired both Downing and Olmsted. The actual landscapes of Capability Brown, such as the grounds of Blenheim Palace, were early experiments in the reality of the manmade picturesque. (Capability's real name was Lancelot, but he is always referred to by the nickname, supposedly because he said he was.)

Bethesda Fountain. Here a gondolier on the lake fulfills the romance promised by Greensward, Olmsted & Vaux's winning competition for the design of Central Park.

Brown's influence had no impact on early America, but his spirit was revived in concert with the paintings of the Hudson River school by Downing and Olmsted.

Central Park's 840 acres, excised from the commissioners' grid, truly fulfilled the dreams of Bryant and Downing. Probably because of Downing's untimely death in 1852 (he drowned in a steamboat accident, attempting to save his mother-in-law), a competition was proposed in 1857, and its winners were selected a year later. Olmsted and Vaux's "Greensward" plan was the clear winner. Calvert Vaux (1824–1895) was Olmsted's partner and architect of many of the park's buildings and other structures. With a major romantic landscape the size of Monaco, New York at one stroke matured into an urbane, not merely urban, city. And its sister city, Brooklyn, followed close suit with the same team's Prospect Park (1866–1874).

Early attempts at attaining the grandeur of European classical discipline came in Olmsted's two great boulevards of the City of Brooklyn, Ocean Parkway and Eastern Parkway. Eastern Parkway was built in concert with Prospect Park, intended as a great armature along which the buildings of import could line. Unfortunately the timing was ill, and the flanks, save for a few blocks east of Grand Army Plaza (the nexus of park, parkway, and the adjoining city) are filled with buildings of suburban scale, unmatching this great way. Ocean Parkway suffered a different fate, lined later with apartment houses for much of its length, with a central roadway separated from, and supplemented by, the service roads at each side. The apartment houses followed sixty to eighty years, however, after the route's construction.

It remained for Park Avenue to fulfill the balanced dream of a great boulevard in symbiosis with buildings of style and discipline that would reinforce the intervening space. In well worn but clear words, here the whole is greater than the sum of its parts. The depression of the railroad into a covered way allowed Fourth Avenue, a dingy place, to be transmogrified into a place of style and gran-

Park Avenue in the 80's. The "compleat" Park Avenue is an orderly place to which the affluent retreat from a seemingly disorderly city. The understatement of its apartment houses is in the spirit of the dour architecture of Florence, where wealth was privately displayed within an obviously large, solid, but soft-spoken shell.

deur. Cinderella's pumpkin stayed in place: the prince did not have to seek the slipper's owner.

The final great boulevard, the Grand Concourse, is in the much maligned Bronx. Here development occurred in the 1920's and 1930's, a modern event that left great lines of Art Deco and Art Moderne apartment houses along this actually grand linear space.

Much of the search for grandeur pursued by Olmsted, and at Park Avenue and the Grand Concourse, had been isolated and symbolized by the Chicago World's Fair. Under the architectural and planning tutelage of Daniel H. Burnham, an American Renaissance was presented, with disciplined classical plan and buildings mostly of classical ancestry (save for Louis Sullivan's Transportation Building) that worked together with uniform cornice lines. The dominance of this event over subsequent building and planning was overpowering, controlling the style of architecture for generations. But aside from "style," it brought to American architect-planners the vision of a planned city, of a City Beautiful, that could be visually organized as a designed grouping rather than by the random organic growth that had worked well in medieval times, when there was a consistent architecture, a relatively small urban scale, and a somewhat monolithic social discipline. But in modern times, when anything seemed possible from a technical standpoint, and when commerce, habitations, and public buildings were in conflict and confrontation, an overall discipline seemed the logical savior. Comparing contemporary Park and Third avenues, one sees the great power and unity of the former and the chaotic and staccato quality of the latter. Order for its own sake can produce appalling regimentation, as in most of the modern housing projects of New York and other cities, where the order achieved has no grand or unifying aesthetic, merely the disciplining of housing units. But order as part of a grand statement, as on Park Avenue, brings, as in the words of Sir Henry Wotton, not only "firmness and commodity" but also delight.

Third Avenue, in the 70's. Third Avenue had no discipline suggested or imposed, save for that mid nineteenth-century order of four- and five-story brownstone and brick aligned in endless rows. The elevated limited further development until it was demolished in 1956. At that stroke license prevailed, and the worst of architecture and planning joined to create the messy auto-route of today.

Broadway, or the Former "Boulevard," 73rd Street. The Ansonia as a powerful presence overshadows the polyglot qualities of what was once *the* Boulevard, when that very word evoked the life and style of Paris, or Vienna, or Budapest.

Broadway in its role as main street of New Amsterdam and early New York cut a swath through the growing city. It served as the central spine of movement and commerce from Bowling Green to Central Park. Broadway now, however, has different roles and characters. Its role at and around Times Square is well known, but north of Times Square and, particularly, north of 59th Street (the juncture with Central Park), it aspired to grandeur. The Boulevard was its sometime name from there to 155th Street (that northern outlimit of the 1811 gridmakers' plan). But the residential infill did not live up to the developers' dreams. Distinguished apartment buildings blossomed here and there (the Ansonia, the Belnord), but the whole never gathered together a form equal to that of Park Avenue. The intensity of its use made it more a place of commercial and cultural life, rather than one of residential repose.

For obvious reasons, Fifth Avenue, Central Park West, and Riverside Drive all afforded, aside from their fashionable postures, places for grand views of Central Park for the first two; of Riverside Park, the Hudson, and the Palisades for the last. Here the permission of zoning merely allowed bulk that made a great conglomerate facade in each case. The sum of the parts, great walls of architecture, punctuated by both higher and lower individual elements, has a certain grandeur en masse but a quality achieved without the benefit of any conscious aesthetic organization. Occasional buildings are of distinguished architecture, but the whole is more impressive as a force than as an integrated design.

The rivers and harbor were gradually barricaded from the people by industry and shipping over the nineteenth and into the twentieth century. In Manhattan, only at Battery Park was there an easy relationship with water. The first serious return of a pedestrian river edge was with Robert Moses' commissioned covering of the old Hudson River Railroad line as part of the new Henry Hudson Parkway (1936), which brought Olmsted and Sons' Riverside Park (1873–1910) to the river's very edge. As a result, the whole West Side was enriched. This WPA-financed event was paralleled on the East Side by the happy interweaving (1940) of the new East River Drive (later renamed Franklin D. Roosevelt Drive) with Carl Schurz Park. The park's edge was lifted like a lid over the drive, bringing its users to a high stance along the busy East River, its tidal waters filled with frequently passing shipping. The drive's construction also provided a narrow pedestrian way on and off the riverside to the Lower East Side; but accessibility is only at widely spaced bridges, making it a more isolated opportunity than the water's edge at Carl Schurz. Thirteen years later, after the intervention of World War II, a more dramatic blend of highway and people was achieved by the same team of Robert Moses and company for Brooklyn Heights. Here the new Brooklyn–Queens Expressway, stacked on three levels over the docks below, provided northbound and southbound lanes, and a pedestrian promenade on top that was the best urban edge to date. The view of Manhattan's lower skyline is so dramatic that it ranks with the Staten Island Ferry as a stance for photographers coming from everywhere. The acts of creating these pedestrian edges were primarily engineering events, consummate solutions for major highways. Their fringe benefits, though conscious, were urban enhancements by happy chance: the automobile that had taken away so much of the delight of this and other pedestrian cities here gave back its due to the pedestrian world.

Most recently, Battery Park City has created another mile of city river edge with elegance from Battery Park northward. Here a sophisticated architectural master plan (Cooper, Eckstut and Associates) included urbane architecture lining a traditional streetscape and complemented with an understated but elegantly designed promenade accessible from numerous city streets. Westway, the nickname for the project to build a new underground and covered West Side Highway, would have created a park and supplementary promenade northward. Unfortunately this vast amenity, which would have continued the pedes-

Lower Manhattan Skyline. Now. It is hard to ignore a spectacle, but when it is before you at all times it becomes an event no more important than a perfectly flushing toilet. The slender towers of the 1920's and 1930's are muted by the vast honeycombed warehouses of banking of the 1950's and later. What was for Maxim Gorky a filigree of "uneven black teeth" here becomes a serrated mountain.

trian way from the Battery to midtown, was scrapped in a battle over financing highways versus mass transit, with a bit of interstate New Jersey–New York political maneuvering thrown in. Its demise is a sadly lost opportunity to bring back the island's edge to that vision which the commissioners had so firmly held.

In counterpoint to the efforts and successes in bringing the island's edges back to the people, planners sought to bring spatial relief to the island's inner grid. The new 1961 zoning resolution provided bonuses to builders, allowing them more floor area for their developments if they provided either indoor or outdoor public spaces. Plazas and arcades, both covered and uncovered, with access most of the time to the general public here became extensions of the existing street and sidewalk system. The Seagram Building plaza (1958, Mies van der Rohe) showed how a new building could provide a grand public space when architecturally oriented enlightened self-interest came into play. Paley Plaza Park (1967), which had been donated to the city by William Paley (Zion and Breen, landscape architects), was the model that many followed: a "vest-pocket" park with an umbrella of trees and with moving water that provided sparkling reflections and sound to mask the city's surrounding noises. The response was a plethora of plazas concentrated where the "action" was, bringing space-confronting space in many instances rather than opening a breathing and sitting space into bleakly dense city precincts. To build a plaza for General Motors opposite the Plaza Hotel and Central Park at 59th Street was a loss to the city rather than a gain: it weakened the Plaza and offered little in return. In contrast, the indoor plaza at Citicorp brings space, life, and activity to a part of town that is packed with office workers sorely in need of local respite. If on Sixth Avenue (officially the Avenue of the Americas) the heavy row of Rockefeller Center–annexed office buildings (Exxon, McGraw Hill, Time-Life, Equitable, Sperry-Rand) had situated their vast plazas behind rather than in front of their bulk, the product would have been far more

Central Park West. This handsome wall of buildings, punctuated with towers, gives Central Park a skyline, and its inhabitants a lovely perch above that great garden. The architecture of apartments here had a common posture that was heads above most of the city.

productive in relieving the pedestrian's life and role. The newest buildings largely are making their public spatial gestures internally, with skylit atria more part of a separate but pleasant world than an island of repose off the street's activity. Among these is the new Equitable Center atrium at Seventh Avenue between 51st and 52nd streets.

With Manhattan's gaudy maturity, planners and builders have graduated from creating mere buildings in the grid to a reassessment and construction of amenities that enhance pedestrian life. Midtown and the financial district have gained a rich share of such projects. Previously, public agencies in the process of engineering traffic needs have equivalently recouped much of the city's edge. All of this has occurred where money talked: supplementing the office buildings of well-heeled corporations as well as the routes of a richly endowed national-highway trust fund. Unfortunately, the densely urban portions of Manhattan and Brooklyn, where no water edges are offered and no corporations lurk, have neither the money nor the opportunity to create many similar pedestrian incisions. In Bedford-Stuyvesant the Restoration Corporation has created a private plaza–enhanced shopping center at New York Avenue. In Harlem and on the Lower East Side the Astor Foundation has financed urbane reworkings of the amorphous space between high-rise public housing. Riis Houses Plaza at 6th Street and Avenue D (1966, M. Paul Friedberg, landscape architect) is the best example. That not only building but also pedestrian space is on the minds of planners, politicians, and architects bodes well for city development. New York is the richer for it. Perhaps not a City Beautiful, New York is an urban center where the new design attitudes for street, building, plaza, and park are bringing an improving richness to city life.

Restoration Plaza, Bedford-Stuyvesant, Brooklyn. The decaying facades of Fulton Street are here spruced up and used as the gateway to a modern business, shopping, and cultural center.

Cornelius Vanderbilt Mansion. Cornelius Vanderbilt II was the grandson of the "Commodore." Vanderbilt railroad wealth fueled the construction of this great town palace, as well as houses for rich relatives such as the Breakers in Newport and Biltmore in Asheville, North Carolina.

10.

The Newly Rich

The inexorable need for the pioneer, even in an urban setting, not only to create wealth but also to advertise its presence, brought to New York some of its grandest buildings and, fortunately, some that have survived those pioneers' successors. A lone remembrance at the Battery, several at Lafayette Street, a smattering on lower Fifth Avenue, a grand set on upper Fifth Avenue, a bunch on Brooklyn's Clinton Hill, an outpost in Queens' Astoria—these are the urban stage sets for the newly sophisticated wealth of Astors, Vanderbilts, Carnegies, Fricks, Rockefellers, Pratts, and Steinways. The Whitneys, of course, came later.

The phenomena that led to the building of New York's mansions are the same ones that, on a grander and longer-termed scale, created the great châteaux, country houses, palazzi, and villas of Europe. The new families in power, largely through the new riches of Renaissance banking in Italy and through the Crown-rewarded estates in the wars and the Protestant-Catholic conflicts of England, built great personal monuments in Florence and Rome, at Blenheim

Blenheim Palace. An impressive acreage of architecture for the son of "an impoverished squire." The quick way to the top before the Industrial Revolution was through military coup or patriotic victory. The Duke of Marlborough seems to have been amply rewarded.

and Hardwick, at Vicenza and Azay-le-Rideau. The Duke of Marlborough, son of an "impoverished squire," was awarded Blenheim in 1705 as a grand prize for victory over the combined French and Bavarian armies at the place of the same name. And Hardwick Hall was proof of the powerful legacy of a woman who married power and money (without any inherited rights). The Medici were Florentine bankers, and what could be more nouveau riche than bankers in a moment in history when banking (and the very upper middle class) were invented as a species?

The early patrons of architectural grandeur in New York in the early 1800's were grand in relation to their neighbors and peers but modest in comparison to the extravagant magnificence of the nineteenth century's last decade in this city. The James Watson house on State Street facing Battery Park is the oldest remnant, from 1793 (now the offices for the Shrine of St. Elizabeth Seton), a lovely but modest palazzo infilling a row of its peers, in the manner of the Massimi in Rome. Now, of course, it is dwarfed by the gigantism of the whole financial district. But at the spectrum's opposite chronological end, the Carnegie Mansion (now the Cooper-Hewitt Museum) attempts to emulate in scale the seventeenth- and eighteenth-century palazzi, houses, and villas that gave it status by symbolic transference.

First after the Battery as a precinct of social and financial elegance was Lafayette Place (now Lafayette Street), where Vanderbilts, Astors, and Delanos built row houses on a place that was, happily for them, short and dead-ended (its southern end was Great Jones Street). This placid and expensive enclave wore four- and five-story town houses on each side, now remembered only by Colonnade Row, a cluster of four Corinthian-columned units (out of an original nine), still seedily holding their position. It was here that the many-styled architect, Alexander Jackson Davis, brought a colonnade that tied the separate buildings together, so that they would jointly seem to be palatial, in the manner of an English terrace, as in a facade on Bedford

Square or John Nash's Carleton House Terrace at St. James's Park. Before their arrival the street was in a neighborhood of more modest houses, largely the late Federal and early Greek Revival ones of the upper middle-income classes described in the novels of Edith Wharton and Henry James. But Mrs. Wharton's Mrs. Manson Mingott was the Astor-Vanderbilt image of her time, who would have scorned the merely elegant brick Federal house in order to build a mansion on Lafayette Place.

In *The Age of Innocence* (1920) Edith Wharton writes about life in the 1870's: Mrs. Manson Mingott "married two of her daughters to 'foreigners' (an Italian Marquis and an English banker), and put the crowning touch to her audacities by building a large house of pale cream-coloured stone (when brown sandstone seemed as much the only wear as a frockcoat in the afternoon) in an inaccessible wilderness near the Central Park. . . . the cream-coloured house (supposed to be modelled on the private hotels of the Parisian aristocracy) was there as a visible proof of her moral courage; and she throned in it, among pre-Revolutionary furniture and souvenirs of the Tuileries of Louis Napoleon (where she had shone in her middle age), as placidly as if there were nothing peculiar in living above Thirty-fourth Street, or in having French windows that opened like doors instead of sashes that pushed up.

". . . The house in itself was already an historic document, though not, of course, as venerable as certain other old family houses in University Place and lower Fifth Avenue. Those were of the purest 1830, with a grim harmony of cabbage-rose-garlanded carpets, rosewood consoles, round-arched fireplaces with black marble mantles, and immense glazed book-cases of mahogany; whereas old Mrs. Mingott, who had built her house later, had bodily cast out the massive furniture of her prime, and mingled with the Mingott heirlooms the frivolous upholstery of the Second Empire. It was her habit to sit in a window of her sitting-room on the ground floor, as if watching calmly for life and fashion to flow northward to her solitary doors.

Colonnade Row, Lafayette Street. Four remnants of an original nine, these were in the style of London's Carleton Terrace: separate houses seeming to be a single palace in their aggregate.

Caroline Schermerhorn Astor House, 65th Street and Fifth Avenue. This Mrs. Astor was without question the social doyenne of her times and, in memory, of times after. Her moves in the social flux of New York broke the geographical barriers and led the wanderers to the promised land of upper Fifth Avenue.

"The burden of Mrs. Manson Mingott's flesh had long since made it impossible for her to go up and down stairs, and with characteristic independence she had made her reception rooms upstairs and established herself (in flagrant violation of all the New York proprieties) on the ground floor of her house; so that, as you sat in her sitting-room window with her, you caught (through a door that was always open, and a looped-back yellow damask portière) the unexpected vista of a bedroom with a huge low bed upholstered like a sofa, and a toilet-table with frivolous lace flounces and a gilt-framed mirror.

"Her visitors were startled and fascinated by the foreignness of this arrangement, which recalled scenes in French fiction, and architectural incentives to immorality such as the simple American had never dreamed of. That was how women with lovers lived in the wicked old societies, in apartments with all the rooms on one floor, and all the indecent propinquities that their novels described."

The geography of Society is always somewhat mysterious, sometimes seemingly unrelated to the physical delight of the neighborhood, being a sometime function of who was there first (whether the prince regent or the Joneses) and whom one has to keep up with. Each new shift in Society's center of gravity occurred in a wave action following a leading pioneer, the prime examples in New York being the moves of Mrs. Astor (Caroline Schermerhorn Astor) and of Andrew Carnegie, and in the building of the Dakota apartments.

Edith Wharton continued in *The Age of Innocence,* speaking of her "hero," Newland Archer, who, in reflecting on his father-in-law to be, "knew that Mr. Welland, who was behaving 'very handsomely,' already had his eye on a newly built house in East Thirty-ninth Street. The neighborhood was thought remote, and the house was built in a ghastly greenish-yellow stone that the younger architects were beginning to employ as a protest against the brownstone of which the uniform hue coated New York like a cold chocolate sauce; but the plumbing was perfect."

Mrs. Astor's moves were those of a grande dame well aware of her own posture and power: the very phrase the Four Hundred related to the size of her ballroom at 34th Street and Fifth Avenue, where only four hundred whirling dancers could be accommodated, a precise stricture on the number of bodies who might count themselves Society. She, the most notorious of the Astors, built next a mansion in the wilds of the north (now termed the Upper East Side) at the northeast corner of 65th Street and Fifth Avenue, where the grand Temple Emmanu-El now stands. Her château, by architect Richard Morris Hunt, brought Society and an increasingly elaborate renaissance style thirty-one blocks north of her last bastion.

Carnegie, on the other hand, arrived in these territories as an immigrant not only from Scotland but also from his own steel precincts (Pennsylvania), an immigrant searching for symbolic land that could give the credence of Society to his immense and sudden wealth. And his château at 2 East 91st Street was as strong a statement of pioneer faith in the relentless blocks of New York's grid as was the Dakota at Central Park West and 72nd Street. The Carnegie mansion (1901, Babb, Cook and Willard) made the Carnegies pioneers in a neighborhood then still rife with squatters. The next year, however, James Burden's house, by architects Warren and Wetmore, rose across 91st Street at number 7, to be followed in 1909 by the John Hammond House at number 9 (Carrère and Hastings).

Carnegie Hill, as we now remember the area, was the last enclave of great mansion construction. The rich were destined for a very different manner of living, for by the time the George F. Baker house, at 75 East 93rd Street, was expanded for his needs (from the Francis F. Palmer House; Delano and Aldrich, 1917–1928), Park Avenue was the site of blooming fifteen-story apartment buildings, palatial multiple dwellings that lined the newly created boulevard in the manner of gargantuan palazzi. The last urban palace for the city was built off Park on 93rd Street,

George F. Baker House, 93rd Street and Park Avenue. Baker's very European arrangements—a carriage court was embraced by the house and its wings—were clad in English Georgian in this late stylistic revival.

William G. Loew House, 56 East 93rd Street. Only a movie mogul would still build a stylish town house during the Great Depression. Such very newly rich were of course looked upon with disdain by the merely newly rich.

across from the Baker house, for William G. Loew (1932, Walker and Gillette); it is usually remembered as the Billy Rose House.

The Dakota (1884, Henry Hardenburgh), a grand early luxury apartment house on the west flank of Central Park at 72nd Street, was so far from Society's center or even frontier that it acquired the nickname Dakota. It seemed to the chic and powerful to bear a similar relation to the fashionable city that that territory bore to New York State (territorial status 1881, statehood 1889). But its patron, Edward S. Clark, heir to the Singer Sewing Machine Company, confounded the skeptics, as the West Side blossomed into the gridded streets in the Dakota's precincts.

In the vigorous city of Brooklyn, across the East River, an equally vigorous social life created enclaves of style and wealth. Brooklyn Heights, in effect founded in 1819 with the subdivision of its farmland into urban building lots, was at first the developing enclave of the well-to-do merchants of New York across the river. Modest Federal houses were soon supplanted by legions of the Greek Revival. And then, with the availability of a vast pool of Irish immigrant labor, servants became economical and houses ballooned into the Renaissance Revival. And with that Revival, not only grander row houses were commissioned on Pierrepont and Remsen streets, but many great mansions lined Columbia Heights, the street along the Heights proper, overlooking the Upper Bay and the four-storied many-steepled skyline of New York proper. On Pierrepont Place, Abiel Abbot Low, the banker and father of Seth Low, who became mayor of Brooklyn and president of Columbia College, built a grand brownstone house next to those of Henry Pierrepont and Alexander M. White (1857, Frederick A. Peterson). These three mansions (now there are two) are the palazzi, in the Florentine sense, of Brooklyn Heights.

But on Clinton Hill, two miles away, Charles Pratt commissioned a freestanding house not only for himself but for each of the first three of his four sons, as they were married; the four mansions show a minihistory of late nineteenth-century architecture for the wealthy along Clinton Avenue. And further into contemporary Brooklyn, on Park Slope, Edwin Litchfield had built his Italianate villa as early as 1857, to be followed much later, and on the completion of Prospect Park, with a line of grand mansions along its western edge, Prospect Park West. The Heights, the Hill, and the Slope fell into decline between the first and second World Wars but have all, in varying degrees, succumbed to gentrification in the 1960's, '70's, and '80's.

In Queens, a less clear image of fashionable leadership emerged. Some grand houses were built among what was then a series of small towns amid rural surroundings. William Steinway (of piano fame) bought and expanded an Italianate granite villa atop a small hill in present-day Astoria, overlooking his nearby factory to the southwest. And here and there the great white houses of sea captains, who sailed in the China trade and to the Caribbean Islands, overlooked their ships' berths along the west end of Long Island Sound. But ship captains were not fashion's leaders, and theirs was a kind of lonely elegance.

In the Bronx, while it too was merely a collection of country towns and farms, there were substantial Greek Revival houses such as those at Wave Hill of 1844, overlooking the Hudson and the Palisades from the heights of Riverdale. And the William E. Dodge residence, Greyston, was a Gothic Revival gem by James Renwick, Jr. The Dodges were not only copper magnates (Phelps, Dodge) but also were related by marriage to the founder of the American University in Beirut. Subsequent generations supplied two presidents to that institution. Aside from the romantic heights of Riverdale, now infilled with ungainly apartment buildings of dubious architecture, the Bronx offered little to the social explorer. An occasional mansion, most impressive of which is the Bartow-Pell house, stood alone in the east Bronx, overlooking Pelham Bay, from "feudal" times (built in 1675, altered into the Federal style from 1836 to 1845, and later "restored").

Charles M. Pratt House, 241 Clinton Avenue, Brooklyn. Now the residence of the bishop of Brooklyn, this wedding present was in the latest style of its time (1893), Romanesque Revival. Charles' brothers were equally grandly housed next door in Georgian Revival, the styles for a wealthy family's urban costumes when their turns had come.

Wave Hill, Riverdale, the Bronx. A large Greek Revival country house with a Gothic Revival hall attached, this was one of a pair of houses of the Perkins and Freeman families. It now shelters a conference center, with grand gardens and views of the Palisades, open to the public.

Sir Edward Cunard Residence, Grymes Hill, Staten Island. Now a Wagner College office building, this once was named Bellevue for its grand ocean vistas. From here Cunard, one of the English steamship clan, could view his liners steaming in and through the Narrows.

Staten Island's Grymes Hill offered a summer retreat for the more reserved wealthy or a rural estate for those more concerned with privacy than a social posture that could be viewed up close by the masses. In the 1830's through 1850's, this hill was covered with Gothic, then Stick, style houses for such as General William Greene Ward or Sir Edmund Cunard. Most are now converted to institutional use, several for Wagner College, which has usurped the east edge of the hill.

Now that the old guard has no more new territory to colonize in Manhattan—let alone other boroughs—it can maintain an austere in-city splendor only among the nouveau riche (or newer nouveau riche) and valiant rent-controlled remnant citizens from all income levels who are the happy chaff among their wheat. And what were once weekend "places" or country "cottages" for the same group's peregrinatory social life are mostly now nunneries, legations, and homes for the unhappy and infirm. A few of these suburban landmarks have found a new life as multiple condominiums where the towns, long holding out their right to the single-family dwelling (even on vast reaches of land), have given in to social realities and allowed the merely affluent to subdivide palaces into grand apartments.

Back in Manhattan, the greater town houses of the sidestreeted Upper East Side have long been honeycombed for the preppies of the 1950's and '60's and '70's. But the new breed of the 1970's and '80's seems more interested in internal style within a bland envelope—square footage and kitchens—rather than architecture or serious design. A Jacuzzi for two, a bidet, perhaps a view, and a marble duet of sinks seem more enticing to the upwardly mobile than an architecturally rich and human-scaled neighborhood. And therefore a high-rise mania has gripped the blocks east of Central Park. To live in an aerie among architectural and urban history and urbane streets has diminished the cohesion and group style of this sector—in a manner not unlike similar previous incursions of cellular life, high- and medium-rised, into Greenwich Village, Brooklyn Heights, and other rich architectural conclaves.

"I was under no illusion that" (said Lionel Trilling) "[Greenwich] Village was any longer in its great days—I knew that in the matter of residential preference I was a mere epigone. So much so, indeed, that my apartment was not in a brownstone house or in a more-or-less reconditioned tenement, but in a brand new, yellow-brick, jerry-built six-story apartment building, exactly like the apartment buildings that were going up all over the Bronx and Brooklyn. Still, the Village was the Village, there seemed no other place in New York where a right-thinking person might live, . . . What is more, my address was Bank Street, which, of all the famous streets of the Village, seemed to me at the time to have had the most distinguished literary past."

Town Houses, East 73rd Street, Manhattan. The side streets housed the less wealthy or the more discreet. Here the Joseph Pulitzer mansion shares the block with the handsome homes of ordinary wealth.

Riverside Apartments, Brooklyn Heights. These bravely experimental apartments reversed the proportions of the typical tenement. The long dimension here was that with windows, bringing maximum sun and air to the interior. To improve matters even more, the open-access corridors allowed all apartments to have true cross-ventilation, sixty years before air conditioning became a popular possibility.

11.

The Populous City

The character of cities as a whole is largely expressed in the built bulk of their housing, form that occupies ten times the volume of a city's commerce and culture, monuments, and parks and that creates the image that becomes a traveler's memory of Paris or Rome, London or New York, San Francisco or São Paolo. Housing determines and is determined by the configuration of streets and public spaces, such as the great boulevards, *places*, and *piazze* of Paris and Rome, the garden squares of London (although, in some instances, these have been usurped by modern infiltrating offices). More specifically, in Paris, there is the Avenue Foch, its Park Avenue, and the Place des Vosges, with shops and restaurants at the ground level. Rome has the Via Sistina, the Corso, the Piazza Navona, all with bulk housing mounted above minor commerce. In London, there are Bedford and Russell squares.

In New York, there is Park Avenue, the tenemented streets of Harlem, suburban Queens, meandering Greenwich Village, the backwaters of Brooklyn Heights, the relentless speculation of Staten Island, and that organic

Christopher Street, Greenwich Village. The street's activity comes in part from an interplay of ground-floor shops and restaurants, with apartments above. The resulting life is in sharp contrast to the bedroom ghettos of housing projects and suburbia.

plan of lower Manhattan, left as a memory of the seventeenth-century Dutch life, now usurped by the gigantism of the world's financial center. On their arrival, the Dutch settlers quickly built a simplified set of Amsterdam houses that shared dwelling space with work and storage. These lined and formed the streets, creating most of lower Manhattan's plan, houses that surrounded gardens filling the interiors of these often immense blocks. The creation of New Amsterdam therefore created the urban plan that in turn financiers, corporate lawyers, and their allies work in today.

In Boston, a somewhat apocryphal tradition claims that cows, grazing on the Common and taking a comfortable route home to or with their masters, set the streets that were later formalized and lined with houses. New Amsterdam's Dutch, however, managed a plan seemingly equally arbitrary or capricious, based upon the island's irregular shape, its topography, springs, ponds, marshes, and adaptability for seventeenth-century defense (water on three sides, the wall on the fourth). In both cities the streets seem to meander without reason, but reasons there were of different sorts, rational to their times. Reasons became reason with the imposition of the grid or commissioners' plan, ordered by the state legislature and promulgated in 1811. The commissioners' plan blanketed the island with blocks 200 feet long north–south and 600 to 900 feet long east–west and with avenues 100 feet wide—but with no central park, which was "not needed" because of the vast water frontage. Later variations added the 840-acre Central Park and inserted Lexington and Madison avenues between Third and Park (Fourth) and Park and Fifth. The new avenues were narrowed to 80 and 85 feet respectively in order to save valued real estate.

This relentless set of right angles was like a brand on the wilderness of Manhattan's forests, hills, springs, and streams, ignoring them so that inevitably the forests were cut, the hills leveled, and the streams seduced into the underground pipery that bore them invisibly from source to sea. And the housing that infilled these two thousand blocks was at first the same that replaced the Dutch city: simplified Georgian brick row houses of two or three floors (plus basement and dormered attic).

Although the Federal houses of Brooklyn rarely attained more than thirty-two hundred square feet, the early New York counterparts housed a family, and perhaps its servants, in a very generous four to five thousand square feet: a basement kitchen and dining room, twin parlors (front and back) on the first (parlor) floor; bedrooms (front, back, and hall) on the second and third (if there is one); the servants in the dormered attic.

Before substantial immigration of the poor of Ireland, Italy, and eastern Europe (largely due to the Irish potato famine of the 1840's, Sicilian poverty, and Russian pogroms respectively), the population was bourgeois pioneers, urban pioneers in relatively sophisticated circumstances but pioneers trading on the resources of a continent colonized and exploited by Europeans for only 175 years by 1800. Housing for the masses did not exist save for a ragged few who shared older, ill-kempt places, remnants still of the Dutch.

The nomenclature of floors differs in different countries and even within the same country. The ground floor of Britain becomes the *rez-de-chaussée* in France but is America's first floor. The first floor of Britain and the Continent, and the *piano nobile* (elevated floor) of the Italian Renaissance, are America's second floor. New York's basement is a legal and liveable space, more than half above the ground surrounding; and a cellar is what is, in turn, below the basement. The best example of a typical basement is that of a traditional brownstone, served by a stoop, where the main reception floor (first floor) is at the stoop's crest; below, with a separate entry under the stoop, were the service areas, servants' workspace and kitchen, less than half under, more than half above street grade. The brownstone evolved in a period of Renaissance Revivalism, and the first floor became a neo–*piano nobile*, positioned

A Grand Stoop, Pierrepont Street, Brooklyn. A drawbridged portal or a triumphal arch are parts of the celebration of entry, of arrival. And so the stoop became the not-so-common man's personal place of reception, enriching the perspective of the street.

imperiously above the streetscape and internally providing high, grand space for reception in a "parlor" of visitors or guests. Hence it was also termed the parlor floor.

The stoop derived perhaps from the Dutch *stoep*, a flight of steps to raise the first level above potential flooding in a country threatened by rising seas or the leaking or breaching of dikes. But it also worked grandly for the concept of the parlor floor, giving posture to that remembrance of the *piano nobile* without consuming the internal space of a limited site and plan (typically, at best, twenty-five wide by 100 feet deep; but often only eighteen, twenty, or twenty-two feet wide). The stoop became an architectural statement in its own right that was, in turn, lopped off in the name of style to make the architecture seem more English, as in London homes entered straight from the street. The stylistic pioneer was Elsie de Wolfe, America's first interior decorator in the modern sense (here, exterior de-decorating), who later managed to Anglicize her own person, becoming, on her marriage in 1926, Lady Mendl. But the stoop railing, or parapet-balustrade, of bronze, cast iron, steel, or brownstone was wrought, carved, cast, and sculpted to form a visual identity within a systemized discipline that often gives to the grid of Manhattan and Brooklyn a variety and rhythm that converts the potential of regimentation to a pleasant discipline, in the way that the human face gives strong identity to most individuals with the same set of parts for everyone.

The first housing, as opposed to houses, for New York's burgeoning bulk population was tenements, now a pejorative word not only because tenements admit minimal light and air but also because of their overcrowding—in reality a problem of use, not architecture. Tenements allowed concentration: the prototypical 25-by-100 site once alloted to a Federal house now supported a tenement, or a tenement was built on a virgin part of the commissioners' grid, five stories (sometimes six plus a basement) built ninety feet deep. This model contained up to twenty apartments (plus a superintendent in the cellar), each with one bedroom, a shared bathroom in the hall, common to four units on each floor. Tenements, in increasingly regulated form, were built from the 1840's to 1929, when, in effect, they were outlawed by the new requirements of the New York State Multiple Dwelling Law, demanding less density and more light and air. Vast numbers of tenements, however, still survive in their original or remodeled form, but many have ended up as the gutted shells of Brownsville or the rubble of the south Bronx.

The Danish-American reporter Jacob Riis wrote in the *New York Sun* in 1922, describing the neighborhood near Washington's official residence in his first year as President: "We stand upon the domain of the tenement. In the shadow of the great stone abutments [of the Brooklyn Bridge], the old Knickerbocker houses linger like ghosts of a departed day. Down the winding slope of Cherry Street—proud and fashionable Cherry Hill that was—their broad steps, sloping roofs, and dormer windows are easily made out; all the more easily for the contrast with the ugly barracks that elbow them right and left. . . ."

In reaction to the tenement's exploitation of land and population, social activists and architects, in a series of competitions and experimental constructions, attempted to bring efficiency, economy, light, and air to the nineteenth-century walk-up apartment still, however, generally called the tenement.

In *Jews Without Money* (1930) Michael Gold evoked the Lower East Side of his childhood: "A tenement canyon hung with fire-escapes, bedclothing and faces. Always these faces at the tenement windows. The street never failed them. It was an immense excitement." Sculptor Jacob Epstein, in his autobiography, *Let There Be Sculpture* (1940), also remembered it: "When my parents moved to a more respectable and duller part of the city, it held no interest whatever for me. I hired a room in Hester Street in a wooden, ramshackle building that seemed to date back at least a hundred years and, from my window overlooking the market, made drawings daily."

Tenement Houses, 135th Street, Manhattan. Where the bulk population lived, the lower middle class and the poor. The facade was appliqué, a false front on these deep and ill lit barracks. A quarter of New York's housing is still in tenements.

In his novel *The City Boy* (1948) Herman Wouk recalled the Bronx of the 1920's, with his building "a brick cliff very much like other brick cliffs that stood wall to wall for many blocks along the less rocky side of the street. It was gray, square, five stories high, punctured with windows, and saved from bleakness only by the entrance, which tried on a little matter of plaster gargoyles overhead and dead shrubs in cracked plaster urns on either side of the iron-grilled glass doors."

With the City and Suburban Homes Company as a client, and Henry Atterbury Smith, Ernest Flagg, and I. N. Phelps Stokes, for example, as architects, buildings were produced that proved the possibility of quality within the economic context that created the typical tenement, a program coincidental with the state-promulgated Tenement House Law of 1901 marking the beginning of the so-called New Law tenement and requiring more light and air, larger light courts, and greater rearyard setbacks. The Cherokee Apartments (1912), 77th to 78th streets east of First Avenue, not only made use of gracious courtyards to produce light and air but thereby, with its tunnel-vaulted entries, provided stylish and elegant access. Windows almost to the floor (triple-hung), with railings to protect the occupants, give a European flavor to the street.

It was Brooklyn that was the site of the first both architecturally and financially experimental housing for the moderate income family. A Brooklyn businessman, Alfred Tredway White, with "enlightened self-interest" (dubiously termed: by his own motto it was "philanthropy plus 5 percent," when 5 percent was a terrific rate for the lender), commissioned architects William Field and Son to create, in the spirit of the then new "sun-lighted tenements" of Victorian London, housing for his workers and their families. The product, at both the Tower and the Home apartments in Cobble Hill, and Riverside in Brooklyn Heights, are six-story buildings originally entered at a series of spiral stairs serving open-access balconies. The apartments are floor-through, with cross-ventilation, and

Tower and Home Apartments, Cobble Hill, Brooklyn. The very best of tenement experiments (with its sister apartments in Brooklyn Heights, Riverside), these 1870's dwellings have light, air, a common garden, and a strong "modern" architectural character.

overlook, from the opposite or living room side, a peaceful central garden court (truncated at Riverside diagonally by the Brooklyn–Queens Expressway of 1951). The catch, however, as an example for speculators to follow, was that Field's use of land provided a much lower and hence less profitable density than tenements of the ordinary sardine variety.

Simultaneous with tenements as the urban infill for the poor and lower middle classes came the brownstone town house, a nomenclature so ubiquitous that it is equally and loosely applied to town houses made of brick. Brownstone, or brown or red sandstone, is a sedimentary rock quarried at the edge of river basins: for New York these were the Hackensack (N.J.) and Connecticut rivers. The brownstone was the inexpensive "developer's house" for the bourgeoisie (mostly petite), faced with soft and easily carved material, veneering the brick understructure, creating a facade with historic allusions to the ordinary family. Tens of thousands filled the streets between the grand houses of the rich and the tenements of the lower economic masses—between Lexington and Third on Manhattan's Upper East Side, in the East and West 40's and 50's, in Harlem's 120's, and in Brooklyn's Park Slope, Cobble Hill, and Bedford-Stuyvesant. The brownstone was larger than the Federal or Greek Revival house, deeper, and usually a story taller. Its arrival on the urban landscape coincided with the great immigration of young, untrained Irish women, fleeing the potato famine and hence available for roles as servants (what else could they do?) to clean and service these sometimes inflated establishments. The more common speculators' brownstone of the then unfashionable Upper East Side east of Third Avenue (1880's) could be as small, however, as fifteen by fifty feet on four floors (three thousand square feet), while the grand brownstones of Brooklyn's Remsen Street or Washington Avenue reached thirty-seven by seventy feet and five floors (thirteen thousand square feet); but the average was somewhere in between.

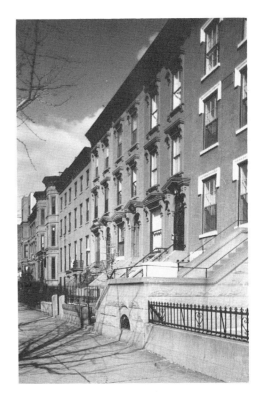

Brownstones, Fort Greene Park, Brooklyn. Brownstones, with independent clients and a free budget, were sometimes presented in clusters of variable grandeur. Easy carving of this soft sedimentary stone permitted virtuosity in details.

First New York "Apartment House," East 18th Street. Richard Morris Hunt not only was trained at the Ecole des Beaux-Arts but also brought Parisian ideas to New York—here in the city's first apartment house—"French flats" to New Yorkers.

Later, these spacious establishments would be reincarnated as the gentrified brown elephants of the 1960's and 1970's, providing as many as five to ten apartments where there had been one family with related servants.

New York's first apartment house was Rutherford Stuyvesant's building on East 18th Street (1869). Apartment housing was a European, both Continental and British, tradition before it blossomed in America. New Yorkers were the first to succumb to its economy of servants and land in the press for convenience of location in time in the preautomobile, presubway city and to embrace it for its fashion ("French flats," they said—and suddenly Paris was in New York). The tenement had been a model of what not to follow, and the elevator allowed not only the grandeur of a high point of view (in the tenement the highest floor was the cheapest) but also the pomp of service by both a doorman (a community butler) or elevator operator (the community footman). Apartment houses ranged from the modest and efficient to the extravagant; there was no limit to their size and grandeur merely because they were part of a larger whole.

Mrs. Marjorie Meriwether Post built an apartment house in 1925 at 1107 Fifth Avenue to provide for herself a town house at its summit: a fifty-four-room triplex that outshone in internal size and splendor most mansions on the ground (compare the James Duke house at 78th Street and Fifth, grand to the street but less flamboyant in its internal facilities).

The West Side, a more European-oriented part of town, led the way in apartment experimentation and construction, the pathfinder being the Dakota (1884), followed by a spate of buildings up to the end of a first wave (1908). In these years the West Side acquired a bevy of grand eclectic "palaces," with large and sprawling plans reminiscent of Paris, Rome, or Budapest, rooms stringing like beads along long corridors or galleries, wrapping around streets and courts.

The West Side, as the goal of the wealthy immigrant,

balanced the East Side, the about-to-become habitat of the apartment WASP after World War I. Buildings followed the street framework, much as if they were but high-rise and palatial cousins (and sometimes replacements) of the town house. West Side brick and limestone town houses, however, developed later than those to the east, that first glut of brownstones that gave way to later apartment houses on the side streets east of Park Avenue.

Symbolic of the West Side is the two-and-one-half-mile-long composite facade of Central Park West, with strong representation from the end of the nineteenth through the first decade of the twentieth century. But its silhouette is punctuated by the boom of the late 1920's and early '30's: the Century (1931), Majestic (1930), San Remo (1930), Beresford (1929), and Eldorado (1931) are blockfront volumes with twin towers fingering the sky over Central Park. These were started at the crest of the economic boom and completed at or after the great stock market crash of 1929.

Apartment building on the East Side largely bloomed in the period during and after World War I, lingering into the late 1920's and early '30's. A major breakthrough was in the creation and renaming of Park Avenue. As Fourth Avenue, it had borne train traffic to the original city terminal at Chambers Street, then to 23rd Street, where the New York Life Insurance Company now stands, and finally to the first of three Grand Central terminals at 42nd to 45th streets. Electric-powered trains were the means to the elegant end-solution—the covering of the railroad right-of-way and yards, the installation of a parklike mall, and the sale of air rights to build over the yards at either side of the avenue between 45th and 49th streets. North of 50th Street, only the railroad tunnels' masonry barrel vaults pass under Park Avenue proper; and the frontage of modest buildings, brownstones, and factories from 50th to 96th streets was largely and slowly replaced by fifteen-story high-rise palazzi, obviously inspired to varying degrees—from lip service to fully quoined and rusticated and corniced—by the fifteenth century of Rome and Florence, as cooled

Grand Concourse. The Bronx, rural during most of the nineteenth century, bore the Speedway Concourse as an escape route to its great parks. That boulevard became truly grand on this alignment for the apartments of the 1930's, the upwardly mobile Art Deco stylish haven of immigrant Jews.

and simplified by London: inflated and understated, frequently individually boring, but servant buildings to a larger whole. Here is housing creating form in concert with a Parisian boulevard in the Haussmann sense, catalyzed, however, not by a military or aesthetic discipline but by the engineering event of submerging the trains.

Baron Georges Eugène Haussmann was the appointed prefect of Paris (1853–1870) under Napoleon III. In the name of mob control, great boulevards were created, impaling medieval sectors in great swaths that were veneered frequently with facades, shallow over existing medieval structures. Six stories was the limit, but the mansarded roofs (after François Mansart) often housed two more floors in an effort to exploit the land to its maximum. Here visual order was given to the city in the name of military order. Today, the remembered vision and color of Paris is largely in its great but scattered monuments and in its later nineteenth-century boulevards.

The discipline and understated elegance of Park Avenue below 59th Street was broken after World War II by commercial buildings that replaced all but one of the apartment houses with new office buildings ranging from banality to distinction—from Colgate to Lever, from American Tobacco to Seagram, a pride of lions needing advertising as their basic food—architecture that related to the seat of sales rather than the seat of some more elegant posture. But, sadly, even the best of the lot (Lever House and Seagram) broke the unity of the Park Avenue building wall with form that was out of concert and space that "leaked" the order of the boulevard. Some bland neighbors were merely fat squatters.

Happily, from 59th to 96th streets, the avenue remains substantially as conceived. A few sparse remnants antedate the boulevard quality of the place, as in the old Lewis G. Morris House at 85th Street (1910), the George F. Baker House at 93rd Street, or the Percy Pyne House at 68th Street (1909) and neighbors on the same block to the north (1917–1926). These aberrants are wonderful, variations that make the system seem right.

The Park Avenue experience was matched in similar experiments in boulevardism, most prominently at the Grand Concourse (Bronx, 1892, as the Speedway Concourse, a route originally planned for Manhattanites to reach the open parks of the Bronx), and lined only with architecture of the 1920's and '30's, Art Deco and Art Moderne periods that make this one of the grand reservoirs of these styles. Later, West End Avenue (Eleventh Avenue renamed from 59th Street to 107th Street) maintains the uniform boulevardism of Park Avenue, but in a narrower place and without the "Park." In Brooklyn, both Eastern and Ocean parkways, laid out by Frederick Law Olmsted, designer of both Central and Prospect parks, were intended as boulevards and still serve as great auto routes without the tall and grand buildings intended in the Parisian manner. Between Grand Army Plaza and Washington Avenue there is one strong section, though with great apartment houses continuously on the north side, and great institutions to the south: Brooklyn Public Library, Botanic Garden, and Brooklyn Museum.

The street, with town house, brownstone, tenement, or apartment house flush and facing it, was served and defined by such housing throughout urban history: whether in classical Rome (Ostia), medieval Strasbourg, Renaissance Florence, Baroque Rome, eighteenth-century London, or nineteenth-century Paris. This pattern, in the inner city, was broken only by the American public housers of the 1930's and 1940's, who grasped with passion the city-planning ideas (without benefit of his architectural thoughts) of the great Swiss-French architect Charles Edouard Jeanneret, known as Le Corbusier.

Le Corbusier's "Ville Radieuse," "Ville Verte," and "Plan Voisin" for Paris proposed erasing vast areas of central Paris, replacing them with a parklike landscape studded with freestanding high-rise towers, some for offices, others

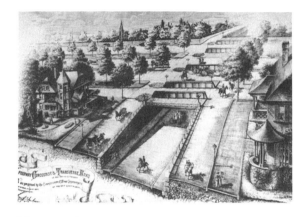

The Speedway Concourse, the Bronx. When only a boulevard without dwellings or boulevardiers, the Speedway was an engineer's dream.

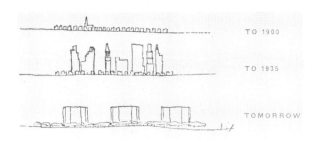

TO 1900

TO 1935

TOMORROW

Le Corbusier's New York. Corbu's sketch plan for New York would "correct," by elimination, the noxious streets, replacing them with freestanding skyscrapers—the existing ones of the 1930's were "too small"—amid parkland and the necessary interconnecting highways.

for apartments. The scale was that of the auto, almost an icon in Corbu's scheme of things. He was fascinated with America: with the highways (not big enough though), with the skyscrapers (not tall enough though), and with the dams that dominated and dwarfed natural landscapes. But of course it should be remembered that this was in the early 1930's, when technology itself was almost a new religion.

Le Corbusier's urban mission, transferred to New York's public housing, embraced the concept of freestanding towers on superblocks amid lawns (untouchables that are chained off from the wear of strollers and children's play) without, however, the benefit of Corbu's classy architecture. Superblocks (clustered blocks of the 1811 grid) were assembled, and six or ten or more red-brick spartan towers were geometrically marched over the landscape. The street was canceled, and, to exaggerate the isolation from the surrounding city, shops were banned. The place and route of urbane city life, the street with shops and windows, was gone, the residents marooned on a bedroom island from which they had to emigrate to the surrounding traditional city.

The exception, paradoxically, to a dogma of freestanding high-rise, shopless public housing was New York's very first project: Williamsburg Houses, built in 1937 in the Williamsburg section of northwest Brooklyn, four stories, continuous, and street-fronted on the perimeter streets with some shops. Here in the low scale of Williamsburg, this project is a modest neighbor (for its vast sixteen-hundred-unit size), where interior courtyards are of a different vocabulary from the streets around but of a character in scale and concert with them.

Housing, as opposed to houses, here in the hands of tender bureaucrats and architects, became nonarchitecture in the name of economy and modernity. In fact, there is reason to suspect that the very symbolic nature of freestanding brick towers among a grass island would assuage the politicians, protecting them from a middle class husbanding its own identity coming from the better tenements of the Upper East Side to Park Avenue: the towering ghetto was clearly separated from the surrounding city.

Much later, after World War II, the middle class got its share of grassed towers at Stuyvesant Town and Peter Cooper Village, built in 1947 with the idea of housing returning veterans and their families, but here in tight juxtaposition with a lively First Avenue commercial strip—still a "ghetto" but of a higher economic level.

Outside the density and bulk of Manhattan (100 people per acre, approximately, in 1980, and in enclaves as much as 600–1,000 people per acre), the other boroughs, excepting the old brownstone city of Brooklyn and the vast tenements of the Bronx, were largely suburban: 35 people per acre for the overall city; 9 for Staten Island; 26 for Queens.

Old Brooklyn, the city of the nineteenth century, was largely a brownstone, brick, and limestone set of row houses, with occasional mansions in grand locations such as those facing Prospect Park, or on the crest of Clinton Hill, or overseeing Brooklyn Heights harbor. It was largely a bedroom city, expanded from its first density at Brooklyn Heights, and had been called New York's first suburb by dint of Fulton's steam-powered ferry that allowed quick and reliable transport across the East River. The City of Brooklyn in the period between 1820 (population, 11,187) and 1898, the year of consolidation with New York (population, 1,000,000+), infilled gridded blocks in areas now named or renamed in the spirit of gentrification—Cobble Hill, Carroll Gardens, Boerum Hill, Park Slope, Prospect Heights, Lefferts Gardens—and neighborhoods that still may be similarly gentrified, such as Bedford-Stuyvesant and Crown Heights, once staunch, still handsome, precincts of the middle class.

Bedford-Stuyvesant, still marked as a ghetto if not a slum, is in fact an area of houses of distinction, largely brownstones, that served the middle- and upper-middle income classes. F. W. Woolworth's mansion at 209 Jefferson Street (1890) is a case in point.

Williamsburg Houses. The best of the 1930's. The exposed concrete structures and corner windows were avant-garde. The low scale with separate entries and no corridors retained the more personal cityscape lost in public housing.

Twentieth-century Brooklyn, Queens, and Staten Island mostly took the suburban route, with freestanding, one-, two- and three-family houses that allowed their lords the feeling of pioneer America: a castle on the ground, with one or two other families that were, of course, subservient to the land lord.

Beyond the "pale," therefore, in-city suburban living blossomed in outer Brooklyn, most of Queens, almost all of Staten Island, and in the west Bronx. The single-family house and then the two- and three-family home dominated these vast areas and populations, mostly housing a modest middle class—with great exceptions in the Bronx's Riverdale and Fieldston; Queens' Jamaica Estates, Jackson Heights, and Forest Hills Gardens; Staten Island's Grymes and Todt hills; Brooklyn's Prospect Park South, and parts of Bay Ridge. All these were pockets of the affluent.

With staunch individualism and conservatism, the skilled working population strove for the identity of a freestanding house, lawn, garage, and garden, while the very affluent and rich were delighted with the convenience and elegance of a central Manhattan high rise. Those born poor in the center city often, when more affluent, moved to the suburbs; those born in the suburbs usually stayed there. And those born to affluence in the city, more often than not, stayed in the city.

Invader of the single-family precincts was the garden apartment, which seemingly provided a cheap alternative to the single family house, while it maintained a semblance of suburban scale and vegetation. Queens, in particular, gave way to numerous two-story rambling units that tended to maintain the staccato streetscape and that were reminiscent of the suburban idea.

In the 1930's through '60's the six-story apartment house was a popular developer's medium because state and city laws allowed an economical package of six levels, at a maximum, to be constructed of load-bearing masonry walls with wood beams, as opposed to fireproof reinforced-con-

Staten Island's New Suburbia. The banal monotony and vulgarity of most of post–World War II Staten Island seems a tragedy. What if an enlightened American developer had concentrated it all in a series of Bloomsburys and left, in contrast, a network of great streets and parks?

crete or fireproofed steel required when buildings were taller.

Ebenezer Howard, the English stenographer, turned his meticulous mind and training to the social planning of cities, becoming, in effect, the soul-parent of "garden cities" and "new towns." His naïve chart of the virtues, evils, lacks, and benefits of city and country inspired him to propose the compromise, the planned "garden" city, as one of a series appended to a major metropolis—in this case, London. Although not an architect himself, his work inspired Sir Raymond Unwin to create the early twentieth-century garden cities of Letchworth and Welwyn. They were to be balanced places of work, dwelling, and recreation, with a need for the center city (London) only for special events, on special occasions. Filled with the vegetation of seventy years and warmed by the patina of age, Letchworth and Welwyn seem comfortable, well-planned suburbs for those who savor a compromise life-style.

Inspired by Howard, Unwin, and their peers, planners and architects of New York's twentieth century gathered in the late 1920's and early '30's to combat the touted evils of the city (tenements, crowding, lack of light and air, speculators' exploitation) with new solutions. What evolved for New York in government-financed housing were First Houses and Williamsburg Houses and, in the private world, Forest Hills Gardens.

Among the leaders in planned communities were critic-writer Lewis Mumford and architects Clarence Stein and Henry Wright, who jointly and with others created the experimental towns of Radburn, New Jersey; Greenbelt, Maryland; and Baldwin Hills Village (Los Angeles), California; all are noted for their clustered housing, common garden areas, and separation of pedestrian and vehicular traffic. Amazingly, this last virtue was incorporated in the park designs of Frederick Law Olmsted at Central and Prospect parks as early as the 1860's. More important to them was the disposition of elements, rather than the char-

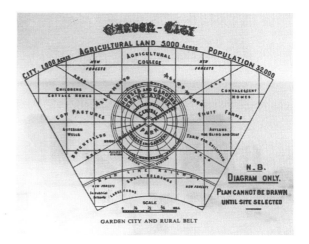

GARDEN CITY AND RURAL BELT

Ebenezer Howard's Diagram. Howard was the surprising theoretician of the "garden city" movement, a balanced plan of work and ordinary life. The resulting suburbias in Great Britain and the United States, however, became bedroom communities, satellite to London and New York, mostly without any business or cultural life of their own.

Sunnyside Gardens, Queens. Here the true middle middle class had a pleasant, tree-filled, small-scale community of row houses surrounding common gardens. This is a pleasant environment without any important architecture.

Forest Hills Gardens, Queens. The gentle curves of Olmsted, Jr.'s plan give a constantly changing perspective to the picturesque architecture of the Gardens.

acter (urban design) of individual architecture. What was missing here was urban street life, because the bedroom and living room were truly isolated from street and shop. More urbane solutions, but still without street activity and vitality, were those blocks of Queens that became Sunnyside Gardens (1924) on cheap mosquito-infested land, two-story street-fronted and alley-fronted buildings surrounding common central gardens. The project was a proven success in that two of its creators, Henry Wright and Lewis Mumford, lived there happily for a generation.

Previous to the work of Stein, Mumford, and Wright, less widely known and less documented, was Forest Hills Gardens (1913–), an enclave in the center of Queens next to the then existing affluent suburb of Kew Gardens. Queens was rural in the 1930's beyond the industrial suburbs of Long Island City (chewing gum, crackers, and warehousing) and Astoria (Steinway and Sohmer pianos) and the suburban former towns of Flushing, Whitestone, and Jamaica. In the late 1940's the surge of returning veterans yearned for that American ideal, the freestanding house, however small, on a lawn, however small, which British writer J. M. Richards termed *The Castles on the Ground.* And in the 1930's, with the advent of the E and F trains piercing this tranquil countryside, development became inevitable. Cows munched where Borough Hall now stands. But the forerunner of any conscious development, as opposed to laissez-faire evolution, was Forest Hills Gardens of 1910:

"Apart from its convenient location, within a quarter of an hour of the center of Manhattan Island, the Forest Hills Gardens enterprise differentiates itself . . . from other suburban development schemes most notably in that its size permits a *unique layout* of winding streets, open spaces and building lots and thus permits the development of an ideally attractive neighborhood, while its financial backing is such that the realization of the well studied plans is assured in advance beyond peradventure" wrote Alfred Tredway White in a promotional booklet of 1911. White would not have been disappointed in the eventual product. This has become Queens' most distinguished and exclusive residential enclave. It is without a doubt a splendid, and unique (for this city), combination of suburban planning and of romantic, picturesque architecture.

At first an island in farmland, Forest Hills Gardens is now an island amid the unplanned commercial speculation that surged down Queens Boulevard from the 1940's through '70's. Romantically planned and lushly landscaped by Frederick Law Olmsted, Jr. (son of the designer of Central and Prospect parks), the buildings are designed largely by Grosvenor Atterbury, neo-Tudor and Arts and Crafts cottages built, however, of tilt-up concrete. A mixed palette of housing types includes single-family houses from substantial to grand, two-family houses, row houses, garden apartments, and medium-rise apartment buildings, all within the picturesquely "painted" master plan of Olmsted and Atterbury. Not surprisingly, the Gardens were the product not of private speculative development but, rather, of the sponsorship of a private foundation, that of Russell Sage.

Alfred T. White, active in the development of Forest Hills Gardens, had built Brooklyn's Tower and Home, then Riverside Apartments in the 1870's. Others who have experimented gratuitously and/or philanthropically in prototypical housing included John D. Rockefeller, Jr., whose Thomas Garden Apartments (1928, Grand Concourse, Bronx), and Dunbar Apartments (1928, Harlem, both by architect Andrew J. Thomas) were attempts to bring housing quality to the middle class. The Astor estate created Harlem's Graham Court Apartments (1901, Clinton and Russell). The Phipps Houses, over seventy-five years, have experimented with housing in diverse sections of the city and varying ways: Phipps Houses, West 63rd and 64th streets (1907 and 1911, Whitefield and King); Phipps Garden Apartments next to Sunnyside Gardens (1931, Clarence Stein); Lambert Houses next to the Bronx Zoo (1973, Davis, Brody and Associates); Phipps Plaza (1976, Frost

Lambert Houses, the Bronx. An experiment in bringing back a gentle scale of street and building to the poor, here at the south entry of the Bronx Zoo. The simple brick buildings have a modulation of form that is enough to give character appropriate to a London street front.

Associates), 26th to 29th Street on Second Avenue, and others.

The Whites, Phippses, and Rockefellers moved into an experimental vacuum, as free enterprise did not: the latter only exploited the city, constrained only by the market and, to a certain extent, by the inertia of tradition, by the grid plan superposed by the commissioners in Manhattan, and by developer-hired surveyors in Brooklyn. Controls of a modest nature constrained, rather than inspired, housing: minimum cubage per person in the 1840's, minimum light and air (Tenement House Law, 1901), more light and air and more safety requirements (Multiple Dwelling Law, 1929). But inspiration, for better or worse, passed into government hands with the advent of public housing in the 1930's: New York was the pioneer American City, with a Housing Authority before the Roosevelt Administration's own program became a reality. The federal Public Housing Administration (PHA) was catalyzed by New York's Senator Robert F. Wagner. This was housing for the poor, designed like a utility's network, warehousing of families out of context with the city. With a bit of exterior decoration (stucco, tile, a bit of stone, a shape or wiggle here and there) it studded ground later across America, surrounded Paris and Rome and Moscow (except with the European panache of shops and hard people-plazas), leaving the center city for the very rich, the tourist, and the very poor—mostly, not always—or the very imaginative. From 1931 to 1968 public housing was social passion, middle-class guilt, and Protestant good works, patronizing the poor.

In the late 1960's Mayor Lindsay attempted, with so-called model cities grants from the federal government, to insert public housing into the context of decaying neighborhoods, which were low-rise and of a friendly scale. The success was limited architecturally, but blockbusting (literally) gave way to block reinforcement, and reemphasis of the street as public space.

Both New York City and New York State also as-

Roosevelt Island. The state Urban Development Corporation commissioned Jose Luis Sert to consummate much of Philip Johnson's master plan for the island's housing. Fingers reach out from Main Street to the river views and breezes.

sisted in creating "limited profit" middle-income housing, where developers, building to certain standards and constrained to modest profits (originally 6 percent, but of what?), built housing mostly little different, unhappily, from public housing (with balconies to console the middle class), until the 1960's, when such projects as Riverbend (Davis, Brody and Associates) recelebrated the street with urbane architecture.

And the refreshing visions of New York State Urban Development Administrator Edward J. Logue brought us a super Main Street at Roosevelt Island.

Metropolitan Museum of Art. If Blenheim could not be replicated in New York as a mansion, its grandeur and scale could house a great museum of art. The modest neo-Gothic structure of Calvert Vaux was here dressed in neo-baroque splendor and reoriented from park to city.

12.

Gentlemen Prefer Monuments

At the end of the nineteenth century New York's plan was largely frozen, its transportation systems in place, its blocks ventilated with the great Central and Prospect parks, its boroughs laced together with bridges. Elevators and steel had brought to it a burgeoning skyline, and the city grew up all over, as its 320 square miles became infilled, and up was the only direction possible in many sectors. The challenge to patrons and architects was now one of creating grandeur—monuments to embellish the architectural engineering that had made the city's largely frozen template. Excisions were to occur, modulating the streets, but with the creation of Central and Prospect parks, of Grand Central and Park Avenue, the opportunities for impact were now in buildings and projects, monuments to the glory of commerce, art, government, education, and individual wealth.

To the gentlemen architects who dominated the profession in those times, the modern architecture born in Chicago and growing in Europe was a joke, a threat, a horror, a bewilderment, perhaps to be embraced for its search for a functional plan but not for its style. These not-so-gentle men basked in the fading light of archaeology, bringing to America and New York buildings of grandeur despised by the modernists of the 1930's through 1960's and beloved by grown-up architects today (post-Modernists included).

In a society where no one of social or financial power and eminence was far from being *nouveau riche* (the Astors were but a few generations from the beaver pelt trade), status—complete with some tangible stage sets for both living and working—was essential. To be a gentleman one would have to appear to be one, and the architectural trappings for that were available for mere money. And thus the mansions of Astors, Vanderbilts, Carnegies, and their peers became powerful architectural presences. But in the waning of these needs, where self-confidence grew and where the private palace was no longer necessary as a prop to one's image and ego (Park and Fifth Avenue duplexes were enough), the wealthy embellished the city with clubs, churches, libraries, and office buildings and extended their dwellings to the country. The aim was to fulfill an image of gracious history, and of course most architects of this era came from countries with a gracious history: Great Britain with a smattering of France and Germany. Thus, remembrances of things past grew mostly in medieval and Renaissance ways, providing grandiose civic scenes and, sometimes, great spaces that could awe the naïve and sophisticated alike.

In New York's urban precincts McKim, Mead and White were builders of neo-Italian palazzi; Cram, Goodhue and Ferguson of great neo-Gothic churches; Welles Bosworth of sprawling and multitiered temples of commerce and learning; Carrère and Hastings a library worthy of Napoleon; Ernest Flagg a Beaux Arts tower that would have that Ecole trembling with jealousy; Cass Gilbert, Roman temples, Gothic skyscrapers, and Beaux Arts palaces, with three towers capped with gold on the New York skyline; John Russell Pope, a painting gallery for a steel

Pennsylvania Station Train Shed, 1910.
A station on the way from Boston to Washington—rather than a terminal—Penn Station outdid its European mentors by its multilevel iron-and-glass train shed, a technology of shelter that Napoleon III had termed the "umbrellas" of his Paris.

mogul; Trowbridge and Livingston, a Parisian hotel; Warren and Wetmore, another palace, this time for the celebration of arrival at the heart of the city.

Charles Follen McKim (1847–1909), William Rutherford Mead (1846–1928), and Stanford White (1853–1906) were joined as McKim, Mead and White. White, the most notorious of the three, lived most of his life in the nineteenth century, shot and killed by a jealous husband, ironically, on the roof garden of one of his greatest buildings, Madison Square Garden, then still at Madison Square. His early work, first as an employee of H. H. Richardson and later independently with partners McKim and Mead, was picturesque, romantic, and suburban, with medieval remnants of wood, stick, and shingle. Later he converted this romance into one of classical white, tan, and yellow parts. But in this city, he and his partner McKim, a stern classicist, created a sober Roman and Italian Renaissance architecture and brought the somberness of Florence to New York. Pennsylvania Station (1910–1966) was the grandest public space ever built in America, unhappily demolished to make way for a cheesy pile in the name of economics. Ironically the replacement, Madison Square Garden Center, is to be demolished in favor of a fourth Madison Square Garden site over railroad yards to the west.

McKim, Mead and White's University, Metropolitan, Harmonie, and Racquet and Tennis clubs are of the Florentine Renaissance: limestone, quoined, and corniced but taller (elevators intervened) and containing, in addition to a grandeur of interiors that the Strozzis would not have scoffed at, such un-Florentine spaces as swimming pools, squash courts, and cocktail bars.

The firm also built Columbia University, the Brooklyn Museum, finishing and flanking wings to Richard Morris Hunt's Metropolitan Museum central pavilion, the Harvard Club (in "colonial" brick, as was also the Colony Club), the Morgan Library (for the fabulously wealthy J. P. Morgan), the Municipal Building, Washington Arch, and

Pennsylvania Station Waiting Room, 1910. Rome's Baths of Caracalla was a vast complex of which this space copied only a small part: its tepidarium, or warm room, for the lounging sybarite of the third century A.D. Here the lounging was limited, but the architecture breathtaking.

University Club, 1899. A high-rise Florentine palace on Fifth Avenue, this beautifully detailed granite club makes the glass architecture of modern incursions such as Trump Tower seem merely the cellophane wrappings of the expensive chocolates and neckties purveyed within.

the Villard Houses. MM&W were eclectic in their overall practice but not in any one building, that might reek of the Via Tornabuoni, or Harvard Yard, or the Giralda, or San Paolo Furoi le Mura, all with hyperacademic scholasticism. New York would be a dimmer place without them. The romantic remembrance of White perhaps shades the dour brilliance of McKim, whose dominance at Pennsylvania Station, Columbia University, and elsewhere was less publicly seen, let alone acknowledged. But the symbiotic interplay between the two produced architecture that makes post-Modernists weep.

Ralph Adams Cram (1863–1942) and Bertram Grosvenor Goodhue (1869–1924) were archaeologic architects once more, without the burden of digging. Sharp-eyed, and familiar with the twelfth through fifteenth centuries in France first, England and Byzantine Italy second, they produced some of the most superacademically detailed buildings of the late neo-Gothic, as opposed to the Gothic Revival of the 1840's. West Point's Chapel and Princeton's Chapel were the outbuildings of a luxurious Episcopal religion that ornately, and with literal and moral incense, wallowed in an architecture that was as decadent to Baptists (Riverside Church excepted) as the work of the Benedictines was to the Cistercians. Included in Cram and Goodhue's roster are also Park Avenue Christian Church (1911), the Cathedral Church of St. John the Divine (1911), St. Thomas Church (1914), the Church (formerly Chapel) of the Intercession (1914), St. Bartholomew's (1919, Goodhue solo), St. Vincent Ferrer (1923, Goodhue solo), the one Catholic venture, and Christ Church (1932).

St. John the Divine is, in that American way, the *largest* "French Gothic" church in the world, its nave, by Cram, leading to a crossing and choir started by the architect Grant LaFarge in the 1890's. The earlier, heavy quasi-Romanesque work was vaulted by Cram; and the nave, worthy of the Ile de France, marched out to Amsterdam Avenue amid a garden close more typical of Ely or Salisbury than of Chartres or Rheims. But Cram, bless

Cathedral of St. John the Divine. Ralph Adams Cram's great nave was spanned in the thirteenth-century manner with ribbed vaults of stone. The nineteenth-century neo-Gothic had commonly simulated such structure with plaster—but Cram built with the architectural piety that only the wealthy Protestants could afford.

St. Bartholomew's Church. St. Bart's is the best of American eclecticism, the joining of varied fragments of historical architecture into a single composition. The need to reuse history was compounded by the need for it to *look* aged, used, and repaired, the brick on its flanks seemingly patched with stone, and vice versa.

Former American Telephone and Telegraph Building, 195 Broadway. Classical columns, in the Renaissance manner, embrace three stories at a time. Temple upon temple, these are the carved limestone of Dorians and Ionians in quantity.

his heart, was immune to such trivial complaints. The moral fiber, real or purchased, of New York's bankers, corporate lawyers, and stockbrokers was renewed at this towering cathedral of the powerful and affluent.

St. Thomas, hard by the Museum of Modern Art, is both externally and internally a loved and loving jewel, intricate and careful, perfect in its scholarly imperfection. It brings to Fifth Avenue a level of twelfth- and thirteenth-century resurrected detail equal to that of the University Club's fifteenth-century vocabulary on the next block north. The earlier Gothic Revivalists never had the means to build such magnificent intricacies, with carving that had become a snap for the machines of the rich. The less affluent had lost carving to cast iron and terra-cotta in the interregnum. Therefore this revival is that of multistyled late nineteenth-century eclecticism, rather than that true Gothic Revival of the 1840's and '50's.

St. Bartholomew's, by Goodhue solo with designer Clarence Stein, graces Park Avenue, the first interruption of those dour Renaissance facades—long before Lever House and Seagram—and in concert with the Racquet and Tennis Club two blocks away. This domed eclecticism is based on an assembly of details, forms, and spaces historically never assembled but seen in parts in Istanbul's Byzantium and Ravenna's early Christian buildings, with bits of Italian and French Romanesque. It is smashing: the post-Modernists will be back. Goodhue's body, however, was veneered with McKim, Mead and White's French Romanesque portal, copied from Arles and transported from the former St. Bart's at 24th Street to soften the uptown excursion.

(William) Welles Bosworth's (1869–1966) only significant New York venture was the old American Telephone and Telegraph building of 1917, at Fulton Street and Broadway. Significant because of its site, it is prominent with Ionic columns that embrace three floors at a time, in tier after tier, on three exposed sides. With its eclectic use of Renaissance parts, it resurrects the stacked orders of the Colosseum and Florentine palaces, and even of the 1836–1907 Citibank on Wall Street, but in a way and at a scale never before considered.

Edward Palmer York and Philip Sawyer's banks are some of the great rooms of the city open to the public, though ostensibly for private business. Included are the Bowery Savings Bank, 42nd Street (1923); the Brooklyn Trust Company (now the Manufacturers Hanover), Montague Street (1915); the Central Savings Bank, Broadway and 73rd Street (1928); and the Greenwich Savings Bank, Broadway and 36th Street (1924).

These again, like many works of McKim, Mead and White, are rusticated Italian palazzi, with various allusions and, on one occasion, a specific palazzo transmogrified. All shelter spaces with vaults, domes, or great timber beams, often coffered, sometimes gilt. The materials are rich down to the very floors, these often inlaid with marbles in the fashion of the Italian early Renaissance Cosmati family. Banks were in search of respect, of an identity of security, wealth, and wisdom, and here sought it directly from the fountainhead of banking, Florence of the fifteenth-century Medicis.

York and Sawyer banks succeeded those of the Greek Revival, which had been mostly large-scale houses lining Wall Street, and preceded, by thirty-nine years, the conversion of banking to a form of fast-money supermarketism, blessed architecturally at the Manufacturers Hanover's vault in the window, 43rd Street and Fifth Avenue (1954, Skidmore, Owings and Merrill).

John Mervin Carrère (1858–1911) and Thomas Hastings (1860–1929) can be remembered many places, among them the Ritz Tower and the great Standard Oil Building at Bowling Green. But more than memorable, at the heart of the city stands the New York Public Library of 1911, an urban palace with its own gardens, Bryant Park, behind, in the manner of a junior Versailles. The white marble library is a temple of books, where their presence, and the process of seeking and reading them in the vast reading rooms, is a ceremony more in keeping with Chaucer or

Manufacturers Hanover Trust Company, 177 Montague Street, 1915. A careful recollection from Renaissance Cremona, this bank's architecture is enriched with iron and bronze metalwork on the street and, within, inlaid marble floors and a smashing coffered barrel vault.

T. S. Eliot than Jacqueline Susann. The building is worthy of savoring for its own sake and certainly is savored as part of the street life of midtown Manhattan: in summer the naughty lions that guard it are joined by resting and munching humans who absorb learning by osmosis through the thick masonry. This, with Cass Gilbert's Custom House, Warren and Wetmore's Grand Central, Richard Morris Hunt's Metropolitan Museum, and McKim, Mead and White's former Pennsylvania Station, are the grandest public buildings New York ever produced. Others are brilliant and exciting, from Louis Sullivan to Mies and Wright and Johnson; but these have grandeur.

Ernest Flagg (1857–1947) had the dubious privilege of designing the tallest building ever to be demolished, the 41-story Singer Tower (1907–1970) at Broadway and Liberty Streets. Its better reputation was in its style, a Beaux Arts mansard roof six stories tall tipped with a lantern at the crest of a slender office shaft. This Singer (there is another, smaller Singer at Broadway and Prince Street by Flagg, equally exciting architecturally in its own way) was the headquarters for America's technological export to the third world: sewing machines, which at first could be operated by foot power in the jungle or desert and that changed the life of many. Flagg also designed an elegant bookstore for Scribners, on Fifth Avenue between 48th and 49th (1913), a two-story groin-vaulted space, elegantly detailed in cast and wrought iron, still more than holding its own in the competitive facades of Fifth Avenue. Here is a place for gentle browsing more with the quality of a club library than a place for vending books. Flagg also designed experimental tenements on 42nd and 79th streets, and the United States Naval Academy, Annapolis.

Cass Gilbert (1859–1934) created one of the five great "palaces" of New York, the Custom House (1907), where, in the English urban manner, it faced a park (Bowling Green) alongside of a park (Battery Park), with architecture of the late nineteenth-century Beaux Arts. Granite, columned, and corniced with elaborate statuary, it boasts

Custom House. Cass Gilbert's great château sits at Broadway's foot, its Beaux Arts facade guarded by sculptures of the four principal continents in trading partnership (from left to right): Asia, America, Europe, and Africa.

major works (the four continents seated before the facade) by Daniel Chester French of Lincoln Memorial Fame. Here shipping and the wealthy gentlefolk of those enterprises were honored in their freight's clearance through customs, as the people transported often by the same shipping lines were honored at Ellis Island, safely separated across the bay.

Gilbert also built the Federal Courthouse at Foley Square (1936), the New York Life Insurance Company Building at 26th Street (1928), and the Woolworth Building (1913); all proving that a gentleman would work with equal facility in styles as diverse as Beaux Arts, Renaissance Revival, and neo-Gothic. His last and most notorious building was the Roman-inspired Supreme Court in Washington.

Benjamin Wistar Morris (1870–1944) designed the Union League Club (for Republican gentlemen) and the Morgan Library Annex to McKim, Mead and White's glorious library proper; both are insipid. But grandeur did not elude him, for at the Cunard Building, 25 Broadway aside of Bowling Green, the interior ticket and freight-lading spaces occupied domed and vaulted halls equal to any Renaissance cathedral (vaults by Ezra Winter, murals by Barry Faulkner). Because of Morris' previous record a brilliant junior designer is here suggested. But Morris caused or allowed it to happen, a reprise of the vast halls of the Custom House down and across Bowling Green.

John Russell Pope (1874–1937) is remembered more for his national works in Washington than for those in New York: that is, the Jefferson Memorial and the National Gallery of Art (originally Mellon Gallery, now demoted to West Wing). However, the Frick Collection, a 1935 addition to and renovation of Carrère and Hastings' 1914 Frick house, was the spatial antecedent of the Mellon. Here a fountain courtyard proves a pleasant oasis in the travels of the serious tourist, a courtyard repeated in plural and grander form in Washington. The building embraces a garden fronting Fifth Avenue that breaks, spatially, the re-

Former Cunard Building, 25 Broadway. The vaulted lobby gives a preview of the much grander dome and side vaults of this passenger-shipping office. The ceremony of luxurious travel began here for the voyager on the *Queen Mary*.

lentless facades fronting the park from 59th to 105th streets. There is another break at the Carnegie Mansion at 91st Street and a formal aberration at the Guggenheim Museum at 88th. Pope's great renderer (draftsman of visions of what was to be built), Otto Eggers, continued the practice after Pope's death, as Eggers and Higgins.

Samuel Trowbridge and Goodhue Livingston were in the second echelon of Renaissance Revival designers, standing behind Stanford White, Charles McKim, and Carrère and Hastings. Creators of numerous town houses for the wealthy, in blocks between Park and Fifth avenues in the 60's and 70's, their chefs d'oeuvre were Fifth Avenue's grandest hotel, the St. Regis (now the St. Regis–Sheraton), and Benjamin Altman's great store at 34th Street, a whole block of high-rise Renaissance Revival. The St. Regis is grand, both inside and out in the manner of the George V in Paris, Claridge's in London, and the Gritti Palace in Venice, and with an enriched architecture to house the elegance of service and Society (or would-be Society). Only the Plaza Hotel has equal architectural and social panache. Here the borrowed style of Europe was inflated for America.

The store is called Altman's, the possessive particularly a part of New York terminology—Macy's, Bloomingdale's. In other places stores are most frequently unpossessed: Neiman-Marcus in Dallas; Jordan Marsh in Boston; Carson, Pirie Scott in Chicago. Altman moved his store to 34th Street from the late nineteenth-century Ladies' Mile around 19th Street and Sixth Avenue and created a palace across from Caroline Schermerhorn Astor's Hotel Astoria, which occupied the site of her former mansion from 1897 to 1931, when it was replaced by the Empire State Building.

Whitney Warren (1864–1943) of Warren and Wetmore, along with codesigners Reed and Stem, honored the Ecole des Beaux-Arts in the area where it truly deserves credit and where credit is often overlooked when critics survey the purely visual aspects of this flamboyant French neo-Renaissance style. *Circulation* is an architect's word for the intelligent and efficient movement of people and vehicles, meeting where necessary but otherwise separated, all with an architectural grace and grandeur as such movement is experienced over a period of time. Grand Central Station is truly grand, but its circulation is a work of genius. Two levels of train platforms (long-distance above, commuters below) are served by the Park Avenue tunnels and by vast yards between Madison and Lexington, from 42nd to 50th streets (under all those buildings). Auto traffic on Park Avenue sails up ramps through barrel vaults, embracing the terminal with its lithe routes, descending again at 40th Street to the avenue's surface. The tunnel from here to 31st Street is not part of this design: it is left from the railroad's former route to the south, before Grand Central and its antecedents were built, and continues the level of the Park Avenue tunnel tracks.

The nave of the station (the waiting room is the smaller space along 42nd Street) is now New York's great ceremonial rooms of arrival since the loss of Pennsylvania Station. The exterior, facing south on Park Avenue, is another "palace," here with Park Avenue at its feet. To the north the New York Central (Railroad) Building, now renamed the Helmsley Building, terminates the grand vista of Park Avenue from 96th to 46th streets, those fifty blocks of instant boulevard (Haussmann's Parisian ones were instant also). Unhappily it is backed by the giant Pan Am building, built on air rights sold by the railroad to raise cash, a sorry story in the railroads' fall from style. What had created the vast fortunes of Harriman, Flagler, and Vanderbilt lapsed into inefficiency and tawdriness when fortunes were no longer to be made.

Warren and Wetmore also gave us the R. Livingston Beekman House (1905), the James A. Burden House (1902), and the New York Yacht Club (1899). These turn-of-the-century buildings maintain a vigor that the firm's later work lost, when simplification seemed to them a substitute for true modernism—nothing added, merely some-

The New York Yacht Club, 37 West 44th Street. Built in the days when "yacht" meant to J. P. Morgan that you can't afford one if you must ask how much it costs. This is where the Americas Cup was born.

**Original Facade, Metropolitan Museum
of Art.** Now indoors, this remnant of Calvert Vaux's original building was the front
door of the infant museum, entered from
Central Park. Hunt's new Fifth Avenue pavilion reversed it all.

thing taken away—as at 927 Fifth Avenue (1917) and the
Consolidated Edison Tower (1926).

Richard Morris Hunt (1827–1895) not only attended
the Ecole des Beaux-Arts in Paris but also worked in the
atelier of his professors Visconti and Lefuel, particularly
on the additions to the Louvre ordered by Napoleon III.
It is said that he was responsible for part of the facade
along the rue de Rivoli attributed to the two. But his
connection with Franco-American architecture is better
demonstrated in a remarkable commission. Hunt's granite
base for the Statue of Liberty is the pedestal for Bartholdi
and Eiffel's great lady, a lesson in scale, as the monument
is one viewed from a distance, telescopically, in contrast
to the tight juxtaposition of his later Metropolitan Museum
with the Fifth Avenue viewer. This lusty granite plinth is
worthy of grand architecture, in an era when statuary was
commonly sited and set by the sculptors' architectural peers.
Compare Stanford White's settings for Augustus Saint-
Gaudens' sculptures of Peter Cooper at 7th Street and the
Bowery or of Admiral Farragut in Madison Square Park.

More important, of course, to New York's urban history is the central section of the Metropolitan Museum of
Art (extended later with north and south wings by McKim,
Mead and White), which fronts a facade worthy of Versailles to Fifth Avenue, with all of Central Park serving as
its palatial gardens—(gardens, however, in the English romantic sense, rather than the French formal sense). The
Metropolitan (its musical peer seems, appropriately, to keep
the popular nickname, the Met) faces a rich section of the
avenue that came to gather at its flanks. In 1880, when
Calvert Vaux created the now invisible corps of the museum, its facade faced west into the park, and Fifth Avenue
was still in the boondocks. The Hunt facade (1895–1902),
reorienting the museum to Fifth Avenue, presented a dynamic neo-Baroque facade with an extraordinary vigor—
a gracious street presence in these hinterlands which were
soon infilled with town houses and minor mansion neighbors.

When historians reflect on this city, the most important events are in its technology of transportation, of construction, of utilities and water, mostly the invisible bones of buildings, the subterranean conduits of travel and service. But the tourist and casual New Yorker seeks and sees the architectural tips of these icebergs, the monuments advertising the glory of that great engineering. These gentlemen archaeologists, as here recounted, gave back to engineering such urban embellishments as made the special place, the separated monument, in contrast to vast, quietly stated blocks of brownstones and apartment houses, the vernacular bulk of the city to which their grand buildings are the counterpoint.

New York Public Library, 1911. The main reference library occupies the site of the old Murray Hill (Croton) Reservoir, and the gardens behind (Bryant Park) that of the 1853 Crystal Palace. When new, this stretch of Fifth Avenue was lined with the mansions of the wealthy in an architecture of equal richness.

Beaux Arts Ball, architects dressed as their buildings. The idea of buildings as fancy dress, as in haute couture or the styling of 1950's Cadillac fins, was perhaps unwittingly presented by these, the most talented architects of their time.

13.

Early Modern

What is modern today becomes tomorrow's style of time past, as each time, each era, in an increasingly accelerated manner, claims for itself the mantle of modernity. The categorizing of periods of architecture was a latter-day event, a kind of self-conscious chronology of ideas about art and architecture. *Classical,* as a term to describe the architecture of ancient Greece and Rome, was first used in writing in English about 1600; *medieval,* in 1827; *Renaissance,* in 1845; but *modern* appeared in 1585, "of, relating to, or characteristic of a period extending from a relevant remote past to the present time" (*Webster's Ninth New Collegiate Dictionary*). Before the very word appeared in print, architects, artisans, and clients of the moment believed that they were creating a new architecture, appropriate to their own times, without name or categorization. In New York's own history early nineteenth-century architect Minard Lafever's great copybook for carpenter-builders was titled *The Beauties of Modern Architecture* (1835), creating buildings that we now look back

Bas-Relief, Condict Building, 1898. Sullivan's organic ornament in cast terra-cotta enriched this curtain wall sheathing a steel frame in the year that Samuel Bing opened his store, L'Art Nouveau, in Paris.

on as Gothic Revival, Italianate, and even Egyptian Revival.

To many, *modern* was technology and the rejection of the built past; who could relate a classical order to a lean and lively machine? To others, modernism was **style** or, better still, **anti**style, to purge the fancy dress trappings of architecture and allow its soul to show. To still others, modernism was **functional**, in that it organized space (at least in the building plan, if not in vertical space) to allow the efficient relationship of parts of a whole (home, office, school) that, in its most simplistic form, expressed, through exterior volumes, those parts, without expressing a very convincing concept of "whole." And, of course, these three, *technology*, *style*, and *function* should have been simultaneously on the mind of any competent architect. Functionalism, by the way, is not an idea invented by modernists. The Roman architectural historian and critic, Vitruvius, coined the triplicity "firmness, commodity, and delight" at about the time of the birth of Christ. His commodity is what we now term functionalism; but Vitruvius also saw equal need in the triangle for firmness (structural integrity) and delight (aesthetic fulfillment). The last is what the battles are now all about.

The stirrings of American modern architecture began with a line of masters and apprentices who marked the nation and, tangentially, New York: Frank Furness (1839–1912), Henry Hobson Richardson (1838–1886), Louis Henry Sullivan (1856–1924), and Frank Lloyd Wright (1867–1959). The latter three each worked and learned in the studio of his predecessor.

Furness influenced Richardson, and Richardson influenced Brooklyn's great eclectic talent, Frank Freeman. Richardsonian Romanesque was a sharp departure from classical form and parts, using the bold scale and power of bulky stone with Romanesque arches to bring impact to the city as, for example, in Richardson's Marshall Field Warehouse in Chicago. Freeman brought the same power, with greater elegance, to the City of Brooklyn Fire Headquarters (1892). Sullivan learned directly from Richardson as his employer. Sullivan's work in Chicago, and the Chicago school's proselytizing, gave to those first skyscrapers an expression that was convincingly modern stylistically, for the internal workings of the Chicago towers were not different from those of the classically draped skyscrapers of New York such as Daniel Burnham's Flatiron Building of 1902, or Ernest Flagg's Singer Building of 1907. Sullivan's work in the 1880's and early '90's reached its apogee (sky-scraping) with the Wainwright Building (St. Louis, 1891) and the Guaranty Trust (Buffalo, 1895). He brought these talents to the modern architectural backwaters of New York in 1898 for Alden Condict's offices on Bleecker Street (note historian Carl Condit's apt quote, "Who would expect an aesthetic experience on Bleecker Street"). It is a vertical terra-cotta expression, admittedly with a classically related cornice but a cornice here with angels rather than classical parts, though they might be thought of as ethereal caryatids. The decoration of panels, capitals, and tympani is realized with a natural vegetative detail invented by Sullivan and prescient of such Art Nouveau intertwines as those of Hector Guimard in the Paris Métro entrances. He had learned at Paris' Ecole des Beaux-Arts about architecture, not merely how to copy cleverly the past as interpreted by another.

Sullivan's star assistant in Chicago was Frank Lloyd Wright. His influence on the city—any city—was minimal, in that his very approach to architecture was that of unique identities that were, in his later years, incompatible with their neighbors. His early work, Chicago's Midway Gardens (beer), Buffalo's Larkin Building (mail order), and Oak Park's Unity Temple (church), all were happy in their context; but elsewhere and later his urban work more aggressively dominated or clashed with the city scene. New York's Guggenheim Museum, a wondrous place, is a flamboyant conch among the staid limestone high- and low-rise palaces of Fifth Avenue.

In Europe, the early work of Wright was widely pub-

Housing, Amsterdam. Dutch society, neat and industrious, and caring of its less advantaged, produced some of the most homely housing of the 1920's and 1930's. Here human-scaled blocks in natural Holland brick trimly house those who in New York might be consigned to true slums.

lished and adored: the Wasmuth edition of Wright's work, published in Berlin in 1910, was a beacon for the youthful modernists of the continent. Le Corbusier was twenty-three; Mies van der Rohe, twenty-four; Gropius, twenty-seven; Wright was already forty-three. Available were the plans, perspectives, and renderings of Unity Temple, the Larkin Building, the Robie house, powerfully modeled cubism in the case of the first two, with a dynamic interplay of planes (horizontal) at the last. Wright's cubism was one not only of volume but also of space. But more important than volume, space, and detail was the inspiration of the New World, still a mysterious place to the average European, particularly before World War I, during which American soldiers gave some inkling of the persons and personalities that inhabited North America.

Aesthetic response and development included such singular works as the houses and furniture of Gerrit Rietveld in Holland; Charles Rennie Mackintosh in Glasgow; Mies, Hans Scharoun, Walter Gropius, and others in Germany; and myriad Dutch housers. Encouraged by social activism, abetted by the facts of Wright's built reality, and hardened by the Protestantism of northern Europe, modernism produced housing in disciplined street-fronted rows; Amsterdam was the field of greatest and grandest success, later modified and softened by the romantic subforms and detailing of such as Michel de Klerk. In Germany the Deutscher Werkbund exhibitions brought experimental architecture to the issue of urban housing, in exhibits that assembled the built talents of Gropius, Mies, Scharoun, Adolf Loos, Le Corbusier, and others in a microurbanization. Here was medium-density low-rise, at a time when New York was also still housing its masses in the medium-density low-rise of brownstones and tenements. Although the West Side had built a clutch of large, Parisian-scaled apartment houses, these were, however, a tiny percentage of the bulk of housed units in the city. Park Avenue was yet to give birth to its housed form.

The new work in Berlin and Amsterdam reflected on

Housing, Siemensstadt, Berlin. It was in Germany that the aesthetic of what came to be known as the International School was refined. Here Walter Gropius, who later taught a generation of architects at Harvard, unrolls a ribbon of white housing.

another group of American architects in a social manner. The latters' passions were in the use of architecture as a tool for social action; for the housing of the poor and moderate-incomed; and for combating the apparent evils of slums: lack of light, air, and sanitation, of play space and dignity. The aesthetic invigoration of Wright, passed to Europe, produced there an original architecture, both aesthetically and socially, that bounded back, refracted, largely as a simplified, schematic solution for social action in the physical act of housing. Aestheticism, to the extent that it was conscious, was in the denuding of ornament, in the glorification of the bare plan, the apartment block, the superblock, the whole city precinct. This combination of an unadorned and ascetic style with social activism meant that "modernism" first influenced New York in a way we now regret, producing the austere, minimal architecture erected for the social warehousing and segregation of multitudes of the poor.

The housing of the upper economic classes, and the office buildings that served their businesses and professions, were modern in their technology but largely classical in their facades. Mostly conceived as parts of streets, as walls of such urban spaces, the facades were not meant as objects to be admired or used in the round, as was the new socially modern public housing.

The Chicago World's Fair of 1893 had made a two-pronged attack of both building and cityscape on the virgin modernism of the Chicago school. Under architect Daniel H. Burnham's autocratic direction a City Beautiful was created, with ornate—even flamboyant—classical architecture to support the city's form, in the spirit of current work at the Ecole des Beaux-Arts, where most of the prominent architects in the late nineteenth century were trained. In Paris, buildings recalling that period are the Grand Palais and Petit Palais, exhibition galleries for the fair of 1900, still in use as galleries for shows, from paintings to automobiles. The Chicago fair influenced New York immensely, setting back the cause (it seemed to be a cause, rather than an inevitable evolution) of modern architecture in the face of buildings limestone-quoined, rusticated, vermiculated, articulated, linteled, corniced, with the apparatus and vocabulary of Greece, Rome, and particularly the Italian Renaissance, as garbled and electicized by the English (softened and simplified, a bland Italianism) and the French (bold and brassy, outdoing the Italians at their own histrionics).

Modernism, as used in the Museum of Modern Art (MOMA) sense—what you see as an object, rather than the experience of use—sank into oblivion with the fair and the simultaneous waning of Sullivan's influence. It was rescued as an idea by MOMA's landmark exhibition, The International Style, in 1932 (curated by Philip C. Johnson and Henry-Russell Hitchcock, Jr.), where *international* meant Europe (to them).

In New York, in 1932, Rockefeller Center was breaking ground, the Daily News Building was in place on East 42nd Street, McGraw-Hill inhabited West 42nd Street—all by, or inspired by, Raymond Hood, New York's first and perhaps only skyscraper genius to match Chicago's earlier Louis Sullivan. Hood had earlier produced the remarkable American Radiator Building on West 40th Street and, before that, his New York counterattack on the Chicago school, winning the competition for the Chicago Tribune Tower with a neo-Gothic shaft reminiscent of American versions of English university gothic (Magdelen College reincarnated at Princeton) or French ecclesiastical remnants (Tour Saint-Jacques, Paris). The modernists entered at Chicago, including a finned and austere tower by Gropius and a second-prize winner by Eliel Saarinen that was the catalyst to draw him to America, to Cranbrook Academy in the dubious suburbs of Detroit.

Modernism as a negative or neutral, or nonforce, aesthetically, and as a positive force functionally (that is, in the efficiency and economy of the plan), was embraced not only by the architects who would be social activists but also by those honestly enthralled at the Puritanism of the

New York Daily News Building. Raymond Hood's early (1930) essay in the language of what was to become Rockefeller Center. The spandrels (panels over and under the windows) have a nice Art Deco brick geometry.

visual product. Among the latter are Walter Kilham (former worker for, and biographer of, Hood), Eric Kebbon, Frederick Woodbridge, John C. B. Moore, Otto and David Eggers, and Alfred Easton Poor. Their work was not necessarily at the chronological beginning of the modern movement but continued in the spirit of bland functionalism until the late 1970's.

Eric Kebbon, architect for the Board of Education in the 1940's, produced a simplified brick-and-limestone architecture that reflected the juxtaposition of major and minor school space: class and gym and auditorium and playground. This was accomplished in a configuration inspired by the International school but in a less convincing and, surprisingly, more bland shell. The buildings neared the streets but broke the streetline in a way that represented neither the gusto of premodern architecture nor the passion of the modernists.

Architecture has rarely been the province of radical patrons, with its innate necessity for a client with the money "up front." While painters and, to a lesser degree, sculptors could create in splendid isolation, from Tahiti to the East Village, architects were seeking their clients before the fact—a commission not for the casual speculation of the middle class but for the wealthy individual, the corporate patron, the governmental agency. In Chicago, the still frontier vitality of the 1890's, compounded by the city's rebuilding from the fire of 1871, gave its patrons a vigor unmatched in staid New York, hanging on to its close and past European connections while Europe was itself breaking radical ground with an architecture of social action. New York patrons sought the imagery of those returned students of the Ecole des Beaux-Arts who could deliver history in packages that enveloped libraries, museums, railroad stations, and, most of all, office buildings. They decried the "businessmen" of Chicago who, working for profit, commissioned the works of William LeBaron Jenney, Adler and Sullivan, Holabird and Roche, Burnham and Root, and Frank Lloyd Wright. New York's snobbery embraced

P. S. 6, Madison Avenue and 81st Street. Bland brick boxes, ornamented with pallid detail, in the hope that blandness would somehow be the essence of modernity.

The Majestic Apartments. The Majestic is redolent more of the sleek modernity of the 1930's than of the Art Deco of the '20's: stylish or modernistic, rather than truly modern.

Former National Title Guarantee Building. A superb example of Art Deco as an enhancement of a modest stepped skyscraper on Brooklyn's Montague Street. Architect Harvey Wiley Corbett joined with architect Hood and others to later create Rockefeller Center.

an imported culture, while the clear, hard noses of Chicago built for profit with a free aesthetic spirit.

Full-blown "modern" in New York is encapsulated in the fifty years from the 1920's to the present, where post-Modern tentatively blossoms. Our "modern" first blossomed as a style, in a way similar to the more fluid changes of style in clothing or, once upon a time, in women's hats, where the girl remained the same while her cornice changed her image.

The style was at first only a cladding, an overcoat anew, rather than any inner change of the nature of a building. America was first stimulated in this way by the Paris exposition of 1925, the font of Art Deco. Remembered for decoration and color more than form, it created a lively geometry of glazed tile and brick, of pattern, and of the right angle in contrast to the Art Nouveau sinuousity that had dominated before World War I. In form, there was a cubism of parts: details, cornices, fins, and buttresses rather than any large-scale remaking of form as a whole. At this level Art Deco can still be seen on the apartment houses of the Bronx's Grand Concourse and in the lobbies of the Chrysler and Chanin buildings. Prototypical, as a whole building conceived in this spirit, is the old National Title Guaranty Building (Brooklyn Heights, 1930) by Harvey Wiley Corbett. Here some of the qualities to mature in the detailing of Rockefeller Center were tried on an orthodox street-fronted building, no different from its peers of forty years before (see the Franklin Trust Company down the street, 1891) except for its cladding and the setbacks generated by the new zoning law of 1916, to provide, ostensibly, more light and air, solutions that worked happily with the hard rectangular forms of the Art Deco period.

Art Deco later became a participant in the more complex "modern" architecture that faced the issues of urban design (relationship with the street and other public spaces) and the form of buildings in a new and vigorous manner: in the detailing of Ralph Walker in the several telephone and telegraph buildings of the 1920's; in that of Raymond Hood, his partners, and coventurers at the Daily News and McGraw-Hill buildings and at Rockefeller Center; in that of Shreve, Lamb and Harmon at the Empire State Building; and in that of William Van Alen for the Chrysler Building.

The Office of Irwin Chanin built, or commissioned, or designed some of the most prominent Art Deco "fingers" on the West Side skyline, punctuating the west park edge with the Century Apartments (1931) at 63rd Street; the Majestic Apartments (1930) at 72nd Street; and a major midtown tower, the Chanin Building (1929, Sloan and Robertson, architects). Jacques Delamarre certainly designed the Chanin's Art Deco lobby and, in the case of the two twin towers, was principal designer for both. The brick articulation and corner windows of the Century bespeak Art Deco, but the streamlining (the fastest tower in the West) of the Majestic is a later and more fluid style prescient of Art Moderne (formalized by the Paris exposition of 1937). Styling is at the heart of such classifications, for a few blocks away at 75th Street another twin-towered blockfront, the San Remo (1930, Emery Roth, architect), places circular Roman temples against the sky—same time, same avenue, similar plans, different costume.

Art Moderne combined speed in a staccato fashion and speed in a smooth and streamlined fashion with a smoothly simplified classicism. Jacques Carlu's Palais de Chaillot (Paris, 1937) presents the latter two characteristics in a symmetrical, columned, austere palace axially disposed on the Champs de Mars and the Eiffel Tower. As with previous exposition architecture (Paris, 1889; Chicago, 1893; Paris, 1925), the Paris exposition of 1937 influenced architecture in the mainstream. In New York the now demolished airline facilities at 42nd Street and Park Avenue (bus terminal) and La Guardia (first passenger terminal) were so inspired. The sole remnant at an airport is La Guardia's Marine Terminal, from the days when flying boats like the China Clipper landed on Long Island Sound.

Palais de Chaillot, Paris, 1937. On axis with the Eiffel Tower, this smooth house of museums, by architect Jacques Carlu, stood at the head of the 1937 exposition in the timid neoclassical modernity of its time.

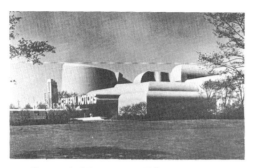

General Motors Building, New York World's Fair, 1939. When buildings met the air as if they were speeding bullets, GM presented its Futurama to a world obsessed with speed as the essence of modernism.

Set from *Things to Come,* 1936. With more fantasy than the 1939 World's Fair—and a better idea of how cities might actually work, as well as look—architect Vincent Korda created an underground utopia for this futuristic movie.

Speed (staccato) was implied in the stepped massing of the German Pavilion at Paris; speed (streamlining), at the General Motors exhibit (Flushing Meadow, 1939). Here the product on display, the car, suggested the attitude of the streamlined building; and the exhibit within, the landscape and city of the future, was one generated by the car, served and created by superhighways, with buildings equally softened by the passing wind.

Streamlining as an idea far surpassed streamlining as a necessity which was largely needed for aircraft, and **very** high speed trains and cars. The Chrysler Corporation, however, invested in an image of speed in its 1934 Airflow cars, which seemed capable of serious racing but were in fact also available (same chassis and motor) with a "traditional" carapace (body). More visually and mechanically avant-garde was the Dymaxion car of Buckminster Fuller (1937), teardropped and three-wheeled, which was redolent of the space age. This was the era of the comic strip Buck Rogers (of the twenty-fifth century), of Flash Gordon and, best of all, of the fantastic underworld city created by architect Vincent Korda for the 1936 movie *Things to Come,* from the book by H. G. Wells. Korda's city was really smooth (both in the literal and slang senses), with glass elevator shafts bearing cabs propelled like pistons by steam—and everything round, smooth, white, and shining.

Movies about Broadway were set on white stairs that ascended to heaven, and whiteness was made the more white by dancing men in black: Fred Astaire's "white tie, top hat and tails." Modern was a style that permeated everything visual, a kind of cult of industrialization, that honored the future at the bottom of an economic depression that could not very happily honor its recent past.

While New York and Paris and London and Rome were toying with fashion, architects in Germany and one architect in France were laying the foundations of what Johnson and Hitchcock were to term the International style at the Museum of Modern Art. Johnson was the museum's first curator of architecture, Hitchcock a historian of the modern movement; cf. *In the Nature of Materials* (1942), the first catalog of the work of Frank Lloyd Wright.

Protomodernists such as Otto Wagner in Vienna, Victor Horta in Brussels, Hector Guimard in Paris (their bright work partially masked by the sometimes more superficial or decorative cachets—Art Nouveau, Jugendstil, Secessionist) gave way to the powerful industrial modernism of the great Berliner, Peter Behrens. From Behrens it was but a step to Gropius and Mies van der Rohe, Marcel Breuer and Hans Scharoun. And in Holland the cause was picked up by Bakema and Oud. But Corbu alone stood in France, and America waited. Here, easy facades of Art Deco and Art Moderne and the survivalism of a watered-down classicism stood their ground in the 1920's and '30's, a ground not too endangered in a depression economy that built little until after World War II.

Only one major work constructed in New York City prior to World War II provides a true symbiosis of function, engineering brilliance, and distinguished architecture and urban design: Rockefeller Center, perhaps the best group of twentieth-century buildings anywhere. Raymond Hood was the inspiration for this glorious group and its equally glorious plaza and channel gardens, but credit is due also to others who separately gave New York some of its finest modern presence. Rockefeller Center is beyond style, in its solution to a whole precinct of the city: building, street, plaza, underground world of arcades.

Land had been assembled by John D. Rockefeller, Jr., for a vast project, Metropolitan Square, relocating the Metropolitan Opera uptown and nearer to its posh patrons than its 1883 building at 39th Street and Broadway, a "warehouse-like yellow-brick structure" according to the 1939 *WPA Guide to New York City*. But the 1929 crash and subsequent depression intervened, drying up the source of contributions for its new construction. Rockefeller, now owning a vast area between Fifth and Sixth avenues, from 48th to 54th streets, seeking to cut his losses, and create

The RCA Building soars, its slender slab carefully modeled with setbacks and reveals to allow maximum light and air to the workers in this pre-air conditioning centerpiece of Rockefeller Center.

Rockefeller Center Site. What Rockefeller bought and assembled for his projected Metropolitan Opera House and related buildings were these hundreds of brownstones, a minicity complex that gave way to the Center we know today.

Rockefeller Center Today. Photographed millions of times and the subject of countless postcards, this complex is, behind that frenetic publicity, a truly great triumph of urban architecture.

construction jobs for the vast unemployed workforce, converted the program to office and other commercial space. The original architect, Benjamin Wistar Morris, had developed a concept that allowed tall buildings to surround the central Metropolitan Square, something impossible under city zoning on the sixty-foot sidestreets of the city but possible with a vast public space at the center of an even vaster assemblage.

Joseph Urban (1872–1933): Urban used his training in stage design for architecture and produced results much happier than those of most architects . . . the New School for Social Research (1930), an early modern monument. Its banded brick facade has graded spacing between its alternate stripes that, in the Renaissance fashion of false perspective, makes the building tallest when the observer is directly opposite. This university-in-exile served and was served by expatriate German intelligentsia fleeing Nazism and was housed in architecture inspired by the Bauhaus of Gropius and Mies, architecture that Hitler hated (he embraced the stripped classicism of Albert Speer and his mentor, Paul Ludwig Troost). Urban's convictions were, however, founded on style, as those of a stage designer might well be: his Ziegfeld Theatre (gone) was "modern" in the way a Cadillac is modern: stylish, willful design. The Hearst Building, at Eighth Avenue and 57th Street, on the other hand, has taken inspiration from the Secessionist movement in Vienna, contemporary with Art Nouveau in France and Belgium.

Russell and Walter Cory and Yasuo Matsui were together responsible for the Starrett-Lehigh Building (1931). Separately the Corys designed a small cousin to this colossus, in the Bronx, the Cashman Laundry (1932). And Matsui was coarchitect of the 40 Wall Street Tower, with H. Craig Severance (1929), the former Bank of the Manhattan Company. (Remember the Manhattan Company, Aaron Burr's subterfuge to acquire a banking charter?) Here at Starrett-Lehigh is a sinuous 22-story industrial warehouse built over the Lehigh Railroad's yards, originally

Hearst Building, Eighth Avenue at 57th Street. Hearst was an appropriate client for any fantasy of an architect playing stage designer—or the reverse, in this case Joseph Urban. Hearst's famous medieval-Renaissance castle, San Simeon, in California, had been designed by a normally very serious architect, Julia Morgan.

Starrett-Lehigh Building, 1932. Sleek ribbons of glass and rounded corners in this immense warehouse. The Lehigh Railroad's barged freight made this a portal of bulk to the city from the tracks across the river.

serviced by barged freight cars from their New Jersey lines. The continuous strip windows, serpentlike in seemingly endless bands, recall some of the sinuousity of Mies's office buildings drawn and proposed, but never built, for Berlin.

William Lescaze (1896–1969) is a name engraved in the history of modern architecture and the International style by his creation, in association with George Howe, of the Philadelphia Savings Fund Society Building (1932) in Philadelphia, an avant-garde affair, floors cantilevered at their ends, the windows like industrial sash. But in New York two houses mark that era: his own house and office at 48th Street (1934), a house on 70th Street (1941), and one on 74th Street (1935). The last has been called "a handcrafted version of the machine aesthetic, common to most Bauhaus-inspired design and architecture; where the idea of the machine or machine-made product is more important than the fact that it is made, or not made, by a machine."

Lescaze lapsed into a pallid phase with the Civil and Municipal Courthouse (1960) and then into a banal phase with 1 New York Plaza (1969). He was, however, very influential upon a generation of architects after 1932.

Philip Goodwin (1885–1958) and Edward Durrell Stone (1902–1978): Stone, as an "international" stylist in the 1930's, was equal to the best. Here, at the original Museum of Modern Art (1939), he and Goodwin brought to New York its first major radical modern public building, modern in tune with art it displayed. Now that art has become the history of modern art, and the Museum's architecture the history of modern architecture, with its various Philip Johnson and Cesar Pelli changes and additions. He later went on to a more fanciful architecture, first at the New Delhi embassy (1958) and the U.S. Pavilion at the Brussels World's Fair (also 1958). The grillages there developed became his trademark, on subsequently clad dormitories (University of South Carolina), atomic energy laboratories (Islamabad, Pakistan), a whole university (State University Center, Albany), and on his own house on 64th

New York City Cultural Center. When a would-be patron seeks to update his "retardataire" tastes in art, he is fated to get the same level of architecture. A&P heir Huntington Hartford hired Edward Durell Stone to do this kitsch.

Street. His alternate obsession, white marble, fulfilled his General Motors Building (1968) at 59th and Fifth Avenue and the Huntington Hartford Gallery of Modern Art (1965) at Columbus Circle.

Stone's transition from the austerity and elegance of his International style (seen also at the A. Conger Goodyear house at Old Westbury, Long Island) to a more confectionary attitude seems a kind of emotional rejection of the past rather than a true renewal. What was lost was the baby and the bath water, both building and principle. What was gained seems to be only something easily marketable, salesmanship in a context that had lost its convictions, before the newer convictions of the much later post-Modernists. Goodwin was better known for his writing in *Brazil Builds* (1943), which brought that country's early and radical modern architecture to the attention of America.

Wallace K. Harrison (1895–1981) is remembered particularly for his ability to mediate between competing talents in later years, such as at the United Nations where the cast was dominated by Le Corbusier (for France) but where, nevertheless, there was a field of competing international egos. He extracted a compromise solution and, as "architect of record," converted the schematic idea into the finished product. At Lincoln Center his chairmanship allowed compromises again—this time, however, with a building for each (his is the Metropolitan Opera). But with Jacques André Fouilhoux (1879–1945) he built the Rockefeller Apartments, a light, lovely, and graceful glassy building overlooking the Museum of Modern Art gardens. It was on a strip acquired by the Rockefellers at the time of assembling land for Rockefeller Center: an assembly that also included the later Esso Building site, that of the Donnell Library, the Museum of Modern Art—all the midblocks north to 55th Street. One conjectures that Fouilhoux had a major hand here, for it is very unlike any of Harrison's other work.

Harvey Wiley Corbett (1873–1954) gave us the Tombs, New York's Criminal Court and Prison (1939); Brooklyn's

Rockefeller Apartments, 17 West 54th Street. New York's most handsome and thoughtful apartment house of the pre–World War II years. The gracious window bays have the luck of overlooking MOMA's garden. The two sections of this through-block complex share a central garden court.

240 Central Park South, 1941. The bold massing of this luxury building overlooks Central Park and Columbus Circle. The stepped shops along Broadway merit a second look.

National Title Guaranty Building (1930), and the North Building of the Metropolitan Life Insurance Company at 25th Street (1932). His work was largely inspired by, and inspiring of, Art Deco and Art Moderne. Corbett ranks second only to Raymond Hood in the pantheon of New York's early modernism.

Raymond Hood (1881–1934) was to the urban skyscraper and its surrounds as Frank Lloyd Wright was to suburbia. In this sense he was the true heir, if not pupil, of Louis Sullivan and the Chicago school, whose brilliant works bejeweled Chicago's Loop in the 1880's and 1890's. In New York he is remembered for two unique skyscrapers, the Daily News Building (1930, Howells and Hood), and the McGraw-Hill Building (1931, Hood, Godley and Fouilhoux). But his legacy becomes monumental in his leading role in creating the vast multibuilding complex of Rockefeller Center. In the notorious movie, *The Fountainhead*, the hero's idol is based upon Hood, portrayed as the unsung hero in his time.

Albert Mayer (1897–1981) and Julian Whittlesey's (1905–) 1941 apartment house at 240 Central Park South (at Columbus Circle) is one of a sequence of luxury buildings created by this firm and its successor(s): Manhattan House (1950, with Skidmore, Owings and Merrill), Butterfield House (1962, Mayer, Whittlesey and Glass; William J. Conklin, designer), and the Premier (1963, same cast as Butterfield). Mayer was known more as a planner, in the sense of large-scale arrangements of urban life. Inspired by the socially concerned planning of the 1930's at Radburn (New Jersey) and Greenbelt (Maryland) and sensitive to the successes of the English architect, Raymond Unwin, at Letchworth and Hampstead garden cities, he was given opportunity to crossbreed it all with distinguished architecture at Chandigarh, the new capital of the severed Indian portion of the Punjab (Pakistan took with its half the ancient capital of Lahore). His work, in concert with architect Matthew Nowicki, was aborted when Nowicki died in a plane crash; they were replaced by Le Corbusier and his cousin, Pierre Jeanneret. 240 Central Park South ranks as one of the great apartment houses of New York. Sited at a knuckle of the city, it enjoys and reinforces the space of Columbus Circle, while savoring views of Central Park. Its crisp steel corner windows and rounded stepped-back stores along Broadway are elements of great style.

Richmond Shreve (1877–1946), William Frederick Lamb (1883–1952), and Arthur Loomis Harmon (1878–1958) (Shreve, Lamb and Harmon) together were architects of the Empire State Building, symbol of New York finance opened at the bottom of the depression by a corporation that had planned it all in the booming 1920's. Under the leadership of former governor and presidential candidate, Alfred E. Smith, it was touted with a carnival of publicity (including the 1933 movie, *King Kong*) that may have made it the world's most famous or perhaps notorious building. The stainless steel vertical banding and black cast-aluminum panels between floors give it a "curtain wall" kind of styling prescient of Rockefeller Center and the spate of all-glass walls cladding speculative office buildings of the 1950's and '60's.

Harmon's great work was the old Shelton Towers Hotel (1924), at 48th and Lexington, another exuberant experiment in the making of form in concert with the relatively new (1916) zoning resolution. This influenced the form of later architecture as much as the work of Ralph Walker at the Barclay-Vesey Building and the Irving Trust Company Building.

Former Shelton Towers Hotel. This and Ralph Walker's Barclay-Vesey New York Telephone Company Building were the two greatest experiments in the aesthetic exploitation of the 1916 zoning resolution. The setbacks were required for light and air, here raised to a cubist game.

Horseback Dinner. When potential patrons mount horses for dinner, the resulting architecture commissioned may recall "The Charge of the Light Brigade."

14.

Patrons

Architecture is capital. It is the conserved and displayed energy and resources of a culture or civilization, whether a cathedral as the communal efforts of a Gothic town, the dour but imposing palace of a Florentine banker, a vast housing project for the impoverished, or a Madison Avenue corporate symbol. Obviously separated from most other arts by these facts, architecture requires a client or patron, and that patron may well not only give opportunity but also provide inspiration to the architect. That latter patron should frequently be honored for his or her role in the shaping of physical New York City, just as is the architect, landscape architect, or planner responsible for those individual works. Many design talents were never fulfilled by the realities of building due to lack of such patronage, and many mediocre abilities were summoned to bore us. Where would Ictinus be without Pericles (the Parthenon), or the history of baths without Caracalla and Diocletian, Michelangelo and Michelozzo without the Medici, Hardouin-Mansart without Louis XIV (Versailles), Haussmann without Napoleon III (boulevarded

AT&T Building. Never has an American corporation received so much publicity about something unrelated to its product. Here communication is housed in the now notorious Chippendale skyscraper. Architect Philip Johnson is perhaps the oldest *enfant terrible* of our time.

Paris), Domenico Fontana without Pope Sixtus V (Baroque Rome), McKim, Mead and White without Alexander Cassatt, Frederick Law Olmsted without William Cullen Bryant, Eero Saarinen without the Ford Foundation, Raymond Hood without John D. Rockefeller?

Individuals sometimes, corporations frequently, enlightened governments on occasion, have become modern Medicis, giving opportunities to architects and planners to create realities at a scale that has impact and meaning in the landscape of the metropolis, both qualitatively and quantitatively.

Nothing of the financial scale of Central Park had ever been even casually suggested before William Cullen Bryant's campaign to create a great public park for New York (which comprised only Manhattan at that time). As early as 1844 his fame and popularity gave him the stage of public opinion, an opportunity that was embraced by mayoral candidate Ambrose C. Kingsland and fulfilled with honor upon his election in 1850. Bryant and Washington Irving later became members of an advisory committee to the Board of Park Commissioners, which first bought the land for $5 million, and then arranged for clearance of squatters and debris and its survey by Egbert Viele. A competition in 1857 for the park's design was won by Frederick Law Olmsted and Calvert Vaux, with their proposed Greensward. Twenty years later the park was complete, largely the reality that we still enjoy today. But the *scale* was the bravest product, for the park, with 840 acres, was larger than the whole principality of Monaco and four times the size of old New Amsterdam. Bryant, although not the sole patron, was the catalyst to action and then member of the board, which, as a group, acted as client. Engineer, farmer, nurseryman, and journalist, Olmsted's career coalesced into that of a landscape architect through Central Park, and he went on to sometimes equal, sometimes more brilliant, works in the city, including Brooklyn's Prospect, Fort Greene, and Tompkins parks and Manhattan's Riverside and Morningside parks. Opportunity won through the impetus of Bryant allowed his immense talent to flower.

Next to Central Park the greatest nineteenth-century event in New York's physical history was the conception, financing, planning, design, and construction of the "Great East River Bridge," officially called the New York and Brooklyn Bridge and later only the Brooklyn Bridge after consolidation had made Brooklyn part of New York. Old New York then became Manhattan, and an almost parallel bridge to the Brooklyn, the Manhattan, was completed in 1909, twenty-six years after Roebling's marvel. The Brooklyn Bridge was many things to many people. It promised convenient and uninterrupted access to their workplaces for thousands of Brooklyn residents. It offered the opportunity for land speculation on the part of Brooklyn property owners. It was a symbol of progress as an idea before it became an icon in a mental triptych with the Statue of Liberty and Central Park.

Henry Murphy and William Kingsley were the Brooklyn leaders of a combined business and political movement to create the bridge through a state-authorized private enterprise. Murphy, an ex-mayor, ex-congressman, and ex-ambassador, was the leading Brooklyn Democrat in the public eye; Kingsley was a millionaire contractor who had done significant work in the construction of both Central and Prospect parks. Together they sought John Roebling as chief engineer of the bridge, as the only one sufficiently competent and with sufficient public reputation to be entrusted with so vast a financial and engineering enterprise. Roebling died horribly from gangrene contracted in an accident at a pierhead, crushing his foot. His son Washington, who carried on the work, was crippled for life with the bends, a common divers' problem little understood at the time, caused by too rapid ascent from underwater pressure, here similarly effected by the change of pressure from the underwater caissons that support the bridge's great towers to the open air. The bridge was, therefore, both the peak of and the farewell to the Roeblings' contribution to urban monuments.

Bethesda Fountain and Bow Bridge. A view from the time of their construction that recaptures the restored details of Jacob Wrey Mould's and Calvert Vaux's architecture in Olmsted's landscape.

John Jacob Astor lived in Colonnade Row on Lafayette Place (later extended into a street) in the 1830's. Here on Lafayette Place the Astor Library opened its first third to the public in 1853, to be followed by north and south additions in 1859 and 1881. This was New York's first free library, to be followed by the Lenox Library (on the site of the present Frick Collection) and the Tilden Collection; the three ultimately joined as the New York Public Library's 42nd Street palace in 1911. Astor's philanthropy inspired the later benevolence of Andrew Carnegie, whose libraries covered America in the 1920's. The Astor Library's building still remains as the Public Theater, its mid nineteenth-century architecture a prominent relic of Lafayette Place.

Alfred Tredway White became New York's first enlightened houser upon his commissioning of architects William T. Field and Son in the 1870's to produce inexpensive housing for his workers. He described it as "philanthropy plus 5 per cent," in effect anticipating "limited-profit housing" of the state Mitchell-Lama Law by ninety years. The Tower and Home apartments, designed in what is contemporary Brooklyn's Cobble Hill, were inspired by the "sunlighted" tenements of London and enjoyed floor-through apartments with cross-ventilation, served by open-access balconies and overlooking a central garden courtyard. As with many great architectural prototypes, it was never emulated in Manhattan because of the cost of land exploited by speculators for rental to the poor and middle class, who would live in almost anything not too distant from their work. Remember that in 1879 (the date of the Tower and Home apartments' completion) the elevated train had just been born (1870); transit was limited to the Harlem and Hudson railroads, horsecar lines, and the Ninth Avenue El. Movement was a precious asset, and those of moderate income had to necessarily live within walking distance of their work, with some at horse-drawn omnibus or trolley distance. If White's project as interpreted by Field had

Tower and Home Apartments. These were built in what the nineteenth century would term "enlightened self-interest," housing for workers. The patron, Alfred Tredway White, accepted only 5 percent profit on his investment.

become the basic vocabulary of housing, Brooklyn would have remained an airy, sunlit place.

Henry Pierrepont was the son of Hezekiah Pierrepont, whose lands had been surveyed and subdivided in the 1820's in what was to become Brooklyn Heights. The father's name (originally Pierpont, respelled by him in the fashionable French manner) is still remembered at Pierrepont Street, the northern boundary of his original tract. Henry Pierrepont was the developer of Green-Wood Cemetery, a handsome park that preceded Brooklyn's Prospect Park by some thirty years, and is about the same size. It afforded grand views (and still does) of the harbor and ocean from Brooklyn's highest topographic point. The residents were entombed with architectural grandeur; among them were painter-inventor Samuel F. B. Morse, philanthropist Peter Cooper, and abolitionist preacher Henry Ward Beecher. Lacking public space for the formal Sunday strolling that Victorians were wont to pursue, they embraced Green-Wood until the less morbid Prospect Park became available in the 1870's. Pierrepont's lovely topography was, therefore, the first major recreational place—by use, if not by original intent—in the metropolitan area. Its most striking architectural feature is the main gate, a late Gothic Revival confection of 1861 by Richard Upjohn, architect of New York's Trinity Church and Brooklyn's Grace Church.

Peter Cooper, a self-made industrialist, owned iron mines, wrought railroad rails, commissioned the Tom Thumb locomotive, manufactured glue, and was partner with painter-inventor Samuel F. B. Morse in the first transatlantic cable. Cooper's patronage and philanthropy commissioned the Cooper Union for the Advancement of Science and Art. With Architect Frederick A. Peterson he created its highrise brownstone at the junction of Third and Fourth avenues, the apex of the Bowery. But most telling here is not the external architecture of the building, although it reinforced the streetshapes with its strong triangular form, but

Classical Tombs, Green-Wood Cemetery. The Goths greet, but the Romans house the dead in marbled splendor. These were certainly stylish years in which to die.

Peter Cooper. Here shown in his later years as a venerable patriarch, Peter Cooper was a patron of technological wonders that included the Atlantic cable, railroad rails, the Tom Thumb locomotive, and the early use of iron in architecture.

a construction of masonry bearing walls with wrought-iron railroad rails used as beams between them. In turn small brick vaults sprang between the vails, a technique that with some modifications became the standard for floor construction in multistoried Manhattan. Elevators had been invented, but the safety elevator was not installed in a building (the nearby Haughwout Building) until 1857. Yet Cooper's construction allowed for a round elevator shaft for the future elevator in his belief that elevators, like pistons in a cylinder, would achieve a cylindrical shape.

Commodore Vanderbilt created the first Grand Central Terminal in 1871 as the apogee of his railroad empire and as a celebration of arrival and departure from the greatest city in the country. This Second Empire structure by architect John B. Snook backed against a vast cast- and wrought-iron train shed of the sort still common in Europe, sheds that could accommodate surface-running steam-powered trains. Its 1913 successor, interrupting and uplifting Park Avenue, was the corporate commission inspired by a great engineering vice-president of the railroad, William Wilgus. This colossal and complex palace honored in two ways the American architectural legacy of the Beaux Arts, font of late nineteenth-century American architectural education: by its lush external architecture and grand internal spaces, and by the brilliant separation of pedestrian, auto, and train traffic in a multilevel set of conduits and orifices, vast circulation spewing through each. Architects Warren and Wetmore, with Reed and Stem, share the composite design responsibility, but it was Warren who carved the great space and clad it with Roman pomp. Warren supplied a tenuous familial connection to the Vanderbilts as cousin and friend of the Commodore's great-grandson, William Kissam Vanderbilt, Jr. That Vanderbilt's sister, Consuelo, married the Duke of Marlborough, thus subsidizing Blenheim Palace through the Vanderbilt fortunes. One wonders whether William Kissam and Whitney Warren had tarried at John Vanbrugh's great Baroque pal-

Commodore Vanderbilt's fleet of river steamers created his "naval" title and his first fortune, a financial foundation that was the basis for his later vast wealth in a railroad empire. That wealth, through his son and grandsons, decorated New York, Newport, and Asheville (North Carolina) with a half-dozen of the greatest mansions of the nineteenth century.

ace and to what extent that exuberant classical architecture inspired the powerful face of Grand Central.

Alexander Cassatt, president of the Pennsylvania Railroad and brother of noted impressionist painter Mary Cassatt, commissioned Charles McKim of McKim, Mead and White to create the equivalent of Warren's Grand Central. Whereas Grand Central was a retreat from deeper penetration into the city, Penn Station was a new stop on what had been a discontinuous railroad. Electricity allowed trains to travel easily in long tunnels, here under the Hudson River from New Jersey to the station, and then under the East River. They emerged in the Sunnyside yards of Long Island City, then rose on a trestle across Queens, spanning the Hell Gate tidal connection between the East River and Long Island Sound with a bridge of great elegance, and proceeded on to Connecticut and Boston.

The station, over its own modest passenger yards, covered two blocks from 31st to 33rd streets, Seventh to Eighth avenues, on seven acres of land, and housed two levels of trains (local and long-distance), a level of circulation meshing with the subways, and a level of ticketing and arrival. The main ticketing hall was a full-size reproduction of the tepidarium (warm bathing room) of the great third-century Roman Baths of Caracalla; and the train shed for departures was a steel and glass greenhouse, domed, ribbed, and glorious, staidly surrounded with more Tuscan Roman columns, cribbed from Bernini at St. Peter's, giving a conservative demeanor to the street and Eighth Avenue. Cassatt's commission created the greatest building New York ever knew; and his successors, having switched their money from railroads to air routes, let it founder, fade, and be demeaned and destroyed by real estate exploiters. It bore a grand nobility "until that structure was converted by its thoughtful guardians into a vast jukebox" in the words of Lewis Mumford, speaking of its temporary successor, the third Madison Square Garden.

Thomas Wolfe writes in *You Can't Go Home Again*:

Alexander Cassatt. President of the Pennsylvania Railroad, Cassatt commissioned the late Pennsylvania Station. A complex of interior open spaces, it served as New York's sometime piazzas, as well as celebrating the wondrous joys of transcontinental train travel.

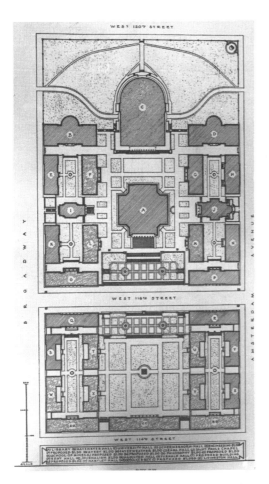

Columbia University Master Plan. Charles McKim rewarded patron Seth Low with this classical enclave on Morningside Heights. It is a fortress of learning with entry gates at its 116th Street flanks.

"The station, as he entered it, was murmurous with the immense and distant sound of time. Great, slant beams of muted light fell ponderously athwart the station's floor and the calm voice of time hovered along the walls and ceiling of the mighty room, distilled out of the voices and movements of the people who swarmed beneath. It had the murmur of a distant sea, the langorous lapse and flow of waters on a beach. It was elemental, detached, indifferent to the lives of men. They contributed to it as drops of rain contribute to a river that draws its flood and movement majestically from great depths, out of purple hills at evening.

"Few buildings are vast enough to hold the sound of time, and . . . there was superb fitness in the fact that the one which held it better than all others should be a railroad station. For here, as nowhere else on earth, men were brought together for a moment at the beginning or end of their innumerable journeys, here one saw their greetings and farewells, here, in a single instant, one got the entire picture of human destiny. Men came and went, they passed and vanished, all were moving through the moments of their lives to death, all made small tickings of the sound of time—but the voice of time remained aloof and unperturbed, a drowsy and eternal murmur below the immense and distant roof."

Seth Low, as president of Columbia University, became patron in 1897 of its new Morningside Heights campus. Columbia, originally King's College, had been founded on a site in lower Manhattan, now two separate blocks bounded by Murray and Barclay streets, West Broadway and Church Street. On valued land as the city grew and in need of more space, the college first moved to the "north woods," Madison Avenue between 49th and 50th streets (former buildings of the New York Deaf and Dumb Asylum). And in the same manner that the residential center of wealth moved, the department store district moved, and the theater district moved, education moved ahead of them all to find substantial tracts of land at modest prices: City

College migrated similarly from 23rd Street to 138th Street in 1907. Columbia's final site after 1897 was at the former Bloomingdale Insane Asylum. President Low commissioned McKim, Mead and White's master plan, a dense series of courtyards subsidiary to a central tight quadrangle (smaller than the great open space now extant). The architecture, excepting the Low Library, is bland, and one wonders how the hand of McKim, who was concurrently designing Penn Station, could have been responsible; or was the firm so busy (it was) with commissions nationwide that attention was too often diverted and talents spread too thin? The walls of buildings that confront Broadway and Amsterdam Avenue would have been happier if the ground floors had contained shops or other activities relating to a local street life. But the neighborhood was new in 1897 (the Broadway subway didn't arrive until 1904), and Columbia and McKim may have thought of the campus as a contained and fortified minitown on these sparsely settled Morningside Heights.

After Low's retirement in 1901, his successor Nicholas Murray Butler oversaw the infilling of McKim's formal plan by McKim himself and a variety of supporting architects and artists, including sculptor Daniel Chester French's *Alma Mater,* presiding over the steps of Low Library, and the great Guastavino-vaulted St. Paul's Chapel by Howells and Stokes, Columbia's greatest single building.

Coney Island's George C. Tilyou and his peers, creators of vast enclaves at Luna and Steeplechase parks, were promoters and entertainers in the spirit of a stationary P. T. Barnum or Times Square-by-the-Sea. In the 1900's through 1920's their parks housed amusement rides that rollercoasted, twirled, and whirled, centrifugal and centripetal terrors for the hardy surpassed only by the arrival in 1941 of the parachute jump from the New York World's Fair at Flushing Meadow. Tilyou provided, at the end of the newly penetrating subway, recreation for the masses, whose dulled senses in the tenements and on the Els of New York yearned for excitement and stimulation of heart

Luna Park, Coney Island, 1906. The Marriott Hotel may be mad with light bulbs, but Coney Island excelled in this almost Sicilian display of sparkling filaments. After all, what good was Mr. Edison's recent work, if it couldn't be so honored?

and body. Now they are thrilled by outrageous television, which excites only the eyes, not the whole person, as did the rollercoaster loop-the-loop. Steeplechase was the namesake of its most famous ride, with wooden horses mounted by visitors that raced on parallel rails in, out, around, and through the vast building that housed myriad eating, drinking, and entertainment events, including Coney Island's second most important elephant, the "Acme of Architectural Triumphs" (a five-story hotel within its colossal lead-sheathed hide had succumbed much earlier). The park was demolished in 1966, in anticipation of a still unbuilt housing project, one of many that now have usurped the space of this seaside pleasure land. Luna Park, remembered only in the name of Luna Park Houses (New York City Housing Authority), was a theatrical version of the 1893 Chicago World's Fair, the Great White City. Domes, cornices, and towers were festooned with light bulbs, giving an image that also recalled the elegant pleasure gardens of Europe, including Copenhagen's Tivoli.

The Russell Sage Foundation, in an attempt to explore economic possibilities for housing the average New Yorker, employed landscape architect Frederick Law Olmsted, Jr., with architect Grosvenor Atterbury, to create both master plan and buildings for a great site in central Queens, then awash in farmland. Forest Hills Gardens took much from the neoromanticism of English garden cities of the turn of the century, and in 1913 opened its doors to a new satellite population, tied to the city by the Long Island Railroad (there is still a Forest Hills stop at the community's shopping and hotel plaza; subways did not arrive until the late 1930's). Handsome and desirable, it became a community for the affluent upper middle class, attracting surrounding development of lesser quality, or sometimes sheer banality. It has survived, however, as one of the great examples of thoughtful planned suburban patronage, worthy of emulation for a flusher group than that of Alfred Tredway White's Brooklyn Tower and Home and Riverside apartments. White was part of the development team at Forest

Luna Park, Coney Island. In the daytime, stucco and metal ornamentation made Luna Park an outlandish and wonderful fantasy. Never tawdry, it was an architectural ensemble as well as a place of rides and games.

Hills as well, one of the consistent "good guys" in the history of New York's housing.

With an architectural vocabulary both coherent and varied, the Gardens' architecture is stylistically in the spirit of English Tudor, crossbred with the late ninteenth-century Arts and Crafts. Softened by the rich counterpoint of vegetation, including vast and numerous trees, it is almost a fantasy of suburbia, too good to be true near the heart of New York City.

Robert Moses not only brought the tablets down from the mountain, but also used them as license to dominate the city's public construction for a long generation and with puritanical zeal. His works are legion, the product of grand engineering, extraordinary politics, Machiavellian finance, middle-class values, and sometimes dubious planning principles. Moses hated cities in their traditional dense pedestrian sense and loved cars, although he couldn't drive one. His political territories included both the city and Long Island parks (he was commissioner for both), housing (he was in charge of "slum clearance"), highways (mostly to and from Westchester, Connecticut, and Long Island), and bridges and tunnels (Triborough Bridge and Tunnel Authority). No American—and no one anywhere in the twentieth century—has had such control by delegated authority, or by default, of such great changes in the physical environment.

Aside from the nature of his works, and their quality as bridges or parks or buildings, they followed his cardinal principle: dispersion and landscaping. Dispersion by bridge and tunnel and highway allowed the development of the million single-family houses that have peppered Long Island since World War II: an auto-served heaven for the breeding of postwar babies (they and their peers could go to postwar-baby schools free from the dangers of the "asphalt jungle"). The highways were parkways, handsome routes restricted to the passenger car (no trucks or buses, for the latter were vehicles of the lower classes). The Northern and Southern State parkways are handsome, green-

Riis Park bathhouses present vigorous brick architecture fronting a stretch of Atlantic Ocean beach saved for the New York citizen at the end of public transit. Here a work of the much-criticized Robert Moses is an urban joy.

lawned, and treed, sinuous roads that bring the traveler to home or park or seashore. And most famed as both park and seashore is Jones Beach, a whole island barrier beach that could redeem Moses' fame and reputation almost regardless of his sometimes inappropriate works. Jones Beach is a magnificent seashore, handsomely tended, ornamented with a serene Art Deco architecture, again unfortunately out of range of economical city transportation. Riis Park, however, on in-city transit-available Rockaway beach, offers at a smaller scale similar facilities of equal quality— also by Moses.

In town, Moses' marks are largely in the vast excisions of "slums"—of Harlem, the Lower East Side, Bronx and Brooklyn tenements—creating islands of high-rise red-brick housing amid a landscape of trees and token lawns. Although not created by Moses, the architecture and planning, based on a loose and unhappy interpretation of the maxims of Le Corbusier, were under his patronage; and in the same manner that the Long Island parkways excluded the poor from that suburbanization, Housing Authority architecture marked the poor as a breed not only geographically but architecturally apart. Carver Houses, Riis Houses, Vladeck, Pink, and Fort Greene houses are islands in such excisions. His other Manhattan works are at the island's edge: the East River (Franklin D. Roosevelt or FDR) Drive and the Henry Hudson (West Side) Parkway. The former was less difficult both in engineering and politics; it followed the mild gradient of the river's edge mostly through Harlem (90th to 125th Streets) and the industrial belt from 14th to 50th streets through the Lower East Side, but with enclaves of grand housing and wealthy residents at Beekman and Sutton places (49th through 58th Streets) and at East End Avenue–Gracie Square (79th to 92nd Streets). Not surprisingly, the wealthy had picked promontories for their turf that happily worked for them with the elevations of the drive; at Gracie Square (Moses maintained an apartment there), Carl Schurz Park became a lid over the drive, extending the park and creating a promenade for pedestrians at the river's very edge. At Sutton Place, where the drive's space intercepted gardens to the river, those closest to the river bank were replaced with a deck (still private), with a point of view accessible at the end of 57th Street for the rest of us. In Brooklyn Heights the promenade overlooking lower Manhattan's skyline and the harbor was achieved by Moses again. It consists of a top platform cantilevered over three lower levels: a local street, and the stacked south and north lanes of the Brooklyn–Queens Expressway (BQE). Moses is a book (*The Power Broker* by Robert Caro), but he is also remembered visually in the daily experience of the city—in its bridges, drives, parkways, highways, expressways, parks, and beaches.

Moses attempted in housing what Le Corbusier had so misguidedly propounded in *When the Cathedrals Were White*: to replace the dense streets and buildings of Manhattan with a highway-served City in a Park, a promised land. Save for Corbu's reference below to "glass" skyscrapers, the principles followed blindly in Moses' "slum clearance" efforts were established here: "The Cartesian skyscraper [one can assume that he meant the mathematically and philosophically perfect skyscraper] is a miracle in the urbanization of the cities of the machine civilization. It makes possible extraordinary concentrations, from three to four thousand persons on each two and one-half acres. It does so while taking up only 8 to 12 per cent of the ground, 92 to 88 per cent being restored, usable, available for the circulation of pedestrians and cars! These immense free areas, this whole ward in the business section, will become a park. The glass skyscrapers will rise like crystals, clean and transparent in the midst of the foliage of the trees. . . . the tonic spectacle, stimulating, cheering, radiant, which, from each office, appears through the transparent glass walls leading into space. Space! That response to the aspiration of the human being, that relaxation for breathing and for the beating heart, that outpouring of self in looking far, from a height, over a vast, infinite, unlimited expanse. Every bit of sun and fresh, pure air furnished mechanically.

Do you try to maintain the fraud of hypocritical affirmations, to throw discredit on these radiant facts, to argue, to demand the 'good old window,' open on the stenches of the city and street, the noise, air currents, and the company of flies and mosquitoes?"

Where Moses was without doubt the greatest patron of urban public works the country has ever known, the Rockefellers, largely through Nelson Rockefeller, and then Nelson solo, were the greatest patrons of architecture. Rockefeller Center was originally projected with a new Metropolitan Opera House as its centerpiece, a project that failed. In its place is the magnificent RCA Building, perhaps the best skyscraper ever built, centerpiece at the feet of which is Rockefeller Plaza, New York's most exciting urban space. At RCA's flanks are buildings that further honor that space, supplementing the plaza's amenities with the Channel Gardens and rooftop formal greenery, doubly an enjoyment in a towered city, where rooftops are frequently unsightly tarred places marred by the pipes and paraphernalia of heating, or cooling, or plumbing—or whatever.

Sketch of the Proposed Metropolitan Opera House, 1928. The opera house was the catalyst for the creation of Rockefeller Center. When the economic bubble burst in 1929, John D. Rockefeller found another use for his assembled land: Radio City, the original name for the whole complex.

Nelson Rockefeller was twenty-three at the birth of the Center, and the bug of architecture bit him. His cousin by marriage, Wallace K. Harrison, was one of its team of architects, of whom the brilliant trio, Raymond Hood, Harvey Wiley Corbett, and J. André Fouilhoux were the stars; artwork was by Isamu Noguchi, Paul Manship, and others. Noguchi is represented in the "tympanum" of the Associated Press Building, and Manship's *Prometheus* sculpture is a tourist symbol, an integral part of the lowered fountain-plaza. The Center was, therefore, a happy integration of the arts and architecture, unlike more current efforts where the architecture and the sculpted object cooly distance themselves across a barren plaza. Think of Richard Serra's brilliant *Tilted Arc* at Foley Square's banal Federal Building.

Rockefeller Center was an avant-garde work for the 1930's but happily remains a classic event for the city today—not stylish but with style. Interrupted by World War II, Nelson's passions were rekindled by the search for a site for the United Nations, where he persuaded his father, John D. Rockefeller, Jr., to option, offer, and then purchase a site preassembled by real estate tycoon William Zeckendorf. It was 1946, and Nelson had already been assistant secretary of state, no disadvantage in the politics of housing a new world organization founded at San Francisco in 1945 with Nelson in attendance. The site was largely occupied by wholesale meat markets, in a low edge of the city at the tidal East River's shore, bounded to the north by the bluff of Beekman Place, to the south by a Consolidated Edison power plant, to the west by Tudor City. This latter was Fred F. French's middle-class housing enclave (1928) by H. Douglas Ives, architect; few windows overlooked meat-packing to the east, it being apparently so noxious a sight that the residents' river view was forsaken. The UN appointed a committee of international architects including Le Corbusier for France, Oscar Niemeyer for Brazil (the two most influential), Sven Markelius for Sweden, and Wallace K. Harrison for the United States. Harrison acted as chairman and, better still, translated the bulk concept into detailed drawings and then into drawings for construction. The committee had only diagramed the proposal, largely in clay models suggesting the bulk forms.

Nelson's brother, David, as an officer of the Chase Manhattan Bank, was the pioneer in revitalizing lower Manhattan after World War II. The act of rebuilding its new headquarters on Pine Street, and building it in what was then very avant-garde dress to a Wall Street banker, seemed an act of great nerve. In fact, for this Rockefeller it was a cool, intelligent, and successful business decision. Of course, Nelson applauded the aesthetic event. The bank and plaza forestalled what had promised to be wholesale migrations of money management and corporate lawyering to midtown. This catalytic action inspired a whole renaissance of building on this edge of old New Amsterdam's street system.

Another Rockefeller brother, John D. III, led a powerful group of citizenry devoted to the performing arts to create Lincoln Center (1962–1968); the chairman of the architectural committee was Wallace K. Harrison. Here that committee could divide the spoils, and individual buildings were commissioned to Harrison himself (the Metropolitan Opera), to Harrison's partner, Max Abramovitz (Philharmonic Hall, now Avery Fisher Hall), to Philip C. Johnson (the New York State Theater), to Eero Saarinen (Vivian Beaumont Theatre), to Eggers and Higgins (the Damrosch Park and Guggenheim Bandshell), to Pietro Belluschi and Eduardo Catalano (the Juilliard School). Here the whole is greater than the sum of rather mundane parts: the plaza is a great space, unfortunately an open-air antechamber to the arts performing at any given time, rather than a vibrant part of city life, as is the Piazza San Marco, although it is based vaguely on the Roman Campidoglio of Michelangelo, where the active piazza is flanked by buildings of civic rather than cultural interest. Lincoln Center's individual buildings were termed by *Times* critic Ada Louise Huxtable as "conservative structures that the public finds pleasing, and most professionals consider a failure of nerve, imagination and talent." To be fair, few cultural buildings or enclaves of the twentieth century have summoned that "nerve." Perhaps the least crass of the three interior spaces is that of the State Theater; but all are damned with a kind of expensive kitsch that sells well to a public that wants its architecture to be as much of a placebo as its music. Architectural exceptions outside New York include avant-garde halls such as those built by Hans Scharoun for the Berlin Philharmonic, by John Johansen for the Indianapolis Symphony; by Jorn Utzon for the Sydney Opera House; and best of all such gracious and serene ones as that of Denys Lasdun for London's National Theatre.

Lincoln Center's larger function was in seeding the renewal of the West Side, in particular that portion from Columbus Circle to 96th Street. Urban renewal then removed a vast population of the poor, cleared immense blocks of tenements, and replaced them with "middle-class" high-rise construction along the spine of Columbus Avenue. These events have in turn caused the gentrification of most of the brick and whitestone town housing that surrounds the Center and Columbus Avenue, converting these recently timeworn and deteriorating blocks into a neater and more affluent enclave.

Like a child in a toy shop, Nelson Rockefeller loved all that was new, for the sake of newness or for the sake of the unusual; whereas Robert Moses hated modern architecture, with that not uncommon attitude of the 1930's that embraced modern expression for engineering but kept historic style for personal life. Moses particularly abhorred the elegant parabola at the FDR Drive and 91st Street, now "Asphalt Green," once the municipal asphalt-preparation plant for the city's streets and considered by the profession as one of the major modern monuments of New York (1944, Kahn and Jacobs).

To his great credit, Nelson Rockefeller appointed a surrogate patron, who for a while brought an architecture of housing to New York of a quality rarely seen in its history: Edward J. Logue. Logue had been chairman of the Boston Redevelopment Authority and director of New Haven's urban renewal, both with resounding success from a planning and architectural point of view, although with some social backlash from the displaced poor. Rockefeller's newly created New York State Urban Development Corporation (UDC) was a vehicle for large-scale experimental housing that could ignore local zoning and building codes and could condemn land for its projects. Principal constructed precincts are at Coney Island West, the Twin Parks area of the Bronx, and Roosevelt Island.

Architects who would never have been commissioned by a private developer—and rarely, if ever, by a public agency—were here given opportunity at a wondrous scale. And architects with established practices, who had had little experience in housing as a program, were opened to

Roosevelt Island. As if they had floated a new town up the river, Roosevelt Island's development rose triumphantly in an architecture experimental, handsome, and quite foreign to New York up to that time.

Rutland Plaza, Brooklyn. A handsome experiment in revamping the ordinary and housing those of modest means, this Urban Development Corporation–organized project was designed by Donald Stull of Boston.

that opportunity. Only Davis, Brody and Associates and Sert, Jackson and Gourley had elsewhere already created housing of quality. Here were added Richard Meier; James Stewart Polshek; John Johansen; Hoberman and Wasserman; Prentice and Chan, Ohlhausen; Giovanni Pasanella; James Doman and Emil Steo; and to round off the group, Skidmore, Owings and Merrill, New York's most creative firm of commercial architecture in the 1950's. The lesson illustrated here was that experience in housing might squeeze maximal rents for developers but that good architects, experienced in the reality of any architecture, might present new work that would grace the city, provide equal or better delight for the tenant, and accomplish it at a larger scale of urban design, making possible elegant newly created precincts for the city.

Most comprehensive as a total design was that for the relatively virgin Roosevelt Island, whose northern and southern tips were swarming with city hospitals but which had a largely undeveloped center. Formerly Welfare Island (and originally Blackwell's Island), it housed quarters for those with apparently uncurable or contagious diseases, separated from dense urban life by the fast-moving tidewaters of two arms of the East River. A master plan by architects Johnson and Burgee established form that contained a high-rise Main Street, with shops and restaurants, cascading east and west to fingered wings embracing gardens at the river's edge. The saving grace for this severed part of the city was the great stroke of constructing an aerial tramway to the island from Second Avenue and 59th Street. The island's architecture is unique in New York (mostly Sert, Jackson and Gourley; and Johansen and Bhavnani). The architecture's form is here new for New York but conservative both in materials and detailing: Main Streeted, with fingered plazas of privacy toward the water, a fresh experience.

At Brooklyn's Coney Island and at Twin Parks in the Bronx, large blocks, sometimes superblocks, were assembled for housing that is of considerable variety in form and type, from row housing to high-rise slabs. Access in the elevator buildings is through open corridors that serve duplex apartments, producing a lively facade of shade and shadow. The buildings at Coney Island, in a light gray brick, are less overbearing than the earlier public and publicly assisted housing in this seaside place. In the Bronx, Twin Parks units bore a palette changed to somber brown brick among the dour tenements, and the buildings are more part of a vast continuous city in all directions, whereas at Coney Island they seem the end of an urban line.

Grover Whalen was a name of the 1930's as renowned as that of his boss, Fiorello La Guardia. The Congressman of the people, La Guardia, turned exuberant reform mayor, appointed Whalen his official greeter—(what in a national sense, at the White House, would be termed chief of protocol). Whalen, the supersalesman of smooth and elegant dress and demeanor, was a perfume executive in his private business world. But, more important for history, he was the force behind (and then president of) the New York World's Fair of 1939–1940, a needed vision of a real or apocryphal future in those bleak depression years when desperate countries were about to be locked in war. The fair was planned from 1936 to 1939 and opened in the spring of 1939; four months later Germany invaded Poland, instigating the war that fall.

The fair was a white wonder. Its symbol, the Trylon and Perisphere, a prismatic wand and orb, were in the true spirit of the Moderne (the Paris 1937 exposition was at its peak when the fair was being planned). The countries of the world were mostly present in national pavilions, samplers of foreign cultures, flavors, opportunities for business or tourism, in a time before populous economical travel was possible. Travel to Europe, and even more so to Asia, was reserved for the most affluent, both in terms of time and money; for the voyage to Liverpool or Le Havre and return alone—without setting foot on the Continent or British Isles—was a time of almost two weeks, a whole annual vacation for most in those days. An outpost at the

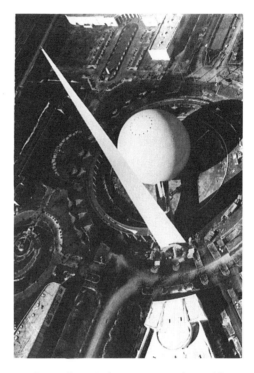

Trylon and Perisphere, New York World's Fair, 1939. A more satisfying symbol than the Geosphere of 1964, and certainly less spectacular than the 1889 Paris fair's Eiffel Tower, these were perfectly attuned to their time. The perisphere housed a giant model of "the world of the future."

fair was therefore a vicarious substitute for the real thing. More impressive, however, were the buildings of American industry, their sleek forms in large part created by "industrial designers," a profession of the 1930's that had taken the ideas of the Bauhaus. Forks, radios, fountain pens, and furniture were now part of the design world, as well as the traditional arts of architecture, painting, and sculpture. They were overlaid first with the stylish demeanors of Art Deco and then Art Moderne and Streamlining. Raymond Loewy, Walter Dorwin Teague, and Henry Dreyfuss were names that conjured up an image of style to the world of industry, as did those of Coco Chanel and Mainbocher in the world of women's fashions. The General Motors Pavilion was called Futurama (you were given a button saying "I Have Seen the Future"), with a ride composed of a serpentine, segmented continuous sofa passing around a suburban city plan with sleek highways snaking between tall towers, in the manner of (but not with the architecture of) Le Corbusier—a not surprising vision for the world's largest auto maker.

Inside the Perisphere was the blood brother of Futurama, an urban-suburban model viewed from a rotating ringed balcony at the sphere's equator. The future was vended everywhere, for who, in a depressed depression city that had discovered the reality of its own slums, would want to contemplate the past? Whalen's fair was a journey to fantasy, a never-never land of exoticism and plenty, where one could watch Coca-Cola being bottled instantly and relentlessly and Hostess Cupcakes being disgorged on endless machines, for a nickel for either, at a time when beggars were asking, "Brother, can you spare a dime?"

The fair was also a pantheon of ideas for patrons, architects, and planners and gave opportunity for some architects to gain a leg up in the profession: Skidmore and Owings, Harrison and Fouilhoux, William Lescaze were here represented. The fair had been abetted by Robert Moses in his role as park commissioner. Its site was the former Corona ash dump at Flushing Bay, filling marsh-

General Motors Futurama, New York World's Fair, 1939. To see this sleek white pavilion, and experience within its believable fantasy of the future, was an antidote to depression during the Great Depression.

land. The fair contributed fill and stability to that acreage, which, as part of the contract, was converted to Flushing Meadow Park after the fair's closing. F. Scott Fitzgerald in his classic novel, *The Great Gatsby* (1925), described the "Corona Dump," which would become the fair site: "This is a valley of ashes—a fantastic farm where ashes grow like wheat into ridges and hills and grotesque gardens; where ashes take the forms of houses and chimneys and rising smoke and, finally, with a transcendent effort, of men who move dimly and already crumbling through powdery air." A successor fair in 1964–1965 was organized on the same site and with the same plan (they could use the same water and sewage piping), mostly with more banal architecture. An exception, and the architectural star of the fair, was the Belgian Village, a complex where one passed through simulated urban history in search of Belgian waffles. One single building shone as distinguished design, the Spanish Pavilion by Javier Caravajal. Gone was the Great White City, streamlined and consistent, of 1939, replaced by the staccato egos of 1964 (the fair at Chicago in 1893 was nicknamed the Great White City because of its white stucco, simulating Renaissance fantasies, while 1939 simulated futuristic fantasies). Moses was the president in 1964 but gave little leadership in its conceptual design and allowed no surrogate to do so either; the result, of course, was an architectural zoo, but so, with much greater style, were the expositions of 1967 at Montreal and of 1970 at Osaka.

Abraham Kazan's name is not a household word, but as president of and driving force behind the United Housing Foundation, he was patron of more housing quantitatively for New York than any individual save Moses, and Moses was more responsible for the excision of "slums" than for the specific housing that replaced them. Kazan was also experimental, at least in his earlier days. Amalgamated Dwellings on Grand Street (1930) by Springsteen and Goldhammer had a European respect for street and contained, as its public space, a central courtyard. The same architects' Hillman Houses (1951) were the more popular

Ruins of the New York State Pavilion. It has been said that the best ruins of modern architecture are those Frank Lloyd Wright houses burned to their rubble stone foundations. Here New York weather has treated this oval painted-metal New York State pavilion no better than its companion 1965 auto. It and the Spanish Pavilion were the fair's two bits of semiserious architecture.

"blocks on a lawn" scheme that had been embraced in the city's public housing. Here the housing was financed by subsidy to a private, nonprofit developer: in effect the foundation was an arm of the Amalgamated Clothing Workers of America (men's clothes) and the International Ladies Garment Workers Union (women's clothes), pioneers in forcing the sweatshops of the needle trades to provide safe working conditions and decent wages and, then later a pioneer in providing decent housing for its members.

Kazan's empire mushroomed in the 1950's and '60's, first with Corlaer's Hook Houses at the foot of Grand Street along the East River (fantastic views) with his staff architect, Herman Jessor, next with Rochdale Village in Queens, on the site of the Jamaica Race Track (5,000 units, where at Corlaer's, there had been 5,000 people). And finally, on filled swampland along the Bronx River he created Co-op City, with 15,500 units: a stultifying dreamland of towering, endless behemoths, it houses a modest middle-class population that in large part vacated the Art Deco apartments of the Grand Concourse. This act, in a prototypical manner, a kind of negative blockbusting, caused that neighborhood's degeneration and decline.

Kazan will be remembered, however, as someone who "got things done," not a bad reputation for a passionate tailor in a city where anything takes forever and quality is demeaned by the bureaucratic obstacle course. Here there is some debate about the quality of construction, but it is superior to most speculative ventures. The apartments are more spacious, more rational, better planned than most; in effect, from an architectural point of view, the best place to be at Co-op City is inside.

Single buildings with an urban posture that has raised them above the state of "building" have given the city delight and inspiration, and urban parks, contributed by philanthropy, have given a pleasant and restful pause to life in midtown. Their patrons have had, on occasion, more

Co-op City, The Bronx. The good works of garment workers' housing here became a near-monster Topsy. Good intentions have, alas, frequently produced banal and boring environments. This is the biggest example of the latter.

impact on the quality of life (as example, not event) than many vast urbanizations: here included are Lever House, 375 Park Avenue (usually called the Seagram Building), the CBS Building, the Ford Foundation Building, and Paley and Greenacre parks.

Charles Luckman's career was extraordinary. Graduating in architecture from the University of Illinois at the bottom of the depression, he was employed as salesman and then as executive of Lever Brothers (now the American branch of the multinational, largely Dutch-English corporation, Unilever). At thirty-seven he was president, sited near MIT on the Charles River across from Boston, a handsome and serene place but far from the advertising action of New York. In the soap business (read Herman Wouk's *Aurora Dawn*) advertising is of perhaps equal importance with production. Luckman led his associates to New York, buying a Park Avenue location. He employed the rising commercial architects of the day, Skidmore, Owings and Merrill, whose design director, Gordon Bunshaft, hereby became a legendary figure in those naïve days where any spirited or unusual modern architecture was enshrined. Lever House was both spirited and unusual: a slab, hovering over a plane, all raised above the pedestrian street, light penetrating to a flowered courtyard. Not only was it a foreign excision of Park Avenue's street wall, but it also offered a dynamic interplay of form of an order that New York had never seen. Such constructivism was a modest child of Mies van der Rohe's great German pavilion at the 1929 Barcelona fair, a total anathema to the neo-Renaissance stolidity Park Avenue had aped. Luckman departed from advertising and soap to return to architecture, and, unhappily, he was less successful as a practitioner than he had been as a client (that is, in the qualitative, as opposed to the financial, sense). His Madison Square Garden Center and adjacent office block are a shoddy and banal drum of concrete and bland tower; his United States Pavilion for the 1964–1965 World's Fair, a dull box. Sleek in his

Ford Foundation Building. When you can't site a building in a garden, put a garden in a building. This handsome interlock of offices and greenhouse is unique. Here experiment in the hands of a private *pro bono publico* foundation was a rich success.

ability to sell toothpaste and architectural services, his talents peaked only when he sold the services of talented others to his own Lever Brothers board of directors.

The Seagram Building was the second scheme for this whiskey company founded by Canadians who smuggled precious liquids into the United States during Prohibition. The first was a scheme by the above cited Charles Luckman, a chunky building that filled the Park Avenue site. Seagram's chairman, Samuel Bronfman, was persuaded by his daughter, Phyllis Lambert, to reject this scheme and to allow her to interview potential distinguished architects who might bring to Seagram honor through architectural distinction. Mies van der Rohe was chosen, and in turn he chose Philip Johnson as his New York design alter ego with Kahn and Jacobs to do the nitty-gritty construction drawings. The product is one of the most widely aped postwar buildings of New York, its plaza as important as its body, in materials of a richness not attempted for a generation: marble-block balustrades on a granite plaza, with bronze mullions (vertical members between glass) and bronze panels developing the elegant facade. Luminous ceilings at the perimeter give it a night life and form perhaps more dramatic than that in daytime. Seagram set a standard of quality both of building and urbanity that, unfortunately, influenced the new zoning resolution of 1961. A plaza unique in New York gave promise of an urbane street life, and thence zoning was modified to give bonuses to those who would dedicate plazas to the people (bonuses allowing more rentable floor area—in effect, usually a taller building). The Bronfman-Lambert patronage gave opportunity for Mies to vend this design elsewhere; and so Baltimore received its neo-Seagram, and Montreal would have received one as well but for the untimely death in a plane crash of its sponsor. Mrs. Lambert, who had been trained in architecture at Vassar at a nonprofessional level, went on to a formal architectural training and practice.

The CBS Building had more traditional patronage, that of corporate president Frank Stanton, interested in

Paley Park. Small size can be an advantage. There is more delight in this minipark, set in the space of a single town house, than in all the plazas of the Avenue of the Americas combined. The waterfall is a stroke of genius, masking the city's noise behind its rushing foam.

the arts (CBS was concerned with both audio and video arts, in theory if not in the programming of its stations), and he extended that interest to the architecture that housed his offices. Ironically, the creative staff of CBS is housed largely in a converted milk company warehouse (very far west on 57th Street), while the more Brooks Brothers-Tripler-Sulka group is at Sixth and 52nd, hard by the Museum of Modern Art (architectural osmosis?). This is the only high-rise building by Eero Saarinen and one of his three in New York (the other two are the Vivian Beaumont Theatre at Lincoln Center and that great bat of a building at Kennedy Airport, TWA.) The latter was designed, according to one apocrypha, at breakfast with the aid of a modified half grapefruit. The CBS Building is New York's most serene and dignified modern skyscraper, clad in a roughened dark granite, set in a somber plaza. Another of those buildings that should have inspired children and grandchildren, it has never been matched.

The Ford Foundation Building (1967) on East 42nd Street crossed an urban greenhouse with the foundation's offices, a building whose form reinforced the street, aligned with its neighbors, but with visual space penetrating that frontage as a square garden roofed in glass. It was a Renaissance idea to complete a building-garden symbiosis with walls of masonry or iron grillage, as in many a Paris *hôtel*, de Lamoignon or de Soubise in the Marais. The concept was resurrected in modern architecture by Le Corbusier at the Villa Savoie, where the main floor (upper level) presents a facade to the landscape that is partly enclosed space, partly open to the sky, all within a rectangle similarly perforated for windows and windowlike openings. How much better the proliferated plazas of the city would be with such architectural enclosure and discipline. Here the patron was patronage sublime: the richest foundation in the world created architecture as one of its many good works.

William Paley, founder of CBS, commissioned a small but elegant urban plaza (1967, Zion and Breen, landscape

Greenacre Park. Bigger and more elaborate than Paley Park, Greenacre is styled as a lady with an extravagant hat, too much costume jewelry, and Lucite heels. Paley, on the other hand, is the Paris model: the superbly cut black dress with a string of real pearls.

architects) in memory of his father, Samuel Paley. Zion managed, in the tight confines of two twenty-one-foot brownstone lots, to give a sense of isolation, an urban oasis from noise, softened by a canopy of trees. The noise was masked by what might be called white sound, the rush of water over a pebbled waterfall. Paved, treed, and watered, this cul-de-sac is inevitably jammed in mild weather, a far more attractive place (small-scale, enclosed) than the open, chairless Seagram Building plaza or those Sixth Avenue horrors built in the name of a Rockefeller Center "annex": Time-Life, Exxon, McGraw-Hill, Sperry-Rand. The small spaces at the rear of these monoliths are much more humanistic than the avenue plazas themselves. Ironically the park was the site of the Stork Club, hangout of Café Society and other affluent elite in the 1920's and '30's. The club had such panache that it had an exclusive room within where the famous and notorious could contemplate each other without harassment by the merely rich. A fine place to memorialize a tailor.

Mrs. Jean Mauzé, another sister of John, Laurance, David, Nelson, and Winthrop Rockefeller, contributed Paley Park's peer and successor, Greenacre Park, on East 51st Street, larger and more complex than Paley (1971, Sasaki, Dawson, DeMay Associates, landscape architects; Goldstone, Dearborn and Hinz, architects). Its waterfall is bigger, louder, and more dynamic; its levels, three; its detailing, elaborated. Less serene than Paley, it provides, nevertheless, welcome urbane relaxation. There are probably no more impressive memorials than these urban voids, space given to the people that affect them far more memorably than most grand, distinguished buildings.

Richard Ravitch, a second-generation New York builder, entered the field of housing development with Riverbend Houses (1967, Davis, Brody and Associates, architects). This was the first serious attempt in New York City by a concerned client and architect to jointly create architecture and urban design of distinguished quality since Williamsburg and Harlem River Houses, both of 1937.

Waterside, 25th to 30th streets at the East River. Waterside went to sea to find its place, on piles over the tidal river flowing below. An urban island, it is umbilically connected to the city by a pedestrian bridge. Slender towers leave the river view unobscured.

The client-architect symbiosis moved on in 1974 to Water-side, in the East River between 25th and 30th streets, slender towers leaving the river views open to the city behind. These commissions brought Davis, Brody credentials that led other clients to them, bringing a high order of architecture to projects in the Bronx and Brooklyn as well as Manhattan. Ravitch went on to serve the civic public in other ways as longtime chairman of the Metropolitan Transportation Authority.

Richard Kahan, head of the New York State Urban Development Corporation after Edward Logue, took on the additional responsibilities of the Battery Park City Authority in 1979. This fortuitous event saw him commission Cooper-Eckstut Associates as master planners. The revised scheme converted the Nelson Rockefeller–commissioned Wallace Harrison scheme, a series of towered islands, into a true extension of the adjacent city. Streets continued from the financial district to the east, and apartment buildings now line a grid that gives the pedestrian the feel of the best of the Upper East Side reincarnated on what threatened to be a lonely landfill.

Rector Place, Battery Park City. A recreation of the spirit of the street-fronted Upper East and West sides, this product of talented architects working within a common discipline promises to be the modern architectural sector of the greatest quality in two generations.

World Financial Center, Battery Park City. The four towers, each uniquely capped, have a simple skyline charm. Up close the granite lower flanks are a welcome relief from all that glass.

15.

Glass Boxes and Fancy Dress

The image of change in New York since World War II has been largely in the architecture of commercial building, the offices of midtown and lower Manhattan that are participants in the most mobile and remembered skylines of the world. The slender towers of the 1920's and '30's were masonry finials, inflated remembrances of the many-steepled city of the eighteenth and nineteenth centuries. Now prismatic boxes grow among those towers, fat and thick boxes made possible by the newly available air conditioning that relieved the developer of the need for windows for all personnel, deploying the masses within the central portion of a vast floor area, with the elite at the windowed circumference.

The history of the packaging of these boxes is, largely, the history of New York's most studied architecture in these four decades. But first we must take a reprise to the birth of the skyscraper.

Unfortunately for New York's ego, the skyscraper as modern architecture was created in the penultimate years of nineteenth-century Chicago by engineer William Le Baron

Lever House. Its crystalline cubism, the single diamond on a formerly dour and subdued Park Avenue, is now awash in a sea of rhinestones.

Jenney, architects John Wellborn Root, Louis Sullivan, William Holabird and Martin Roche, and others. The most noted of these creators, Sullivan, brought one sample of his talent to New York, the Condict (or Bayard) Building on Bleecker Street. New York's skyscrapers were otherwise high-rise versions (same internal guts and behinds as Sullivan) of historical styles: Woolworth Building (Gothic Re-Revival); Flatiron (Fuller) Building (Italian Renaissance Revival). Forty years after Chicago's early brilliance, New York belatedly created the Empire State Building (Modern, Art Moderne Division) and then Raymond Hood's Rockefeller Center (Modern, Really-up-to-Date Division) plus the McGraw-Hill and Daily News buildings. Of these, only Rockefeller Center concerned itself with the urban landscape outside the bounds of buildings proper. More about that elsewhere.

But aside from these great works, little to whet the appetite of a modernist *seemed* to rise, particularly in the center city. The Grand Concourse of the southwestern Bronx was a show place of Art Deco, and glass-block pumping stations graced Coney Island, but the Downtown of All Downtowns was immune to the Modern of the then honored masters: America's own Chicago school, plus Wright, Mies van der Rohe, Le Corbusier and their disciples.

Finally, in 1951, architectural students, faculty, and critic Lewis Mumford in the *New Yorker* joined ranks to cheer Skidmore, Owings and Merrill, a firm born at the 1939–1940 New York World's Fair, whose only mark on New York's more permanent landscape had been Toffenetti's restaurant in Times Square (currently Nathan's). The cheers were for two modern "monuments" of the moment—clear, pristine prisms that juvenated the parched spirits of the theorists and architects-to-be: Lever House (1952) and the Manufacturers Hanover Trust Company (1954). Manufacturers was such a remarkable event in its time that it even played a major part in an ephemeral novel, *Native Stone* by Edwin Gilbert, that seemed to be a rudder for architectural students: a soap opera with only architects for stars. But with a hiatus of eighteen years since completion of Rockefeller Center—even that restrospectively major monument was looked upon as dowdy by the 1950's students—the young profession thirsted for events. Lever House—in 1952 a crystalline force on dour Park Avenue and the only glass in its time—was doubly powerful. Sleek glass walls reflected the rich texture of Renaissance Revival Park Avenue stonework, a sparkling jewel amid the somber understated elegance of its neighbors. Later insensitive copycats created a herd of glassy buildings, ill formed and proportioned, and worst of all they reflected each other's banality. The glass building had been born to the city, and developers embraced its simple skin, a wrapping paper in which they could package their profits—akin to the slender model's Chanel dress worn by a vastly overweight woman.

"Manny Hanny," as Manufacturers Hanover is now flippantly called, created the first New York supermarket of banking: all-glass with luminous ceilings to strongly define and emphasize the full space. The glass bank displays its security to the public—depositor or burglar—the safe is in the window, up out of the cellar, as in "The Purloined Letter." A cube on the avenue, the bank is no skyscraper but added to the vocabulary of glass envelopes for the lower strata of later skyscraper building.

The United Nations Buildings were a similar step in the public acceptance of modern architecture as a real event, a much larger and more complex challenge than the single buildings preceding. An interconnected group, the ensemble was articulated by special functions: the glassy Secretariat's slab housing the vast office staff, the General Assembly a shape to state its auditorium function. Connecting the two are three major subsidiary council chambers: Trusteeship; Economic, Social, and Cultural (Unesco); and Security Councils. Although not "commercial" office space, the Secretariat was in that new vocabulary of sleek glass and offered new support to the developers' modernists who would emulate this style in the name of a new

The Manufacturers Hanover Trust Bank brought its vault to a show window on the street.

United Nations. A promised future was housed in a new prism and sheathed in sparkling glass. International intelligent conversation, if not peace, here was prescribed by an international architectural committee.

contemporary aesthetic. The conceptual design was the product of an international committee that, happily, did not produce a camel in their quest for the perfect horse. Many young architects found opportunities within this gigantic project to have their first adventure in "modern" architecture, among them George Dudley, later to be Nelson Rockefeller's chairman of the New York State Council on Architecture.

But for the public this great freestanding (in a park) symbol of man's quest for peace was overwhelming: "modern" architecture for New York here received its formal blessings. Although flawed in many ways, the UN's design and construction proved a much braver event than that for the League of Nations in 1927, where competition jurors hostile to Le Corbusier disallowed his entry on the grounds that it was not drawn with proper ink and paper.

Lever, Manny Hanny, and the UN grew at a moment when modern architecture needed built form present in the city to mark "modern" as a step out of World War II into the first steps of a future and elusive peace. To make a second step, an icon was created by Mies van der Rohe; the Seagram Building (1958) brought the much studied elegance of Mies to Park Avenue catty-corner to Lever House. And more important, it set the great bronze-and-glass shaft back, to form a vast (for New York) plaza of granite and fountains. Seagram, the icon, was emulated in other cities by Mies himself—and in many places worldwide by many other architects. Clean shafts, freestanding, sprouted across the land (and other lands), prisms that broke from a traditional tight cityscape in Boston and San Francisco but merely extended the spirit of sprawl in such places as Detroit or Houston.

In the late 1950's and all of the '60's buildings blossomed downtown, midtown, and out of town, but their commercial intent was to deliver great areas of rentable space to those craving it in this time of burgeoning economics and short supply of office space to serve it. Aesthetics or city planning or good sense seemed not the route

The Seagram Building. The details, simultaneously so rich and simple, raise this simple form to its now honored architectural status. Materials of permanence—bronze, marble, granite in alliance—make this one of the least transitory buildings of the "modern movement."

for capitalism. The boxed curtain walls (at this time signifying glass and metal assemblies à la Lever) were stretched over forms uncared for, the vestiges of zoning laws without benefit of any true or architectural act.

Two Broadway and the Colgate-Palmolive Building (300 Park Avenue) are two prominent vacuities on the urban scene, glass without subtlety, form only by default, big for the sake of square footage not scale, and as a double insult they replace respectively the great Produce Exchange (1884, George B. Post) and an apartment building of style worthy of the Place Vendôme, housing Sherry's Restaurant. Sherry's was a Society restaurant of great style; but the Exchange was one of New York's great nineteenth-century landmarks. Its demise economically as an institution was perhaps inevitable, but its replacement—let's say "with needed functions"—was made with banality, not minimal architecture but nonarchitecture.

In addition to Sherry's, Colgate and its mushrooming Park Avenue neighbors occupied the sites of the Marguery, the Park Lane, and others, elegant places of residence and play for the idle and not so idle rich; and so the rich were zoned out in the name of progress, unprofitable housing of grandeur yielding place to commerce, with advertising agencies as the principal tenants. Lever and Seagram are isolated moments of distinction in a sea of commercial boredom. The Park Avenue vernacular of 1910 and onward that allowed some neo-Renaissance zest in a continuous facade was here debased into what might be termed architectural nihilism.

Some attempt was made to expand Rockefeller Center along Sixth Avenue (officially the Avenue of the Americas) in the 1950's and '60's. The results were a grim march of giant slabs offering "plazas" to the avenue without any attractive activities and filled with tricky fountains and changes of level, pretentious, inflated, and poorly crafted children of Seagram lined up in soulless regimentation. The avenue, as a result, seems a stark place for the pedestrian, a place to leave in order to enter the vast buildings

Avenue of the Americas Extension, Rockefeller Center. The architecture is big and boring, but more important, the space in front, around, and between the buildings has none of the sophisticated charms of Rockefeller Center and its Channel Gardens. Here Rockefeller Center has been used as a trademark sheltering inferior products.

CBS Building. A small skyscraper of nevertheless lusty parts, CBS brings style to an avenue that hasn't had any since the faded department stores of Ladies Mile, a mile and a half to the south. The building blocks marching down from Central Park across the street are a sad commentary on Fiorello La Guardia's vision of an avenue of the *Americas.*

it bears at its flanks. Time-Life, Sperry-Rand, McGraw-Hill, Exxon, Equitable, and New York Hilton—all share that blandness which seemed to inspire other antiurbane disasters, seemingly exported to most middle American cities and, unfortunately, to those of countries that sometimes ape the worst of New York.

The star, however, of New York's postwar modern commercial architecture is the CBS Building (1965, Eero Saarinen), a strong tower, with its structure articulate, sheathed in a rough granite. It has the stolid serenity of the Renaissance, powerful in a way the glass box could never be. Only modestly set back from the street, its tiny front plaza is in scale with the building proper, the city, and the street.

The World Trade Center (1962–1977, Minoru Yamasaki) is certainly the largest, tallest, and most expensive "modern" project New York has ever "enjoyed." Superlatives, therefore, are here related to light, square footage, and cost; for as a participant in the city it is both an island unto itself and an island internally. Its great plaza, devoid of the activity natural to its European ancestors, is a barren, ill-populated void between objects that are intensely occupied with office work and workers, rather than an active civic space embraced that would serve as a meeting place for occupants of the surrounding buildings, as does the Piazza Navona in Rome or the Piazza del Campo in Siena. The towers are bland shapes and of such colossal size that their very blandness reinforces their lack of scale.

The New York skyline lost its delicate silhouette of slender towers after World War II, when air conditioning made possible interior offices far from a window, and great fat boxes were plunked down among the finials. The World Trade Center was the crowning blow, giants overpowering even relatively distinguished box-buildings that had come to blur the skyline, such as the Chase Manhattan Bank and 140 Broadway. Perhaps it is a kind of aesthetic justice, where the fat boxes are strangely tamed by the two greatest towers of them all.

No matter how carefully the Landmarks Preservation Commission husbands buildings and districts, it tends to be concerned with architecture and the street at ground level. The profile or long view is beyond possible control, for that would constrain the vitality of the financial economy (in this lower Manhattan case); but it does not constrain the quality of architecture, so that we can still hope for contemporary buildings that will become a historic modern of the future. Will we ever again have towers equal to the Chrysler, RCA, or CBS buildings? The economies of modernity have proved false, and post-Modernists have successfully counterattacked, but their attack is largely one of license, freedom to be anarchists, rather than honing their joint talents to enhance the city's landscape.

The mid 1980's have become a time for serious architectural reflections, for architects of note now are commonly hired to fill the needs of commercial developers. Whereas governmental and foundation patrons and an occasional corporate Medici commissioned some rare moments of architectural style and occasionally grandeur (Police Headquarters, Ford Foundation, and CBS Building), speculative builders at the "cutting edge" of profit-making now find the need to deliver stylish buildings to their potential clientele. One hopes they will be buildings of style, and not merely colossal passing fancies. Buildings by Kevin Roche, Helmut Jahn, Cesar Pelli, Philip Johnson, and John Burgee are beginning to blossom in midtown, like an outbreak of fancy hats. Fifty-third Street is a special alley of fashion, and Times Square is threatened by an invasion of bulky matrons in the guise of a kind of Protestant Reformation: clean up the pornography but stamp out life. The four dowdy concierges of the square will be enough to scare away not only the lurid residents but also those seeking that healthy sense of Coney Island at 42nd Street. These are from the office of John Burgee (with Philip Johnson), one who knows better but has been carried away with the mystique of a kind of post-Modern exterior decoration that Johnson has so carefully promoted in the archi-

World Trade Center. Megalopolitan megalomania, or has the "big, brassy, and best" spirit of Dallas now infected New York? The best of this is in the engine room: the shopping arcades interweaving subway concourses and trans-Hudson trains are real urban events, while the static towers overhead are tombstones looming over the street and plaza.

Citicorp Building and Plaza. This building has a notable profile in the skyline and a wonderful interplay of street, subway, and indoor glass-covered plaza. It is a superb citizen whose architecture between its hat and its knees is, perhaps, appropriately bland.

tecture of younger peers, such as Michael Graves and Robert A. M. Stern.

The AT&T Building (American Telephone and Telegraph Company) is the shoe housing the fantastic family of Ma Bell. Here, the "old woman" now maintains a high-style container that breaks seriously with the glass envelopes of speculative Manhattan and brings some stolid, dour granite to 56th Street and Madison Avenue. The office spaces are much like everyone else's, glass box or not; but the entrance lobby, sky lobby, and skyline profile—often accused of being the world's first Chippendale skyscraper—bring a stylish architecture to this avenue, long chic in wares but superficial in housing them. AT&T does its best number with the street as opposed to the skyline, although the somber "arcade" along Madison is heavy-handed and out of the street's scale. The "galleria" behind is in the spirit of midblock indoor and outdoor pedestrian ways as at Olympic Tower, Harper and Row, and Park Avenue Plaza. It is more honorable for its function than its architecture.

One New York street, 53rd, can give an observant traveler opportunity to study a broad history of commercial design blossoming along a route long distinguished by one prewar modern monument, the original Museum of Modern Art (1939, Philip Goodwin and Edward Durell Stone); a postwar minipark, Paley Plaza (1967, Zion and Breen); and two great archaeological revivals, St. Thomas' Church (1914, Bertram G. Goodhue) and the Racquet and Tennis Club (1918, McKim, Mead and White). All are embraced within five crosstown blocks from Third to Seventh avenues. Here also are John Burgee and Philip Johnson's 885 Third Avenue (nicknamed the Lipstick Building); Hugh Stubbins' Citicorp; Edward L. Barnes' 599 Lexington Avenue; Mies van der Rohe's Seagram Building; Skidmore, Owings and Merrill's Lever House; Skidmore's Park Avenue Plaza; Philip Johnson and Cesar Pelli's additions and alterations to the Museum of Modern Art; Cesar Pelli's Museum Tower; Kevin Roche's E. F. Hutton Building;

Galleria, AT&T Building. More urban resting places and byways have proliferated in New York in the past two decades than in the past two centuries. So this through-block galleria is a welcome, if not perfect, addition to the growing roster of plazas and arcades.

E. F. Hutton Building. A neo-Persepolis? Roche and his mentor, Eero Saarinen, have given us some of the best and the worst. The UN Hotel is distinguished; the exterior parkfronts of the Metropolitan Museum of Art additions, gross. Here we have an assemblage of a dyspeptic supper at an architectural smorgasbord.

and Eero Saarinen's CBS Building. Citicorp has stolen the skyline north of the Chrysler Building. Its tilted hat is a jaunty profile originally intended as a south sunning surface for solar energy, but when that proved impractical the slope was so endearing to the architect and client that it was preserved for its shape rather than function. Inside the building's bowels is, however, the liveliest public place in town, a skylit three-story plaza filled with people, shops, and vitality. Here the architecture is made live by the people it envelops, unlike the many failed attempts at putting a south European plaza in New York, at the World Trade Center or even Seagram, which is fine for summer sunning but bleak at other times.

The Lipstick Building snubs the rectangular grid with its elliptical plan. The sleek skin had promised more before the reality of construction; it succeeds, therefore, in being more bizarre than distinguished.

Park Avenue Plaza (1982, Skidmore, Owings and Merrill) is neither on Park Avenue nor confronting a plaza. But such is the assumed magic of words with which its developers advertise its hulk. It consumes the air rights of the adjacent Racquet and Tennis Club, thus reinforcing the preservation of that palazzo, while giving to the public an open arcade through the block, two stories with waterfall, that is skylighted if not skylit. The glass roof is in such gloomy surrounds that light barely penetrates.

The E. F. Hutton Building (1986, Kevin Roche), the latest entry on the street, is in full fancy dress, neo-Egyptian columns parading an arcade facing the rear plaza of CBS, the work of Roche's mentor, Eero Saarinen. The costume is of a fabric somewhat thin, its granite skin many-seamed to allow an inexpensive cladding. Certainly strange, with cultural allusions garbled, it may be the first on the block to be looked upon as the Edsel of its time.

There is little question that this is not the end of the street's development, particularly in its further western reaches. And what is to come is as unpredictable as the spate of post-modernism expressed in the shape of the

Lipstick Building and the granite-clad E. F. Hutton. But one day, perhaps fifty years hence, historians will reflect on style. I suspect that the office buildings remembered with love will be Seagram and CBS, classic but not classical, with an understated elegance worthy of time.

Downtown, an equivalent excursion might be made along Liberty Street and its continuation, Maiden Lane, river to river. Here, at the Hudson, are Battery Park City's commercial towers (World Financial Center, 1986, Cesar Pelli), four great blocks transitional from the glassy modernism of the 1950's to the masonry-clad and top-hatted post-modernism of the 1980's. The street flanks are stone, punched with small windows, a relationship that reverses as the buildings rise, ending in all-glass skins crowned with four differing profiles: one domed, one a pyramid, one a truncated pyramid, and one a ziggurat, all prismatic geometry. From a functional viewpoint, glassy tops and small-windowed bottoms are illogical, for in the deep canyons of space at street level one would seek maximum natural light, and at the buildings' crests light is plentiful where windows here are continuous. But from a pedestrian's viewpoint the city is enriched with stone at street level in concert with the neohistoric stone architecture of the whole financial district.

At Church Street, 1 Liberty Plaza (1974, Skidmore, Owings and Merrill) attempts a forbidding and financially secure image with its structural bones exposed, here the actual perimeter beams shown for the only time in a New York skyscraper. It is a direct evolution from Mies van der Rohe and one of the few buildings following the master that he might himself recognize and praise. The plaza opposite is the open space provided to make the bulky building legally permissible.

At 140 Broadway the Marine Midland Bank (1967, Skidmore, Owings and Merrill) is as sleek as 1 Liberty Plaza is cadaverous. As dour in chroma as its neighbor, it is enlivened by the small but gracious plaza fronting Broadway with a sculpture, a vermilion cube by Isamu Noguchi.

Manufacturers Hanover Trust. The vault in the window was a daring move, considering that banks have historically buried money in the cellar. This marketing gesture, as in the phrase "come and get it," was a far cry from the reverent silence of neo-Renaissance banks, where the meek didn't dare to venture—let alone inherit any earth.

88 Pine Street. This and the CBS Building are the city's two most elegant post-Seagram modern office buildings. Its crisp white exterior is in fact aluminum, painted cladding for the insulated steel frame within.

Here understatement is again a winning asset of this simple building.

Opposite 140's north flank is the extraordinary Beaux Arts palace for the New York State Chamber of Commerce (1901, James B. Baker), a rich foil for the sleek new prisms of its neighborhood.

The Federal Reserve Bank (1924, York and Sawyer) is a giant Florentine palace inflated by the possibilities of steel and elevators. It is a foil once more, this time to the Chase Manhattan Bank across the street to the south.

Construction of the Chase Bank's headquarters building is the act that stimulated the whole post–World War II revival of lower Manhattan. The space given to the public as a plaza here was of equal import to the building proper (1960, Skidmore, Owings and Merrill).

And on Maiden Lane, Liberty Street's continuation, is I. M. Pei's one New York office building: its address 88 Pine Street. The structure is again expressed cleanly, sheathed however in white enameled aluminum over its fire-insulated steel frame. Within this crisp grid, glass stretches without any separating members. The glass is butted and sealed with silicone, creating the ultimate jump in aesthetic scale from the building structure to the office within, as if the whole were a glazed steel cage. It is close in spirit to those "Chicago windows" of Louis Sullivan, such as at the Carson, Pirie Scott store on State Street, a reprise to very early modern, rather than the common reprises of Wall Street to preindustrial architecture.

At the edge of the commercial island is 180 Front Street, perhaps one of the last gasps of glass architecture. Its base is a flared hoopskirt, a greenhouse lobby surrounding its shaft, gold trusswork acting as its squared hoops.

Of this cross section through the island perhaps only Battery Park City will provide a symbiosis of architecture and urban space equivalent to those of Rockefeller Center. It took fifty years for that sound juxtaposition of solid and void to be fully savored and appreciated. Let us hope that more equally urbane complexes bless the city in much less than the next fifty and bring many more sectors with a sense of place, rather than another stylish object on display on the city's fashion runways.

Galleria, World Financial Center. Penn Station was this volume magnified five times—this is where glass really sings—in a transparent urban umbrella for people. More of these indoor winter palaces would be welcome.

Lewis Mumford is perhaps the most venerable observer and critic of modern cities and their architecture still around. But for New York he holds a special memory: as by-lined critic in the *New Yorker* from 1931 to 1963. His "Sky Line" essays opened the eyes and ears of many long-dormant observers in and out of the architectural and planning professions.

16.

Critics and Do-Gooders

It was not until the end of the nineteenth century that a flowering of sophisticated public and critical interest in the environment occurred. Paris fairs of 1867, 1878, and 1889 had gripped the attention of the increasingly transatlantic attitudes of America. And in 1893, the influence of American architectural students trained at the Ecole des Beaux-Arts culminated in the Chicago World's Fair. Names that later dominated monumental places and objects (streets, buildings, plazas, boulevards) in all great American cities were represented there by buildings and sculpture in legion: Richard Morris Hunt, the first American to go to the Ecole des Beaux-Arts, John Carrère, Lloyd Warren, Cass Gilbert. Louis Sullivan was there, heretic modernist of the time, who had also attended the Ecole but had broken with its stylistic discipline and extravagance. The profession had then thought of itself as one only for thirty-six years in New York and twenty-six years nationally, as the American Institute of Architects, or AIA. The focus on architecture as an urban art blossomed as the profession assumed a greater identity and self-consciousness; and the professional unison of the fair showed both the possibilities of a flamboyant neo-Renaissance monumentality and a cooperative architectural discipline that allowed the whole to be greater than the sum of its parts: to allow buildings to jointly make a city—here the Great White City. The fair's concern with a unified architectural design—and that one of majesty (in plaster and wire lath)—was reflected in the new urban architectural dream: the City Beautiful. Where New York had grown into its relentless grid without any larger architectural design, the fair alerted its citizens to the possibilities of orderly grandeur and a common denominator of quality (rigid, but organized, disciplined without gusto). Thirty years later Park Avenue fulfilled this vision with a grand whole, but composed of understated architectural parts, here the simplified Renaissance Revival apartment house.

In the 1890's critic Montgomery Schuyler and architect-critic-lexicographer Russell Sturgis were serious contestors of architecture they thought failing and exhorters of that which they felt to be of quality and distinction. In effect they were the first regularly published architectural critics in and of New York.

William H. Jordy introduces Schuyler (in the 1961 edition of *American Architecture and Other Writings*) as one who "left an extensive body of architectural criticism, which constitutes the most perceptive, most revealing, and most urbane commentary on American architecture to emerge from the critical tenets of progressive nineteenth-century architectural theory. . . . His writings . . . bulk larger than those of any other contributor, except possibly for those of Russell Sturgis."

Schuyler wrote in 1899, on the Bayard-Condict building by Louis Sullivan: "There is nothing capricious in the general treatment of this structure. It is an attempt, and a very serious attempt, to found the architecture of a tall building upon the facts of the case. The actual structure is left or, rather, is helped, to tell its own story. . . . Everywhere the drapery of baked clay is a mere wrapping, which clings so closely to the frame as to reveal it, and even to emphasize it. . . . But, at the worst, this front recalls Rufus Choate's famous toast to the Chief Justice: 'We look upon him as the East Indian upon his wooden idol. We know that he is ugly, but we feel that he is great.' We feel that this front is a true and logical expression of the structure. If we find it ugly notwithstanding, that may be our own fault. If we can find no failure in expressiveness, the architect may retort upon us that it is no uglier than it ought to be."

On the 1893 Chicago World's Fair: "Certainly to question the unmixed beneficence of its influence is not to pass the least criticism upon the architects, the brilliant success of whose labors for their own temporary and spectacular purpose has been admitted and admired by all the world.

"In the first place, the success is first of all a success of unity, a triumph of *ensemble*. The whole is better than any of its parts and greater than all its parts, and its effect is one and indivisible."

Schuyler quotes a "distinguished French painter": "I am told that the buildings at Chicago are old [student] presentations from the [Ecole des] Beaux Arts."

"The White City is the most integral, the most extensive, the most illusive piece of scenic architecture that has ever been seen. . . . It is a seaport on the coast of Bohemia, it is the capital of No Man's land."

It was not until Lewis Mumford's "Sky Line" articles in the *New Yorker* in the 1940's and '50's, and finally Ada Louise Huxtable in the *New York Times* in the 1960's and '70's, that New Yorkers again enjoyed intelligent critics. Critics are read largely by the elite and then only by those who are architects, architectural buffs, other professionals, and civic activists. But through these "agents" we earn substantial potential impact for quality of preservation and change.

In his 1947 "Sky Line" article in the *New Yorker*, Mumford speaks of the forthcoming United Nations complex: "The Board of Design Consultants, whose chairman is Mr. Wallace Harrison, is made up of nine architects and one engineer. . . . assisted by seven other architects, a landscape architect, and eight other engineers. Fifteen countries are represented on this panel, and not all the architects speak English, either. Getting even a Tower of Babel out of such a group would have been an achievement. . . . So far, their headquarters is a combination of Le Corbusier's breezy City of the Future and the businesslike congestion of Rockefeller Center, a blending of the grandiose and the obvious.

"But the United Nations jumped at the first fleabite of land that was offered it hereabouts, . . . let us take a close look at this fleabite. It is in the old slaughterhouse district on the eastern edge of the island . . . a dismally blighted area . . . Mr. Harrison was one of the major architects for Rockefeller Center . . . Mr. Rockefeller is Monopoly Capitalism . . . If, when the project is finished, the United Nations headquarters should, by some fatal chance, look like Rockefeller Center, that would produce both a mischievous and a misleading impression."

Later, commenting in 1951 on the completed United Nations complex, Mumford said: "Apparently, though, the Board of Design Consultants were hypnotized by Le Corbusier, and Le Corbusier has long been hypnotized by the notion that the skyscraper is a symbol of the modern age. But the fact is that both the skyscraper and Le Corbusier are outmoded. Skyscrapers . . . are symbols of the way specious considerations of fashion, profit, prestige, abstract aesthetic form—in a word, 'the package' of commerce—have taken precedence over the need of human beings for good working and living quarters." Two years later, commenting on the General Assembly Building, he predicted that "If the United Nations matures into an organ of effective world government, capable of affectionately commanding men's loyalties throughout the planet, it will be in spite of, not because of, the architecture of its first headquarters."

Mumford in 1948 on post–World War II housing: "The greatest and grimmest of these housing developments is Stuyvesant Town, . . . Shall it be the old, careless urban nightmare of post–Civil War New York, planned so that from a third to a half of the interior space of each house and apartment is dark, airless, dismal, so that there is no view worth speaking of from the windows, except by accident, and so that there is a maximum amount of noise from the streets? Or shall it be the new nightmare, of a great super-block, quiet, orderly, self-contained, but designed as if the fabulous innkeeper Procrustes had turned architect—a nightmare not of caprice and self-centered individualism but of impersonal regimentation, apparently for people who have no identity but the serial numbers of their Social Security cards?"

Mumford in 1952 on Lever House: "Lever House is not, of course, the first all-glass building; the famous Crystal Palace, . . . antedate[s] it. . . . But it is the first office building in which modern materials, modern construction, modern functions have been combined with a modern plan. . . . It is a show place and an advertisement . . . Fragile, exquisite, undaunted by the threat of being melted into a puddle by an atomic bomb."

The World Trade Center.

Ada Louise Huxtable on the World Trade Center (1973): "The towers are pure technology, the lobbies are pure schmaltz and the impact on New York of two 110-story buildings . . . is pure speculation. . . . the World Trade Center is a conundrum. It is a contradiction in terms: the daintiest big buildings in the world. . . . the close grid of their decorative facades has a delicacy that its architect, Minoru Yamasaki, chose deliberately. . . . The Port Authority has built the ultimate Disneyland fairytale blockbuster. It is General Motors Gothic."

In 1975, on the 1960s remodeling of the Times Tower (1904) of Times Square: that was "19th-century picturesque in its Gothic detailing by the architectural firm of Eidlitz and MacKenzie, and 20th-century modern in its remarkable, early steel skeleton . . . if the remodeling [into

Woolworth Building, 1913. The Gothic dress of this skyscraper gave a vertical expression to this burgeoning building type—and a grand image to Woolworth's five and ten.

the Allied Chemical Tower] had set out to be artless, banal, and ordinary, it could not have done a better job."

Reflecting on the Woolworth Building in 1975 she said: "The real [as opposed to the Red Grooms sculptured] Woolworth Building is an unparalleled combination of romantic conceit (would you believe Gothic ogival lambrequins, or choir stall canopies, for cornices?) and soaring structural drama. In 1913, the skyscraper was a relatively new achievement, and the steel-framed tower clad in the exquisitely crafted detail of the delicate, creamy-white terracotta that was, briefly, the tallest building in the world. It is still one of the most beautiful and impressive buildings of modern times. Art is alive and well in the Woolworth Building from the brilliant, vaulted mosaics of the richly decorated lobby to the Gothic fancy of the crown at the top. Myth and magic are once again in good architectural repute."

In 1963: "The city's most monumental addition since the Empire State Building—the $100 million Pan Am Building . . . made its official debut with brass-band ceremonies worthy of a Presidential inauguration.

"Of these new buildings, Pan Am has far the greatest impact on the city scene. . . . Bigness is blinding. A $100 million building cannot really be called cheap. But Pan Am is a colossal collection of minimums . . . gigantically second-rate.

"This is no Michelangelesque masterwork from the late and latter-day Medici, promoter Erwin Wolfson, but a super economy package with the usual face-saving gimmick: painting and sculpture in the lobby. In its new role as an architectural cover-up, the builders of New York are turning good art into a bad joke."

The impact of critics influences those citizens, professional and otherwise, who pursue issues that threaten preservation or who suggest new construction, new city plans, new laws contrary to those citizens' belief in the city's potential quality. Civic power, however, rests largely in those groups that collect the joint wrath or praise of individuals and convert it to a common cause. These become, by default, the joint source of plaint and praise for the sophisticated thousands who despair of or honor civic change. First among these is the Municipal Art Society, created in 1892 from the forces of the City Beautiful movement unleashed at the Chicago World's Fair. Richard Morris Hunt, architect of that fair's administration building, combined power as founding president of the American Institute of Architects and architect of the Metropolitan Museum with a role as founder of this concerned public organization. Concerned with the "beauty" of the city, its early years were directed more at promoting civic embellishment in the form of statues and monuments than in the architecture of the city itself. Strangely enough, its elitism was constitutional: membership only for those "put up" by a member and approved by the membership committee on behalf of all. It was considered that only those who might be found worthy might become privileged to join these olympian arbiters of taste. The contemporary Municipal Art Society membership is open to all concerned but tends by its very nature to attract the doers and the watchers—those with the energy and talent to both confront and praise the city and its buildings, and those who want to be around at the kill or the glory, from Society to social climbers, from serious professionals to little old ladies in tennis shoes. The society's base has spread vastly in the past thirty years and particularly in the past ten, resulting in a marked improvement both in the number of members and in its influence for the good—"good" here being the quality of architecture and the environment, both old and new, largely in the center city. Landmarks preservation legislation was strongly supported by the society in the 1960's, and preservation of individual buildings and areas has become its prime lobbying effort. An offshoot, the Landmarks Conservancy, attempts to put together economic packages to buy and recycle endangered buildings.

The society's equally ancient contemporary is the Fine Arts Federation, a consortium of art and architectural groups

Crown Gardens. The City Club rightly favored this exceptional experiment in moderate-income housing in the heart of Brooklyn's Crown Heights. Low-rise apartments surround three sides of a private courtyard.

founded in 1898, in those exuberant Beaux Arts years. The membership (organization) list represents all shades of aesthetic postures from conservative to avant garde, including the Municipal Art Society, the American Institute of Architects, the American Society of Landscape Architects, the American Institute of Decorators, the American Watercolor Society, and the National Sculpture Society. The federation is a less potent force, largely because its most powerful members do their own lobbying at City Hall and at the Landmarks Preservation and City Planning commissions. Another chorus of voices is, however, always a help. The federation is bound into the city charter, in that the mayor's appointments to the art commission must come from a list presented by the federation.

A relative newcomer to the field of honors is the City Club, a good-government (goo-goo) organization that has since the 1920's attempted to fight corruption "ward by ward," district by district. "Goo-goo" was coined as a sarcastic insult but became instead a badge of honor. In 1963 the club began an architectural awards program, at first to honor public buildings. Its jury found none worthy of honor, triggering wails of "Foul!" from the stiffer members of the architectural establishment. In fact the jury was fair and just: nothing of distinction had been built in the city by the city, state, or federal governments for more than a generation.

Since 1963, the Bard Awards have become the most distinguished architectural honors of and for the city. My favorites have been (and there are few of those honored I wouldn't care to support) the Pepsi-Cola (now Olivetti) Building (1964, Skidmore, Owings and Merrill), Chatham Towers apartments (1967, Kelly and Gruzen), the Ford Foundation (1968, Roche and Dinkeloo), East Midtown Plaza (1973, Davis, Brody and Associates), Crown Gardens (1975, Richard Kaplan/Stevens, Bertin, O'Connell and Harvey), Avery Hall extensions (1978, Alex Kouzmanoff), the Woolworth Building restoration (1982, the Ehrenkranz Group), and the Battery Park City Esplanade (1985, Cooper-Ekstut Associates).

Professional organizations are obviously concerned with the quality of architecture and the environment, but as their own membership creates the work to be honored or criticized (positively or negatively), the politics of negative criticism makes serious discussion almost impossible. However, thoughtless urban design and unfortunate programs (descriptions of the architecture-to-be menu) are fair game.

The New York Chapter, American Institute of Architects (or AIA), is the largest and most involved professional organization, boasting more than two thousand members. Architects have traditionally been poor at the politics of civic architecture and design. The talent and training of the studio, seemingly, have not equipped most, individually or in groups (such as the AIA), to exert a substantial political influence on the form and quality of the city's environment. Individual designers, who have conquered the politics of gaining a commission or have won a city-sponsored competition, have contributed buildings and areas of distinction (William Kendall's Municipal Building, completed in 1914 through the office of McKim, Mead and White, was the product of a competition).

Battery Park City Esplanade. A pedestrian edge to a city long barred from the river by industry and highways. Its understated and traditional detailing is a joy.

The average civic building of the 1940's through '70's has been usually bland and lonely in its context, a jewel or wallflower among the dour middle-class or grimy tenement alike. At rare moments a great civic and urbane event is signaled by the happy congruence of politics and talent. Such occurred for the Police Headquarters, a major priority of Major Lindsay and, happily, a distinguished design of building, plaza, and environment from the graceful symbiosis of Gruzen and Partners, architects, and M. Paul Friedberg and Associates, landscape architects. The product is an integrated juxtaposition with the barrel vault of Kendall's great Municipal Building, forming a triumphal arch to enter the plaza's allée.

Police Headquarters, seen through the Municipal Building Vault. The street, Park Row, was depressed, and a plaza created joining the world of the Civic Center with the new Police Headquarters through the great barrel vault of the 1914 Municipal Building.

The AIA annually awards honors to its membership, but the work submitted can be (built) anywhere and occasional city buildings are so honored; but it is not, in principle, a civic-awards program. The chapter, however, speaks out with increasing force on public architectural and environmental issues.

The American Society of Landscape Architects is, by the nature of its profession, a small group in the city, concerned with the nature and ordering of plant materials in gardens, parks, and conservatories. But in New York City, members are also urban landscapers, creating hard indoor and outdoor space with incidental trees and planting. Their small voice speaks to the love of the city's great parks and plazas (most of the latter are, however, private indoor and outdoor enclaves, such as Paley Plaza, Citicorp Plazas, Rockefeller Plaza). Frederick Law Olmsted's legacies to the city, including Central, Prospect, and Riverside parks, are part of the society's great historical environments, which their membership protects, restores, and defends.

The Art Commission of the City of New York, with three ex officio members, seven mayoral appointees (one architect, one landscape architect, one painter, one sculptor, and three laypersons), plus the mayor or his representative, reviews all art and architecture to be built on city property. Its approval is legally necessary to build a building or place a sculpture or painting in question. Its standards have slowly risen over the past twenty years, but the commission is only a negative force, to prevent the dull or tawdry. Architectural (or "artistic") talent must generate the work to be reviewed. To counter its negative image, the commission, starting in 1982, instituted an awards program to honor the best of each preceding year's approved submissions.

The Landmarks Preservation Commission has been charged since 1965 with the designation of buildings and precincts that it believes should be protected—if not preserved—forever. Its creation was largely the positive by-product of the demolition of McKim, Mead and White's great Pennsylvania Station. For the first time citizens made noise about a great civic architectural loss, much to the amusement and amazement of New York's "press."

Any designation of the commission must be ratified by the Board of Estimate, the financial arm of the city legislature, for constraints on alterations and demolition to a landmark building or area are a financial matter. Preservation of anything at all is a relatively modern event. Certainly, Haussmann reshaped the whole infrastructure of Paris in the second half of the nineteenth century (respecting, however, most major monuments), but New York's Landmarks Preservation Commission not only protects minor delights but also has designated the street plan of Manhattan below Wall Street, as the only remnant (it's almost all there) of Dutch New Amsterdam.

The most famous battle, led in public by stars Jacqueline Kennedy Onassis and Philip Johnson, was the defense of the designated Grand Central Station from development proposals that would have removed its southern facade and waiting room (not the great central hall). The courts upheld the right of the city to designate at this grand scale, reinforcing the backs of the commission and its supporters.

In the early 1960's not only the Landmarks Preservation Commission was birthed (1965), but the *New York Times* appointed its first architectural critic in time remembered, Ada Louise Huxtable, in 1963 (Montgomery Schuyler had died in 1914 after a forty-year career with the *New York Sketch-Book of Architecture*, the *Times*, and *Architectural Record*). Her trenchant criticism focused attention on existing controversies, and her original insights happily isolated new issues that had been ignored or overlooked. Mrs. Huxtable wrote some daily, some Sunday signed columns as well as occasional editorial-page invectives against (with grace), and paens for, the good or the bad (*her* definition, but most goo-goos agreed). Philistines drew in their horns. Her influence ranged from editorial assistance in

Subway Plaza at Citicorp. Here the zoning bonuses worked in their most glorious and urbane manner, assisting in the creation of a humane sunken subway plaza. If this quality of access were common, subway travel might well become the premium way about town once more.

Lincoln Center Plaza. The plaza is far more satisfying than the buildings that contain it. Save for Grand Army Plaza at 59th Street and the Police Plaza, this is the city's only truly public plaza.

preventing the construction of a meat market at Brooklyn's water edge, where romantic posters proclaim the skyline of Manhattan (now a state park), to awaking the citizenry to the architectural banality of Lincoln Center:

"By contrast [with the Juilliard School and the Vivian Beaumont Theater], however, the retardataire fussiness and esthetic indecision of the rest became painfully clear: a gift wrap job of travertine trim and passe partout colonnades applied to basic boxes in a spatial composition new with the Renaissance and reworked six decades ago by the Beaux Arts. In a most depressing sense, the Lincoln Center complex has defaulted as contemporary architecture and design.

"It is, after all, by the standards of art that all art must be judged. As entertainment, Lincoln Center promises to be an operational success. By creative measurement, much of its product and most of its plant are an artistic failure. And that is why its expensively suave, extravagantly commonplace presence is making a great many people in the fine and performing arts profoundly uneasy."

The New York City Planning Commission is more of a constraining force than an inspirational or critical one. Zoning, its principal tool, describes the maximum area, bulk, and population concentration for any building site, leaving it as a challenge to the developer and his architect to achieve the most by hook, crook, or bonus. Bonuses occur (at present) when the public receives some benefit or amenity (in the eyes of the law and its interpretation by the commission). Samples include plazas for pedestrians (now out of favor because of the dilution of their purpose: a plaza surrounded by plazas is no longer a plaza but merely a memory of Kansas), arcades within buildings but open to the public in the manner of a plaza, and subway entrances where stations open graciously to a lowered plaza or arcade. Bonuses, often misused, allow the developer to build more in return for the amenities provided. Excellent and positive examples are the plazas at Citicorp, 53rd to 54th streets, Lexington to Third (1978, Hugh Stubbins), one outside, one inside. The depressed outer plaza, by a waterfall, offers a subway entrance more agreeable than any competitor. The act of entering the concourse at the plaza level, instead of first disappearing into a hole like Alice's white rabbit, brings this part of subway travel to the level of civilization. Underground things are also improving, but slowly. The stations are under architectural "upgrading," and even sleek new trains appear from time to time.

Solomon R. Guggenheim Museum. An architectural spectacle inside and out, this was designed when Wright was seventy-four, and was not completed until he was ninety-two. Architecture is not frequently a field for youth.

17.

Public and Philanthropic Works

Public works to modify, strengthen, and enhance the postwar civic scene were imposing individually but, for the most part, had little impact on the nature of the city as a whole. Perhaps the most overwhelming acts were those transportation changes that created negative urban or architectural events. Highways and airports effectively destroyed railroads and passenger ships as means of long distance travel. John F. Kennedy International Airport, conceived in 1942 and born in 1948 as Idlewild on seven and one-half square miles of Jamaica Bay marshland, has grown not only in area but also in intensity and complexity to serve as the portal to national and international travel. La Guardia Airport, its sister facility, handles the same volume of landings and takeoffs but for shorter flights. Together they have driven passenger trains nearly out of business, save for service in the Boston–New York–Washington corridor, where the speed of trains from center city to center city can compete with shuttle air time plus travel time to and from airports. Such air service has delivered, unfortunately, specious architecture to sprawling complexes amid vast parking lots and even vaster airfields. And it has contributed indirectly to the demise of great architecture, most prominently in the demolition of Pennsylvania Station, that grand celebrator of arrival from, and departure to, the nation that was demolished in favor of a new Madison Square Garden.

The Hudson River's edge was fronted with piers for innumerable transoceanic liners and cruise ships in the 1950's. In the 1980's it sees a scant visitor, an occasional cruise ship and the visits of the *Queen Elizabeth 2*. What were piers with the vitality of arriving and departing sea voyagers became moribund. In the late '60's an attempt was made to rebuild four blocklengths of major piers for mostly cruise traffic. These too have become ill used, as those cruising fly to Miami and board their ships there, rather than be subjected to what seemed to be a cold or boring voyage down the Atlantic coastline.

The most monumental efforts in the public sector have been those invisible and powerful tunnels for sewage and water. The two most prominent are the multibillion-dollar Catskill Tunnel 3, distributing water to the city from the Yonkers-located High View reservoir, and the interceptor tunnels gathering the sewage of Manhattan's whole West Side for delivery to the new North River Pollution Control Plant between 135th and 145th streets in the Hudson River.

The Verrazzano-Narrows Bridge (1964, Othmar Ammann) furthered the development and suburbanization of Staten Island and simultaneously moved a vast middle class from Brooklyn's brownstone and row-housed ethnic neighborhoods across its span. A symbol to the arriving ship traveler as great as the Statue of Liberty, the Verrazzano contributed to the social collapse of areas of east Flatbush, Brownsville, and East New York (all Brooklyn). And the collapse ended in abandoned property and burned-out building shells. Populations moved to the imagined idyll in the borough across the Narrows; one city planner referred to the migrators as believing that they "had died

North River Pollution Control Plant. When this is in full operation in the 1990's, the Hudson River and harbor may be close to pristine once again. The vast building is excused by the park to be completed on its twenty-two-acre roof. An arcaded concrete facade attempts to bring some scale to this behemoth.

and gone to heaven." But the endless ranks of jerry-built and crudely designed housing are, sadly, a far cry from the elegance and substantial construction of, say, Crown Heights, that they left behind. The lure of the barbecue and the grass toupee in their yard seemed to be more compelling than the architectural qualities of the brick and brownstone city. Obviously "blockbusting," or fear of black and Puerto Rican immigration, exacerbated negative feelings for their old neighborhoods as well.

New subway lines and extension of existing lines were a postwar vision, and construction began on two major routes: the Second Avenue subway and one to Queens. The former promised to relieve the aged and intensely used Lexington Avenue line that delivered the upper middle class to its midtown and lower Manhattan aeries. The demolition of both the Second Avenue (1942) and Third Avenue (1955) elevated routes had compounded the problem of already mushrooming use. The West Side had both the Broadway IRT route and the Independent Eighth Avenue and Sixth Avenue lines; its populace was, therefore, relatively well served with transit. But the crushing expense of city operation drove New York almost to bankruptcy in the mid 1970's. The Second Avenue line was stopped in its tracks, a vast void under Harlem in the twenty blocks south of the Triborough Bridge. The other proposed line to Queens was to be an extension of the postwar stub of the Sixth Avenue subway that brings tracks from its westward turn at 53rd Street north to 57th Street. From here the line tunnels under Central Park, across East 63rd Street, under the East River to Roosevelt Island, and up to 21st Street in Queens. A route planned to connect with existing railroad tracks, its intention was to serve Kennedy Airport with direct transit. It remains another void, with no plan for its completion.

Commerce and its partner, real estate development, brought towers to Manhattan, an architectural extravaganza of capitalism frequently at its environmental best. The city and state governments languished architecturally

John F. Kennedy International Airport. The scattered airline buildings make this complex difficult to use and chaotic architecturally. Some isolated terminals are distinguished, as were the original TWA and National Airlines buildings.

to the extent that in 1963, the Bard Awards program of the City Club of New York, a watchdog organization, stated that nothing of architectural importance had been built by a governmental agency in a hundred years. But times changed. The city administration of John V. Lindsay and the state administration of Nelson Rockefeller, directly and through related agencies, commissioned architecture and urban design of distinction. The work of the New York State Urban Development Corporation (UDC) and its head, Edward J. Logue, has been discussed elsewhere, as has that of the state Battery Park City Authority (BPCA). The authority's World Financial Center has also been described, although the specific plan for this latter project was consummated by a private developer, Olympia and York, commissioning a private architect, Cesar Pelli. Both the UDC and the BPCA have provided housing and urban precincts of distinction.

Public works with the greatest civic impact, however, have been those of the least monumental building type, housing, where architecture and urban design jointly form not only buildings but neighborhoods. Rector Place at Battery Park City and Roosevelt Island's Main Street are distinguished sectors with strong and unique identities, in which serious architects have restrained their egos so that their buildings might fit into a joint urban context, perhaps not as serene as Park Avenue but giving a rich variety within a larger overall discipline.

Projects more monumental, yet comprehensible to a single viewer as significant architectural statements, include the city's Police Headquarters (1973, Gruzen and Partners), and the Jacob K. Javits Convention Center (1986, I. M. Pei and Partners). The Police Headquarters, in the words of *New York Times* critic Ada Louise Huxtable, is "in the miracle class . . . a solid, sober, brick and concrete structure carried out with skill, sense, and taste . . . It is, as Brooks Brothers says of its sportswear, good-looking, meaning it has quality without flash.

"But the real cockeyed miracle, and the greatest hom-

Jacob K. Javits Convention Center. A glistening daytime skin and a sparkling nighttime image light up what was formerly part of the grim New York and Hudson freight yards. These revitalized far reaches of the West Side will slowly infill with hotels, restaurants, and even dwellings.

age due to the architects, is for the public space that the building creates around it. Here, suddenly, is a civic center . . . where only chaos existed before."

The Convention Center, the product of a state authority, brings a suggestion of greenhouses, more than that of crystal palaces, to the very west side. In a place where freight yards once stood, the center's dour glassiness shines opaquely in the daylight and sparkles with internal incandescence at night. A place of life as well as architecture, it is the display house for wares of many trades and technologies and the meeting ground of professionals conferring, from dentists to dog trainers. It is, in a way, a modern atrium building in the manner of a Regency Hyatt hotel, but inside out. The convention spaces are within internal windowless boxes, surrounded by a glassy envelope for pedestrian movement, skylighting, and the weather.

The City University has, through a state financing process, constructed major new complexes notably at the City College, York College, Hunter College, and the Borough of Manhattan Community College. These are but a sampling of the eighteen-college system, where existing campuses, such as that of Queens College, have also been enhanced with distinguished and not-so-distinguished individual buildings by a wide spectrum of architects.

The City College North Academic Complex (1982, John Carl Warnecke and Associates) is a vast, 600,000-square-foot megastructure looming over west Hispanic Harlem, a beached aircraft carrier amid tenements and houses that have been in turn subdivided into apartments. The most kindly thoughts about this gray behemoth describe it as an inoculation of vitality into a drab and largely impoverished neighborhood. Sleek and modern, it acts as a twentieth-century foil to the neo-Gothicism of the original 1905 campus quadrangle adjacent.

York College is another superbuilding, but in the devastated downtown precincts of Jamaica, once a town, later and for generations a commercial section of Queens. A great sculpted monolith of brick and glass, it is truly a

The City College, North Academic Center. A sleek giant next to the serene neo-Gothic quadrangle and legions of local tenements. This is a megastructure, a single complex housing the multifarious departments and functions of what, in another time, would be the Harvard Yard.

Manhattan Community College, West Street between North Moore and Chambers Streets. Another megastructure, here with its main body spanning a street. It flanks Independence Towers, the crudeness of which makes the college seem even more elegant.

phoenix rising from the ashes of leveled blocks of ravaged buildings (1985, Gruzen and Partners).

Hunter College was once a single block, half an early modern building (1940, Shreve, Lamb and Harmon; Harrison and Fouilhoux) and half neo-Gothic (1913, C. B. J. Snyder). It sprang, thanks to the City University's vast building program, across 68th Street to the south and, in turn, across Lexington Avenue to two sleek towers (1977–1984, Ulrich Franzen), umbilically attached to their parents by bridges spanning the street and avenue. Here the grid is challenged by the lacing of buildings across its intersection.

Manhattan Community College (1983, Caudill Rowlett Scott) was designed by some bright Texans in the era when the city sought talent nationally. The City College architect, John Carl Warnecke, was originally from California, as is Robert Marquis, architect of the new performing arts center at Queens College.

The university's construction program has marked widely spaced city neighborhoods with a quality of architecture that is consistently acceptable, never noxious, but rarely with more style than the best Chanel dress might display in a poor and ill-educated neighborhood (City and York colleges) or that the midwestern preppie would show at Park Avenue (Hunter College additions). Inside all such City University places, one might be on a stage set for education. One hopes the aspirants will follow the stage directions.

Private philanthropy provided New York with several of its major postwar civic monuments: the Guggenheim Museum (1959, Frank Lloyd Wright), the Whitney Museum (1966, Marcel Breuer), the Ford Foundation Building (1967, Kevin Roche, John Dinkeloo), Lincoln Center (1962–1969, Wallace Harrison, Max Abramovitz, Philip Johnson, Eero Saarinen, Eggers and Higgins, Pietro Belluschi, Eduardo Catalano, and Skidmore, Owings and Merrill), and the vast remodelings and extensions of both the Museum of Modern Art (1951 and 1964, Philip Johnson) and the Metropolitan Museum (1975–1986, Kevin Roche, John Dinkeloo). The 1985 Museum of Modern Art's alterations and tower were, however, not the product of philanthropy but, rather, of a sale of air rights and the legislative assignment of real estate taxes produced from those rights: Pelli here produced a subdued building of taste if not experimentation.

The other end of the architectural spectrum from that of Mies was that of Frank Lloyd Wright, at the very center of whose thinking was a kind of vast semirural America, where buildings were cozier (at first) and related to lawns and gardens, served by the car (Broadacre City) to the same extent as the ideal but unrealized supercities of Le Corbusier but at a totally different scale. Mies, on the other hand, was equivocal in city planning, and both Wright and Le Corbusier scattered their buildings, the former at the scale of houses, town halls, and monumental but low-rise town centers; the latter as giant ocean liners on the open landscape, minicities within each entity.

Wright's first designs for the Guggenheim Museum date from 1940, and his final version was identical in spirit but reversed in form (right to left) from that earlier design. He had thought of it as a building in the Park (Central, that is), where its unique and dynamic form would be free of the rectilinear city grid. However this was not to be the case: such intrusions were by then out of the question (the Metropolitan Museum of Art was doubly protected in its infancy: its architect was the codesigner of the park, Calvert Vaux, and its site was an enclave carved from the park's legal bounds, allowing it territoriality within the apparent park borders). The site finally was transferred across Fifth Avenue into the city grid, on a whole blockfront facing the park. The great cream concrete helix is New York's avant-garde conch, where, in true Wrightian spirit, the *space* within the form is as dynamic as the form(s) it- or themselves. The Guggenheim (Solomon R. Guggenheim Museum for nonobjective painting—harborer of a slew of Kandinskys) is another icon, but this time unique, unco-

Ford Foundation Building. Modern commerce has brought plants in pots and planters within its lobbies and offices. Here Ford brought the whole garden into its embrace.

pied. The stern vocabulary of Mies was, of course, much more adaptable to commercial construction and even to museums (Mies at Houston and Berlin; Skidmore à la Mies at Buffalo; Philip Johnson à la Mies *cum* Lincoln Center at Fort Worth). The influence of Wright on subsequent building in New York was negligible in literal translation, but his spirit of space fortunately infected a few.

The Ford Foundation Building was a rare adventure, a solution possible only with a building built for public purpose, not for profit (happily). An almost-cube is penetrated to the sky and to two sides by rich gardens, plants and trees that make this a greenhouse-office symbiosis. Here nature is tamed within the architecture, a far more urbane solution than scattering buildings in the manner of Le Corbusier (or the New York City Housing Authority) over the landscape. The street-fronted form holds the building line along 42nd Street and keeps its garden within its subdued glass wall—a combined building and space exotically interrelated and gracefully inserted into the city's disciplined street system.

The original Whitney Museum was a gift to the city from Gertrude Vanderbilt Whitney, a sculptor related to two prominent and wealthy New York families. First adjacent to her home in Greenwich Village's MacDougal Alley as the Studio Club, it was formalized as a museum building (1931) at 8 West 8th Street behind its parent buildings. In 1954 a new building was constructed at the west end of the Museum of Modern Art garden, presenting the Whitney's collection to a delighted new audience. The resulting mushrooming attendance caused the trustees to commission Marcel Breuer to design the present and aggressive structure at 75th Street and Madison Avenue, along one of the principal city esplanades of private art galleries. This dynamic and overwhelming form (1966) is still insufficient and is to be expanded on the adjacent blockfront to the south, where brownstones owned by the museum will be demolished to make way for additions (Michael Graves) not only from the ground up but also over the Breuer original. Here the original philanthropic Whitney collections and bequest are being expanded and rehoused by a surrogate board of trustees. The Breuer building is within the Upper East Side Historic District and will be subject to Landmarks Preservation Commission public hearing and review before it can be altered and extended. It is an ironic turn of events, as Breuer's design for an office slab replacing Whitney Warren's south facade and waiting room of Grand Central Terminal was rejected by an earlier Landmarks Commission; the same preservationists are assembling now to protect Breuer's legacy.

The original Museum of Modern Art (1939, Philip L. Goodwin and Edward Durell Stone) was enhanced in 1951 with Philip Johnson's magnificent sculpture garden. Soon his fellow board members had him expanding not only to the north and south along 53rd Street but also designing the facade of the adjacent 1954 Whitney Museum that fronted that garden and remodeling simultaneously the guts within. Rockefeller money, which had assembled this as part of a tract with Rockefeller Center, assisted at MOMA, along with a galaxy of copatrons. The growing museum unfortunately consumed the two Rockefeller family brownstones to the east, and a grand mansion to the west.

Experimentation is something with which private development can rarely flirt. The work of philanthropy and government must necessarily provide the beacons that suggest alternative urban complexes, alternative architectural images. Governments, unfortunately and at every level, are most often hampered by the tedium of their bureaucracies, the fear of innovation that might breed criticism. But governments are necessary to make any substantial urban impact. Where they shine, as at Battery Park City, it seems miraculous. Where they fail, as at Times Square's clutch of proposed fat office buildings, we despair. The private philanthropists, single or group, will inject moments of great monumental drama into the larger city context, as at the Guggenheim, but they never can achieve

Whitney Museum of American Art. Although as aggressive and dynamic as the Guggenheim, the galleries within are serene and of a human scale. The granite skin is an appropriate neighbor for these Upper East Side blocks of stone and brick.

the urban scale that will graft a new sector of delight onto the existing city. In short, architecture for New York's public, whether created by governmental or philanthropic processes, is the chancy by-product of our capitalistic system. It is at its best when self-conscious cultural attitudes are absent, and a building or group of buildings is built with what the reformers used to term enlightened self-interest. Such is the bold route taken to produce Rockefeller Center, a great public monument created for private gain. And the convention center, Battery Park City, Roosevelt Island, the Police Headquarters, the Ford Foundation—all created by not-for-profit foundations and not-for-profit government—are distinguished as the products of relaxed clients.

Hats. The shapes crowning the World Financial Center give it a flavor that had been lost in the flat-top modern architecture of the 1950s, 60s, and 70s. This commercial core of the Battery Park City complex shares this landfill's distinguished new urban plan with residential streets.

Museum of Modern Art Additions. In his Miesian years, Philip Johnson added these modest steel bays to MOMA when modern art itself was modest. In its newest reconfiguration the museum now vies with the Trump Tower for traffic.

Mykonos. How to cluster workplaces and dwellings in a whole urban landscape that is greater than the sum of its parts. Mykonos and its sister Aegean islands are lessons in urbane architecture rediscovered by the twentieth century.

18.

Counterculture, a Recycled City, and Tomorrow

Man clusters with his kind for myriad and overlapping reasons: security, commerce, topography, sociability, culture, convenience, family, love, accessibility to farming, fishing. In many instances the idea of location is almost as important as the fact. An urban dweller may appreciate the reflected vibrations from a city's opera, theater, music, and film as much as the opportunity to experience such performances firsthand. But people live and have always lived cheek by jowl, sometimes for a daily portion of the experience, sometimes weekly, monthly, or even yearly. Social removal leads to compensating excess: the sailor denied the better half of the race for six months' sea duty reacts with the traditional binge. No punishment is considered more severe than solitary confinement, in a cell removed from fellow prisoners. The society of others, and the added facts of necessary work for practical existence, determine the reason for, purpose, and location of a town or city.

The clustered, terraced, and now-considered-romantic dwellings of the Greek islands were built for sociability, convenience to fishing fleets, and protection from pirates and weather. Hence they were strewn and stacked up the bowled hillsides of harbors that nestle into sea-bottomed mountain tops piercing the eastern Mediterranean. Simple and austere, their pure whitewashed forms provide a preview of cubistic architecture: all of one material and style, a family of forms complementary, interrelated, and seemingly part of a superform veneering the mountain topography. (Their populations could have been "dispersed," in the twentieth century's suburban sense, in widely spaced freestanding houses; "commuting time" from house to fishing boat would be increased, farmland available for cultivation diminished, costs of streets and sewers greater.) But most important, in a pedestrian and cart-drawn, horse-backed world, dwellings of personality snuggle together as do people, leaving nature and its produce on open land and in open water as the complementary bonus available for all, producing a world of character. Such snuggled proximity offers New Yorkers the best qualities of an urbane city, as opposed to the in-town suburbia of Queens, Staten Island, parts of Brooklyn, and the Bronx.

Suburbanites of the 1980's, in Philadelphia and Montreal, Paris and New York, are flocking back to center cities in a renewed understanding of the joys of concentration, of the street as a vibrant part of social life, of the delightful world of being a pedestrian. Gentrification, the conversion of the blighted housing of the poor into sleek housing for the rich, is without doubt a large and unfortunate social part of this population shift; but vast numbers also are absorbing the non- or underutilized commercial and industrial space of the low- and medium-rise city streets: in Manhattan's SoHo, Tribeca, East Village, central Harlem, and many sections of old, preautomobile Brooklyn.

The last years of the nineteenth century saw the pressures of fashion drain Greenwich Village of its early residents. The meandering streets and skewed blocks of Federal houses were then infilled, first with an immigrant black population from the American South, then with Ital-

Pacific Street, Boerum Hill. A delightful small-scale neighborhood of tiny houses and gracious trees. This is the more pervasive and common face of gentrifying Brooklyn.

ians and Irish migrating from the Lower East Side's dank tenements to these open and light-filled rooms. By the second decade of the twentieth century the black population was leapfrogging to Harlem, and the Village had been discovered by artists in search of an inexpensive freedom in a city precinct of charm and history. The *WPA Guide to New York City* (1939) describes the mood: "A nation, coming into its own artistically after an era of ruthless industrial expansion, of materialism and strait-laced conventionality, seized upon Greenwich Village as a symbol of revolt in the ferment of postwar years. The 'Village' was the center of the American Renaissance or of artiness, of political progress or of long-haired radical men and short-haired radical women, of sex freedom or of sex license—dependent upon the point of view.

" . . . At that period [after 1910] materialism had assumed an unprecedented importance in American life. Ambition not directed toward the goal of a large bank account was almost alien to thought and education, and, like most things alien, was regarded with distrust and scorn. Above all was this attitude adopted toward the struggling artist seeking satisfaction from completion of a poem or picture. . . .

"In Greenwich Village the earliest rebels found comparative quiet, winding streets, houses with a flavor of the Old World—and cheap rents.

"By 1939 . . . the Village tearooms and night clubs, for the most part no longer the haunts of the Bohemian, were patronized largely by out-of-town tourists and sensation seekers from outlying boroughs. Large apartment buildings and rents were rising as the well-to-do and white-collar workers, attracted . . . perhaps, by the glamor associated with the address, moved in."

This conversion of a forgotten section of the city to one of glamour or rejuvenated urban delight was the prototypical event repeated since the 1960's in diverse city sectors. The East Village, SoHo, Tribeca, and NoHo are the children of Greenwich Village, to which artists mi-

Patchin Place. e.e. cummings, who lived at number 4, made this Greenwich Village cul-de-sac a noted name. The buildings are ordinary; the situation, special and charming, as is the case in much of gentrification.

grated, followed by would-be artists or by those bankers or lawyers or used-car salesmen who merely savored the environment recaptured by artistic talent and need.

SoHo is the most architecturally cohesive of these followers but of a character totally different from the Village itself. These thirty-odd blocks were christened Hell's Hundred Acres by onetime (1954–1962) fire commissioner, Edward F. Cavanagh, Jr., and the cast-iron architecture of post–Civil War years housed storage facilities for oily rags and tinderous paper in the 1940's and '50's. But artists discovered the great open lofts and high ceilings in a time when the scale of painting was producing canvases so vast that one couldn't even get them through a Federal front door, let alone paint them in a ten-by-twelve studio room. SoHo offered spaces thirty or forty by a hundred feet, with an eleven-foot clear height, in buildings with facades of cast Ionic and Corinthian columns forgotten and unseen for three generations. In ten years this noxiously described backwater became the center of new artistic city life, of painters, sculptors, and galleries to display their works. Of course the vicarious followed, and in an era when painters frequently are affluent and bankers fill the spaces between them, SoHo is filled with restaurants and shops at which a struggling Greenwich Villager of the 1920's could only stare, sometimes with longing, frequently with contempt.

Tribeca and NoHo are merely peripheral offshoots of the SoHo core. The *tri*angle *be*low *Ca*nal Street is a bizarre acronym for those blocks west of the Civic Center and south of SoHo. Here the architecture is less consistent. Although some cast-iron streets are ranged between Broadway and West Broadway, the majority of blocks are an intermingling of brownstones, whitestones, cast iron, and brick, with a staccato group quality, occasionally with distinguished individual buildings. NoHo merely formalizes the blocks to the north of Houston Street, the forlorn section bounded by Greenwich Village to the west, the

SoHo. Cast iron conjures names like James Bogardus, Henry Fernbach, and Badger & Cornell, designers and fabricators of these precast, knocked-down facades. Prefabrication once brought with it style and even modest grandeur. Today it means something minimal and quick to create.

East Village to the north and the great Lower East Side to the east. NoHo perhaps offers the most for the least to the true artist pioneer, and to the yuppies tagging along behind; although Bleecker Street, between Broadway and Lafayette, honors the city with its great, early Modern, Louis Sullivan–designed Condict Building.

The middle class on its own, however, rediscovered sections of the city not particularly enticing to artists but where solid and spacious buildings of many rooms might accommodate new and growing families. Brooklyn Heights was so rediscovered in the 1960's by immigrants from Manhattan and, later, by new arrivals from out of town. Here the housing quality remains superb, although the depression dealt this prime Brooklyn precinct a powerful blow. Single-family houses could no longer be maintained as such, when the fortunes of their owners declined—or sometimes collapsed. Overwhelming numbers became rooming houses, rather grand but seedy barracks for single men and women confronting the same depression that the house owners attempted to defy by renting rooms. Nevertheless, a stoic core maintained the best of the neighborhood with some style, sometimes husbanding their houses, sometimes separating an apartment for rental; and a few apartment houses intermingling suggested the flavor of Park Avenue life overlooking the skyline and harbor.

In the 1960's, when the influx of young immigrants became serious, many of the great houses had been fortuitously preserved by their use as rooming houses. Without alterations necessary for the kitchens and bathrooms of true apartments, buildings had been used "as is," with family baths becoming group singles' bathrooms. Still in place were the marble fireplace mantels, oak parquetry, elaborate plaster cornices, stained glass, and woodwork of the second half of the nineteenth century. The housing stock then was quickly subdivided into apartments in various sizes and configurations—floor-throughs, duplexes, studios—with gardens or terraces on roofs and on exten-

Duane Park, Tribeca. The stepbrother of cast-iron SoHo, its buildings are mostly later and of a more stolid masonry architecture. Here food distributors lingered along Greenwich Street beyond, until the purchasing power of gentrification persuaded them to relocate. Adieu, Les Halles.

sions that projected with two or three floors into rear yards. A backwater in the urban evacuation to suburbia now became the renewed ideal for young family living.

With the Heights infilled with these new migrants, the equally handsome and urbane brownstone blocks of many other Brooklyn neighborhoods soon became the next territories to be recolonized. Sophisticated metropolitan residents flocked to Cobble Hill, Boerum Hill, Park Slope, Carroll Gardens, and Prospect Heights, whose still great areas remained to be equally gentrified. The poor and modest renters and owners of these precincts moved elsewhere, perhaps to Staten Island if they could convert their pot of gold into what for them was a true suburban dream. And the new settlers rejoiced in their newfound city life, a subway ride from downtown rather than a trek of hours to and from what had formerly seemed the suburban promised land.

Aeries in great towers have attracted Hollywood and the jet set to the Manhattan skyline, and a solid upper middle class has expanded its turf in both the Upper East and West sides; but the more adventurous newcomers are reclaiming, in a sequence of urban dominoes, ever-expanding sectors of the old city. Occasional new construction has brought modern architecture of quality and modest scale to newly formed precincts, such as at pockets of row housing in the East New York and Brownsville sections of Brooklyn or in sensitively planned, publicly assisted housing, as at the Lavanburg Homes next to the Bronx Zoo. But the low-rise high-density city is largely one of a recycled past, rather than of innovative urban design. New Brooklyn or Bronx townhousing that can provide the space and quality of construction of older buildings offers few incentives—and minimal profits—to real estate developers.

The adventurous will continue to exploit structures that no one could imagine for recycling into housing ten years ago: churches, fire stations, pump houses, factories, and warehouses have already become condominium apart-

First Place, Carroll Gardens, Brooklyn. Old South Brooklyn, actually the southern portion of nineteenth-century brownstone Brooklyn, shared gentrification of these deeply gardened blocks in the 1960's. Renamed Carroll Gardens at this time, it has been a center of Italian-Americans.

ments. It seems that nothing is so bizarre that it cannot be inhabited.

For the New Yorker, all this gentrification leads to preservation both with and without the aid of the Landmarks Preservation Commission. A building's guts are reconstituted to accommodate new residents, but the streetscape is largely preserved with the scale and detail of the nineteenth-century city. The horrors of urban renewal, which gutted multiple blocks in the 1960's in the name of slum clearance, replacing the dismissed poor with the middle class in high-rise slabs of mostly dubious architectural merit, are here supplanted by a tender reloving of a city that architects, planners, and builders seem unable to simulate even by a wide margin.

The overblooming congestion of midtown and the financial district has created the job markets that have stimulated the renewal of vast residential areas of Manhattan and Brooklyn, but if the momentum continues, the most desirable areas will be absorbed and renewed to their capacity. Standing behind as reservoirs of future reincarnation are such industrial precincts as Long Island City, parts of Chelsea, and areas of the Bronx.

The overloading of Manhattan's streets and subways at midtown and the Battery has caused thoughtful corporations to finally break through the psychological barrier of the East River that has kept them from Queens and Brooklyn. The first major leap to Queens has been by Citibank, whose Long Island City tower, along the Independent subway line one stop from Manhattan, is a four-minute ride from the aeries of Citicorp Center between Lexington and Third. The address differs, but the convenience is comparable, and this thirty-story tower will undoubtedly be the first of many in an intense commercial center.

In Brooklyn's downtown, contiguous with the Heights, Morgan Stanley's 360-foot blockbuster is the largest single office building in Brooklyn's history, to be complemented by a hotel, further office buildings, and the Metrotech

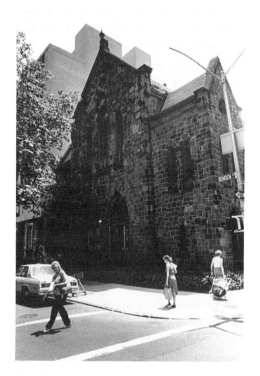

Condominiums, Former Spencer Presbyterian Church. The mind boggles at the virtuosity of architects and developers converting everything into gentrified condominiums. Here a church is subdivided horizontally and vertically to contain seven apartment units.

The Pump House, Joralemon Street at the Brooklyn–Queens Expressway. Fire pumps in a vast space were the former use of this intricate three-dimensional architectural puzzle. Will the unused Second Avenue subway tunnel be the next conversion?

(research) Center annexed intellectually and physically to the higher education centers of the New York Polytechnic Institute and Long Island University.

The New York of the year 2000 promises to be geographically diversified and dispersed in a pattern that will use the improving transit system more intelligently and efficiently. Included in such foresight are great opportunities in new development where one might walk to work at newly created commercial centers near existing housing and, alternately, to existing centers from new residential enclaves. Wall Street has now acquired neighboring housing not only at the wondrous new Battery Park City but also in gentrified Tribeca and such 1960's and '70's projects as Southbridge Towers and Independence Plaza. Brooklyn Heights, Cobble Hill, and Boerum Hill are in place to serve the new office and research complexes of downtown Brooklyn. The lure of the single-family house has paled for many, who first embraced it in a move to emulate the grand nineteenth-century suburbia of the affluent upper middle class, a symbol of social and economic independence.

Let's imagine New York in 1999:

The new Park Avenue supersubway, with its nexus at Grand Central Terminal, using the old Park Avenue tracks and the Lexington Avenue tunnels, speeds at eighty miles an hour on new welded rails from Jamaica in Queens, stopping at Flatbush Avenue, Wall Street, Grand Central, 125th Street, and Fordham Road on its way to White Plains. Cars, forbidden in the center city, can park at either end of this electronically controlled system, which has been submerged north of 96th Street through Harlem, creating a true Park Avenue North. New nodes of activity have blossomed at 125th and 149th streets and along the Grand Concourse, which, in a stylish reincarnation, is fending off a fanatic gentrification. Thousands of former exiles to Co-op City are returning to the grand boulevard of their parents and grandparents.

The West Side's fast transit has allowed sites in the

West Village and Chelsea to be interwoven with business centers from Bank Street to Yonkers. Here the reused Hudson Railroad tracks under Riverside Park have allowed the lovely bluffs of Riverdale in the northwest Bronx to become a new Mykonos, taut and tight housing tumbling down to the Hudson's shore.

And, of course, hovercraft have made possible a whole new microurbanization of Staten Island's north shore, from which it is a four-minute ride to Wall Street. St. George has become a vibrant alternate office center, in concert with the former lower Manhattan financial district, and with equal partners at Long Island City and downtown Brooklyn.

These next decades are those of the renaissance of the inner city, of the taming of the automobile and its lust for highways to unroll before it, of the happy renewal and revitalization of mass transit, of the savoring of the city's past, and of the sometimes faltering, sometimes successful attempt to instill some of the valued qualities of that past into projects for the future.

Westway would have suppressed traffic passing along the city's edge in favor of a pedestrian park. Battery Park City brings us the best piece of remembrance of the Upper East and Upper West sides' qualities updated. The Urban Development Corporation's works at Roosevelt Island offer a modern urbanity that high-rise apartment slabs have mostly missed. Citicorp's subway entrance plaza at Lexington Avenue makes access to the transit system a class act. Examples of sensitive vision perhaps do not yet abound, but the few that do exist are prominent intellectual and design landmarks by which to measure continuing experiments and possibilities for this city's rejuvenation.

To borrow from Mark Twain, "the reports of New York's death are greatly exaggerated." This vulgar and vibrant and lovely place will be around for another three centuries (barring the bomb) and will undoubtedly come to be served totally by foot and transit. Cars will be exiled to its edges as gadgets for escaping to the hopefully still

Lofts? Wouldn't it be smashing to live under the Riverside Drive viaduct, in great lofts overlooking the Hudson River? Why reserve such glorious volumes for storage and service, when they could be wondrous places for people.

existing "country"—some of which might still be preserved from creeping mini-single-family-house exploitation.

The city is the ultimate creation of man's intellect and the fulfillment of his aesthetic needs and, conversely, the crucible of intellectual stimulus. And this city, surprising all its lovers and its critics, seems to have an integrity lacking in its more flaccid American peers—Dallas and Miami, Detroit and Los Angeles—perhaps equaled in its smaller brothers, Boston and Philadelphia and San Francisco.

The watershedding mountains of New York will happily gather their abundance for generations to come, and these crystalline fluids will irrigate the apartments and bodies of New Yorkers with pristine quality forever. Water is the city's greatest natural success, the quiet waters of the distant hills. To demand or use more will not be progress but merely waste. To tap further reaches for greater quantity is to make the city an environmental gourmand, when it needs to be merely a civic gourmet.

Immigrants grace the city again in quantity, ranging from the menial and ill educated to virtuosi who not only garner prizes but also prized themselves. The subways and streets are manned with Indian newsstands. Thai, Vietnamese, Cambodian, and Burmese restaurants abound. Korean greengrocers flourish as luxuriantly as the produce they purvey. Jamaican and Bengali workers reface the historic buildings of Brooklyn and Manhattan. Irish bartenders seem to float across the Atlantic in endless droves. An ethnic Chinese Vietnamese, totally without knowledge of English in 1980, gives the valedictory to his graduating peers at City College in 1985, his perfect academic record marred only by a B in English in his first semester. The immigrants provide brains, brawn, and often a dedication to work that inspires those around them.

Patrons are more diffuse. The single gesture is now replaced by the corporate action and the group efforts of civic boosters who join to create the special moments of architecture new and renewed. The new wings of the Metropolitan Museum of Art and those proposed conversions of the Whitney and the Guggenheim owe their financial future to groups and committees, while those best and greatest impacts on the city are the fruits of government corporation, the Battery Park City Authority and its equals.

The quiet has exited every nook, but peace reigns in many private gardens. Wild, precipitous Manhattan has been turned into a stalagmite maze, its crisp grid a hard matrix to these blocks. But stand again on the west flank of the Cloisters, narrow your vision, and peer once more northwest across Henry Hudson's river to the great bluffs of New Jersey's Palisades. Wipe your mind, and mind-clear, history shelved, you may hear again the sigh of rock, tree, and water.

Noise—the booming, boisterous, vulgar noise of the thriving, lusty city—has replaced much of the quiet. And perhaps the return of the quiet may be one of the great boons of the future. As the pollution of our air has diminished, so may the pollution in our ears abate, with the muting of public radios and the quiet movement of our subways. We all must learn to match civilized behavior to the civilized city's form.

Bibliography

Barlow, Elizabeth. *Frederick Law Olmsted's New York.* New York: Praeger, 1972.

The commissioners' plan of 1811 and Olmsted's Central and Prospect parks were the greatest form-makers of the ultimate city. Only Robert Moses, in later years, matched such impact. Elizabeth Barlow works at the one center of Olmsted's works as curator of Central Park.

———. *The Forests and Wetlands of New York City.* Boston: Little, Brown, 1971.

Our new concerns with environmentalism are expressed for New York City by Ms. Barlow, who reveals the lush pockets of natural life in the sea, marsh, and flyways. Her concerns are noble, and, happily, some of the political promises described give promise.

Berger, Meyer. *Meyer Berger's New York.* New York: Random House, 1960.

Perhaps filled with trivia, but never trivial, Berger's reprinted *New York Times* columns reflect his love and concern for the city and its residents, ranging from tales of Mohawk steelworkers to stories of the Lower East Side, where he was born in 1898.

Blom, Benjamin. *New York: Photographs 1850–1950.* New York: E. P. Dutton, 1982.

A beautiful culling of photographs of New York's buildings and people.

Dunshee, Kenneth Holcomb. *As You Pass By.* New York: Hastings House, 1952.

A curious and wonderful book promoted by the chairman of the Home Insurance Company, Harold V. Smith. The company's fire museum is one of the little-known wonders of New York; and here a history of fire, and of the water to put it out, is intertwined with maps, plans, sketches, and photographs illustrating the city's changing street patterns. This is information unavailable elsewhere, clearly showing how the waterfront of old New York changed and how streets such as Broad Street evolved from the original Dutch canal.

Edmiston, Susan and Linda D. Cirino. *Literary New York.* Boston: Houghton Mifflin, 1976.

A geographical exercise in the game of "who wrote what where" that, concurrently, tells how they enjoyed those respective locales. That Mailer wrote *The Naked and the Dead* at 102 Pierrepont Street in Brooklyn isn't on any plaque. But more impressive is that his friend Arthur Miller was writing *All My Sons* upstairs at the same time.

Federal Writers' Project (including John Cheever). *New York City Guide.* New York: Random House, 1939. Reprint. New York: Pantheon, 1982.

The original WPA guide is one of a series of guides to cities and states similarly covered during the depression through a Works Progress Administration subsidy of writers.

Finney, Jack. *Time and Again.* New York: Simon and Schuster, 1970.

A wonderful fantasy that brings one back in time to the early 1880's. How they do it is pleasant whimsy; what the hero finds, however, is the physical city of that time, its sounds, smells, textures, and rhythms, a far more convincing remembrance of a past world than any history book. Read it.

Fischler, Stan. *Uptown, Downtown.* New York: Hawthorn Books, 1976

A history of transit: streetcars, elevated trains, but mostly a love affair with the netherworld of subways.

Goldberger, Paul. *The City Observed.* New York: Vintage Books, 1979.

The architecture critic of the *New York Times* comments on the major buildings of Manhattan. Sometimes witty, sometimes controversial. One can agree or disagree, but never be bored.

James, Henry. *Washington Square.* New York: Harper and Bros., 1881.

James's descriptions of what we now think of as Greenwich Village and, of course, Washington Square are finely honed, sometimes sarcastic verbal stage sets for his wordy novels. The architecture of the city here looms large.

Kouwenhoven, John A. *The Columbia Historical Portrait of New York.* Garden City, N.Y.: Doubleday, 1953. Reprint. New York: Harper and Row, 1972.

Published in concert with the university's two hundredth anniversary, this takes much of the raw material of Stokes, with some interesting additions, to give a visual history of New York physically and socially. It is a smorgasbord of information, sometimes providing too many random insights. But anyone who cares about New York would have to have this volume on hand.

Lancaster, Clay. *Old Brooklyn Heights.* Rutland, Vt.: Charles E. Tuttle, 1961. 2nd ed. New York: Dover, 1979.

Perhaps New York's first serious architectural inventory of a neighborhood, this helped its dedicatees (Otis and Nancy Pearsall) to further the designation of Brooklyn Heights as the city's first Historic District, now protected by law.

Lockwood, Charles. *Bricks and Brownstone: The New York Row House, 1783–1929.* New York: McGraw-Hill, 1972.

The history of architectural styles and stylish society here is described and illustrated in a handsome articulate book. As in the title, the buildings concerned are houses, not housing.

Marqusee, Mike and Bill Harris. *New York, an Anthology.* Boston: Little, Brown, 1985.

Words written about New York are here carefully collected to describe from then to now in poetry and prose what writers and artists feel and felt about the city. The authors range widely: Trollope, Whitman, Bierce, Gorky, Dos Passos, Fitzgerald, Bellow, Hansberry, Mumford, Runyon, Capote, et al., and more et al.

McCullough, David. *The Great Bridge.* New York: Simon and Schuster, 1972.

A case study of the marriage of New York and Brooklyn, elegantly and elaborately described. It is detailed, thorough, and, as Lewis Mumford commented, "Balzacian": a bridge's creation described as the armature of modern New York's evolution.

Patterson, Jerry E. *The City of New York: A History Illustrated from the Collections of the Museum of the City of New York.* New York: Harry N. Abrams, 1978.

A lovely tour through the collections of this grand museum, with superb photographs of documents, maps, furniture, portraits, engravings, and paintings. A catalog of a permanent New Yorkiana exhibition.

Schuberth, Christopher J. *The Geology of New York City and Environs.* Garden City, N.Y.: National History Press, 1968.

Six hundred million years of geological change in New York's metropolitan region—from an inland sea to Manhattan's tropical rain forest, from glaciers to the rocky foundations for skyscrapers.

Stokes, Isaac Newton Phelps. *The Iconography of Manhattan Island, 1498–1909.* 6 vols. New York: Robert H. Dodd, 1915–1928. Reprint. New York: Arno Press, 1967.

The Bible without apocrypha. Stokes was a serious architect whose work ranged from model-tenement designs to St. Paul's Chapel at Columbia. His life's labor, however, was in these millions of words published over thirteen years. Included are almost every map and view of seventeenth-, eighteenth-, and nineteenth-century New York in high-quality reproductions carefully described as to content and provenance. The index is staggering, comprising almost 400 pages of dense and precise information; and the chronology recounts virtually every event in New York's history up to 1909—in 2,000 pages! It is obviously an encyclopedic source book without comparison for any city in the world, not to be read from A to Z but to be delved into by the serious and the curious alike.

Tauranac, John. *Essential New York.* New York: Holt, Rinehart and Winston, 1979.

His unusual attitude discusses New York's architectural history chronologically, rather than geographically. Again here is someone with real and intelligent opinions at work.

Wharton, Edith. *The Age of Innocence.* New York: D. Appleton, 1920.

This won the Pulitzer Prize in 1921, a devastating fictional account of the social life and values of late nineteenth-century New York Society. And in the process the physical environment of the city is beautifully rendered.

White, Norval and Elliot Willensky. *AIA Guide to New York City.* 2nd ed. New York: Macmillan, 1978.

The first comprehensive guide to an entire American city, this book includes copious information on New York's history and architecture as well as numerous maps, walking tours, and illustrations.

Willensky, Elliot. *When Brooklyn Was the World*. New York: Harmony Books, 1986.

A succulent remembrance of Brooklyn. New York's most populous borough has been drained of some of its wondrous glories by the flight of the Dodgers, the dominance of TV, and the false lures of suburbia.

Wright, Carol von Pressentin. *Blue Guide, New York*. New York: W. W. Norton, 1983.

A first-class tourist guide that incorporates much of New York's physical history.

Wurman, Richard Saul. *NYC Access*. Los Angeles: Access Press, 1983.

A complex and frenetic guide that would appeal more to the yuppies' idea of New York than to those concerned with its reality. It is a morass of wondrous information, a guide to which one needs a guide.

Index

Illustration Credits

xv courtesy MOCONY; xvi courtesy Brooklyn Educational and Cultural Alliance, Pratt Institute; xxiv photo by Gottscho-Schleisner, courtesy MOCONY; xxxi courtesy MOCONY; xxxii collection of NW; 2 collection of NW; 4 from New York Rapid Transit Company, *The New York Subway*, New York 1904; 5 *Amériquain* by Nicolas Bouquet 1764, courtesy Bibliothèque de l'Opéra, Paris; 7 courtesy NYPL; 8 from Stokes; 11 courtesy MOCONY; 12 collection of NW; 15 courtesy Brown University Library; 18 collection of NW; 19 from Stokes; 20 courtesy NYPL; 21T & B from Stokes; 22 from Stokes; 23 courtesy MOCONY; 24 by SK; 26, 27 by SK; 28 by NW; 29 from Stokes; 30 collection of NW; 31 by Ewing Galloway; 32 by NW; 33, 34 by SK; 35 collection of NW; 36 courtesy M. Knoedler & Co., Inc.; 38 collection of NW; 39, 40, 41 from K. H. Dunshee, *As You Pass By*, New York 1952; 42 courtesy NYHS; 45 from Citizens Union Foundation, *Thirsty City*, New York n.d.; 46 courtesy MOCONY; 47 from an old advertisement c. 1848; 49 collection of NW; 50, 52 courtesy of MOCONY; 54 courtesy Sprague Library, Electric Railroaders Association; 55 courtesy NYHS; 56 courtesy MOCONY; 57 by SK; 58 courtesy MOCONY; 59T & B courtesy MOCONY; 60 courtesy Cityana Gallery; 61 courtesy NYHS; 62 from New York Rapid Transit Company, *The New York Subway*; 63, 64 by SK; 68 courtesy Cityana Gallery; 70 *The Iron Bridge at Coalbrook*, engraving by J. Fitler after G. Robinson, 1788; 71 courtesy Cooper Union for the Advancement of Science and Art; 72, 73 by NW; 74 courtesy

Library of Congress; 75 by NW; 77, 78 courtesy MOCONY; 80 collection of NW; 82T & B courtesy MOCONY; 84, 85 courtesy MOCONY; 86 courtesy Chicago Historical Society; 88T courtesy Collection of Plino Nardecchia, Rome; 88B by SK; 89 from S. E. Rasmussen, *Towns and Buildings*, Copenhagen n.d.; 90 from Stokes; 91, 92 courtesy NYHS; 93 photo by J. S. Johnston, collection of the Library of Congress; 94 by NW; 95, 96, 97 by SK; 98 by Chie Nishio; 99T & B by SK; 100 courtesy MOCONY; 102 by Kerry Dundas; 103 by NW; 104 courtesy MOCONY; 105, 106 by SK; 107T by NW; 107B by SK; 108, 109 by SK; 110 by NW; 112 by SK; 114 by NW; 115 by SK; 116 by NW; 117 by SK; 118 courtesy MOCONY; 120 by SK; 121 courtesy MOCONY; 122 from Le Corbusier, *When Cathedrals Were White*, New York 1960; 123, 124 by SK; 125 from E. Howard, *Garden Cities of Tomorrow*, London 1965; 126T by SK; 126B by NW; 127, 128 by SK; 130 courtesy Cityana Gallery; 132 courtesy MOCONY; 133 courtesy Pennsylvania Railroad; 134 by SK; 135T courtesy Archives of the Cathedral of St. John the Divine; 135B by NW; 136 by SK; 137 by NW; 138 by SK; 140 by NW; 141, 142, 143 by SK; 144 courtesy Cityana Gallery; 146, 147 by NW; 148 from W. Gropius, *The Architecture and the Bauhaus*, Boston n.d.; 150 by SK; 151T & B by SK; 152 by NW; 153 from I. Gournay, *Trocadero*; 154T photo by Gottscho-Schleisner, courtesy MOCONY; 154B National Film Archive, London; 155 by SK; 156T courtesy MOCONY; 156B courtesy Rockefeller Center; 157T by SK; 157B courtesy Cityana Gallery; 158, 159, 160, 161 by SK; 162 courtesy MOCONY; 164, 165, 166, 167T by SK; 167B courtesy Cooper Union for the Advancement of Science and Art; 168 collection of NW; 169 collection of Miriam and Ira D. Wallach, Division of Art, Prints, and Photographs, New York Public Library, Astor, Lenox and Tilden Foundation; 170 Plate 46 from *A Monograph of the Works of McKim, Mead & White, 1879–1915* ed. by B. Blom, New York 1973; 171, 172 courtesy Cityana Gallery; 174 by SK; 176 courtesy Metropolitan Opera Archives; 179 by SK; 180 by NW; 181 courtesy Cityana Gallery; 182 courtesy General Motors; 183, 184 by SK; 185 by NW; 186, 187, 188, 189 by SK; 190 by NW; 192, 193T & B, 194, 195, 196, 197, 198, 199, 200, 201, 202, 203, by SK; 204 courtesy Sophia Mumford; 209 by SK; 210 by NW; 212 by SK; 213, 214, 215 by NW; 216 by SK; 218 by NW; 220 by SK; 221 model by Eero Saarinen; 222, 223, 224, 226 by SK; 227 by NW; 228, 229 by SK; 230 by Dimitri Haytalis; 232, 233, 234, 235, 236, 237, 238, 239 by SK.

Abbreviations Key

MOCONY Museum of the City of New York
NYPL New York Public Library, Astor, Lenox and Tilden Foundations

NYHS New York Historical Society
NW Norval White
SK Suzy Kunz
Stokes I. N. P. Stokes, *The Iconography of Manhattan Island, 1498–1909*,
6 vols.
T top
B bottom

NORVAL WHITE was born in Manhattan, received his B.S. from MIT and his M.F.A. from Princeton, and has been a resident of Brooklyn for over twenty years. He has taught both design and history at the Cooper Union, and was chairman of the Department of Architecture and professor at City College, where he currently has a design studio and teaches both general architectural history and the history of New York's physical development. Among his works are New York City Police Headquarters and Essex Terrace, a unique housing project in the East New York section of Brooklyn. He is the author of *The Architecture Book*, and co-author, with Elliot Willensky, of the *AIA Guide to New York City*.